Doris Stokes was a celebrated clairaudient who confounded sceptics with the uncanny accuracy of her readings. In Australia she filled the Sydney Opera House and was mobbed in the streets. In America, 'Charlie's Angels' was removed from a prime television slot to make way for her. In this country her appearances on radio phone-ins caused an avalanche of mail.

In this omnibus of two of Doris Stokes' extremely successful books, *Innocent Voices in My Ear*, and, *Whispering Voices*, bestsellers in the early 1980s, she tells the stories of her 'spirit children' and her amazing gift that over the years of her extraordinary life brought joy and comfort to thousands of people. She died in 1987.

DORIS STOKES

A Host of Voices Omnibus

Innocent Voices in My Ear

&

Whispering Voices

WARNER BOOKS

A *Warner* Book

This edition first published in Great Britain by
Warner Books in 2000

A Host of Voices Omnibus Copyright © Doris Fisher Stokes 2000

Previously published separately:

Innocent Voices in My Ear first published in Great Britain by
Futura Publications, a Division of Macdonald & Co (Publishers) Ltd
in 1983
Reprinted 1983, 1984 (twice), 1985 (three times), 1987
Copyright © Doris Fisher Stokes 1983

Whispering Voices first published in Great Britain by
Futura Publications, a Division of Macdonald & Co (Publishers) Ltd
London & Sydney in 1985
Copyright © Doris Fisher Stokes 1985

A CIP catalogue record for this book
is available from the British Library.

ISBN 0 7515 3059 X

Printed and bound in Great Britain by
Clays Ltd, St Ives plc

Warner Books
A Division of
Little, Brown and Company (UK)
Brettenham House
Lancaster Place
London WC2E 7EN

INNOCENT VOICES IN MY EAR

AUTHOR'S NOTE

Doris Stokes would like to apologize to the parents of all those children who are not mentioned in this book. Vital tapes containing the details of many case histories were stolen in transit, and she has been unable to recall them all. She can only hope that the person responsible will feel thoroughly ashamed when he or she listens to the heartbreak and tragedy recorded.

I dedicate this book to one of
nature's gentlemen, Dick Emery,
who loved children as much as I do.

I would like to thank all those who have
so kindly provided me with photographs
of their children – and only wish that
all could have been printed in this book.

'Death is nothing at all. I have only slipped
away into the next room. I am I and you are you.
Whatever we were to each other, that we are still.

Call me by my old familiar name; speak to me
in the easy way which you always used; put no
difference in your tone; wear no forced air of
solemnity or sorrow; laugh, as we always laughed
at the little jokes we enjoyed together; pray,
smile, think of me, pray for me; let my name be
ever the household word that it always was;
let it be spoken without effect, without the trace
of a shadow on it.

Life means all that it ever meant; it is the same
as it ever was; there is unbroken continuity.
Why should I be out of mind because I am out of
sight? I am waiting for you, for an interval,
somewhere very near – Just around the corner.
All is well.'

*With thanks to Mandy's mother, Jill,
for the comfort her words have given to
parents over the world*

CHAPTER 1

The boy appeared almost immediately. He was a small, neat child, maybe four or five years old, with dark brown hair that waved softly round his head and a pointed little face like that of an elf.

He grinned at me and I smiled back, but then my attention was diverted by something his relatives were saying. Moments later a flash of movement caught my eye. I glanced round and there he was – stripping off his clothes. Off came his jumper, off came his jeans, off came his socks, off came his underwear, and as he finished with each garment he flung it to the floor. Finally, when he was naked as the day he was born, he stood in front of me, pink, dimpled and pleased with himself.

I started to laugh.

'What's the joke?' asked the boy's father because, not being a medium, he couldn't see what had happened.

'The cheeky young beggar!' I chuckled. 'He's just taken off all his clothes and thrown them on the floor. He's standing there in the nudie!'

But, to my surprise, the man didn't laugh. He started to cry. 'That's the only evidence I need,' he said. 'Paul was mentally retarded and we used to apologize to guests in advance because if he thought he was being ignored he used to take his clothes off.'

Little Paul had died or, as I would say, passed on some months before, but, although his family could no longer see him, he wasn't very far away. He hadn't changed. He wasn't mentally handicapped any more, of course, but his personality was still the same. He thought he was being

11

ignored when I talked to someone else, so off came his clothes!

I've always been daft about children and I think that's why, even today, my communications with the other side are particularly vivid if there's a child involved. Even as a child myself I loved the little ones smaller than me and I genuinely thought all babies were beautiful. From the earliest age I would beg to cuddle them and change their nappies. Dolls didn't interest me if there was a real live baby around.

'Pol,' young mothers used to say (for some reason everyone called me Polly in those days), 'come and hold our so and so's bottle.'

And I'd stand there beside the pram, barely tall enough to see over the side, proudly holding the bottle until the baby had finished. Then, standing on tiptoe, I carefully wiped its face and mouth.

Even in those days I was getting a helping hand from the spirit world, although I was too young to realize it then. I remember the day I met a neighbour trundling her heavy old pram along the streets of Grantham where I was born. The sight of that pram was like a magnet to me and I was at her side in seconds. The baby was sitting there in his frilly sun bonnet, tiny fists waving, and I'll swear he smiled when he saw me. I skipped along with the pram for a while, shaking his rattle and pulling funny faces to make him laugh, but in the end I could contain myself no longer.

'Oh, can I have a push?' I burst out, and the woman laughed.

'Go on then, Pol,' she said, probably glad of a rest, 'but just mind what you're doing, that's all.'

She moved aside and I took her place on the handle. Proudly, and with infinite care, I manoeuvred the pram over every crack and bump and soon I was bowling along as if to the manner born. It was all going well – I'd even managed the kerbstone smoothly – when suddenly the baby began to cough.

At first his mother smiled and patted him indulgently on the back, but as the coughing grew worse and he turned scarlet in the face, she became seriously alarmed.

'Whatever's the matter?' she cried, unstrapping him and shooting me an accusing glance as if she suspected it was my fault.

Frightened, I stared at the sobbing child. I was only pushing the pram but could I have done something wrong? What's the matter with him, I wondered guiltily. Instantly, as if a voice had spoken in my head, came the answer. He's got a peanut stuck in his throat.

'He's got a peanut stuck in his throat,' I blurted aloud, without pausing to question how I knew.

The woman stared at me, then put her finger into the baby's mouth. A split second later out came an unchewed nut. Apparently she had been eating peanuts a little while before and, thinking the baby was old enough to cope with them, she'd given him a couple. He must have kept one unchewed in his cheek and forgotten about it until it went down the wrong way.

At any rate, my answer had been right.

'But, Pol,' said our neighbour as she settled the baby back in his place, 'how did . . . ?' Then she stopped, her expression uneasy. 'Yes, well I think I'd better carry on pushing now,' she finished briskly and sadly I was forced to relinquish the pram.

Throughout my childhood I came to know that expression very well. I would say something quite innocent, intending to be helpful, and an adult face would change from relief to suspicion and then wariness. You could almost hear them thinking, 'But how does she know these things?' Had I not been an ordinary, down-to-earth child, good old Sam and Jenny Sutton's little girl, I think they might have been frightened of me. As it was, they were uneasy but I did have some reassuring saving graces. I was a proper little mother and that they approved of, although my involvement with the little ones didn't always do me any good.

When I was a little older I used to take out baby Hazel Hudson, the youngest of our neighbours' children. I went for long walks with the pram, chattering away to Hazel who couldn't understand a word but who gurgled obligingly as if we were having a proper conversation. So when Hazel's brother and sister, Kenny and Joyce, caught scarlet fever and were sent to the isolation hospital it was only natural that Mrs Hudson should ask me to take Hazel to visit them when she wasn't able to go herself.

I didn't mind a bit. The hospital was outside the town, and it was a pleasant walk. As it happened it was a lovely day in the early spring with the tips of crocus just showing above the ground. It was so nice, in fact, that my sister Edna and her friend Peggy decided to come with me.

It was an enjoyable outing. Hazel was well behaved as usual and the rest of us were in high spirits. We knocked on the door of the hospital to hand in the sweets and comics Mrs Hudson had packed up, then we walked round to the window of the children's ward. We weren't allowed inside, of course, but we waved and shouted to Joyce and Kenny through the glass, and I think we cheered them up.

That should have been the end of my good deed. But the following week I began to feel unwell. My head ached, my temperature soared and, by the weekend, I was being raced back to the isolation hospital by ambulance. As they carried me up the path on a stretcher I pushed the blankets off my face.

14

'Don't do that, love,' said the ambulance man, pushing them back again.

'I only wanted to see if the crocuses were out,' I muttered.

But it was too late. We were through the door and heading for the children's ward where I'd be able to cheer Joyce and Kenny from the inside this time. Of the four of us who'd set out that spring afternoon to visit the Hudson children, I was the only one who caught scarlet fever.

I suppose I picked up quite a few childhood illnesses that way but it didn't deter me. As I grew up I was always surrounded by children and when I eventually married it came as no surprise to anyone that I wanted a baby right away.

Well, I got my wish. I had my baby and that baby was to change my life for ever. As I explained in my first book, *Voices in My Ear*, my little John Michael was taken from me when he was just five months old. Blockage of the bowel, they said. They operated on him but it was no use. He died soon afterwards.

It was the tragedy of my life. When you lose a mother or a father or even a much-loved husband it's bad enough, but when you lose a child it's the worst thing that can happen. That child is part of you and when the child dies part of you dies with him.

Sadly, I was unable to have any more children though I was lucky enough to adopt a little boy called Terry who is with us still. Yet, out of that tragedy something wonderful happened. Inconsolable with grief I drifted from church to church until I ended up at a spiritualist meeting. There, at last, I got proof from the medium that my son was not really dead, that he was happy and well and being looked after by his grandad on 'the other side'.

Naturally, I wanted to know more. My mother had always been very much against 'they spiritualists' and continually warned me about them. I'd end up in a mental home if I had anything to do with them, she reckoned. But they were the only ones who'd been able to offer me any comfort and I was determined to find out what their organization was about.

That's how it all began. Gradually, I realized that I was a natural medium. Hundreds of strange little incidents over the years fell into place and I began to develop my powers. If I hadn't lost John Michael my gift might have remained unused and undeveloped. Though I would gladly have traded all my powers just to hold my baby in my arms again it was nice to think that his life hadn't been in vain. Through John Michael I was able to help hundreds, and eventually thousands, of people all over the world.

Today I work on all sorts of cases, from haunted houses and unsolved murders to public meetings in vast stadiums and private sittings for bereaved relatives. Yet I've noticed that, without exception, over the years my most successful sittings have been with mothers who've lost children.

I am convinced this is because of John Michael. Unless you've lost a child yourself you can't truly understand the complex emotions that tear you apart.

When I got back from the hospital that terrible day the first thing I said was: 'What have I done to deserve this? I must have been very bad somewhere.' You feel you're being punished. You feel guilty. You think, Was it my fault? Was there something else I could have done?

No matter how the child died and no matter how illogical it sounds, you blame yourself.

Of course, everyone tells you that time is a great healer but the months wear on and the guilt gives way to desolation and the grief lies like a block of ice right across your solar plexus. If you smoke, you smoke too much; if you drink, you drink too much; nothing does any good. Every morning I woke up thinking it was all a nightmare,

16

that I'd glance across and see my baby playing happily in his cot waiting for me to rise. Then I'd remember and it would hit me all over again. There was no baby, the cot was cold and empty, and the nightmare was real.

At the time it all seemed so senseless and there were days when I wanted to die. But now, years later, I know that it did make sense, there was a purpose to my suffering. Now, when a sitter walks through my door, I can tell immediately if she's lost a child and that common experience strengthens the psychic power. Often I see the child before the mother's even got her coat off.

This sense of affinity was particularly strong when I met recently a young woman called Denise. I knew she'd lost a child, but there was something more than that and it puzzled me. The feeling nagged as I went into the kitchen to put the kettle on for our usual cup of tea before the sitting. When I went back into the living-room I had the sensation of a baby being put into my arms and I realized what that something was. Denise, like me, had lost a baby boy, at five months old. What's more, being particularly sensitive, she'd had a premonition about his death weeks before, just as I did about John Michael.

Denise was divorced and looked after her new husband's three children as well as her daughter from her first marriage, but, apart from that difference in our lives, I could have been meeting myself thirty years before.

After the sitting Denise explained what happened before her baby died. Like me she hardly dared talk about her fears in case people thought she was mad.

'My first husband died unexpectedly just a few weeks before Nathan was born,' she said. 'It hit me pretty hard because, although we were divorced, I was still fond of him. Anyway, Nathan was born and I forgot about the shock because there was a lot of worry over him. He was

17

a perfect little boy but he was premature and only weighed three pounds.

'It was a difficult start for him but he seemed to do well. I brought him home and he was settling down and the children were fascinated by him. Then one day a few weeks later I was sitting by the fire when from nowhere the thought suddenly came into my head: "Len had to go so that he could look after Nathan". I hadn't even been thinking about my ex-husband. It sounds crazy but instantly I just knew that this idea was right. I was so certain, I burst into tears, ran in a panic to check Nathan and then when I was sure he was all right I phoned my sister.

' "Nathan's going to die!" I sobbed.'

Denise's sister obviously thought Denise was suffering from the strain and worry of the premature birth. She made soothing noises, pointed out how healthy Nathan had become and told her to calm down.

'I felt I'd been silly,' said Denise, 'but I couldn't get the idea out of my mind. Yet the weeks went by and Nathan was fine. In the end I thought I must have been imagining things.'

Like John Michael, Nathan was an exceptionally good baby. He never cried. He was always happy. He'd let anyone pick him up. He seemed to need an unusual amount of sleep and he rarely woke of his own accord. Most mornings Denise had to wake him for his feed, but when she mentioned this to anyone else they just said she should think herself lucky. With four other children to care for as well, she soon forgot the strange premonition. Or at least her conscious mind forgot.

'Over the next few months I kept having this weird dream,' said Denise. 'Usually I dream in colour but this dream was in black and white, like an old photograph. There was a group of people standing around chatting

18

and laughing as if they were having a lovely time. But as I looked at them I realized they were all dead. They were people I'd known in the past who'd later died. But as I watched I had this strong feeling of being pulled up -- as if they were pulling me up to them to join the party. I shouted out, "I can't come." Then I'd wake up.

'About this time I was looking through a shopping catalogue and I decided to buy a black suit. Now, black is a colour I never wear. I look really dreadful in black and for that reason I haven't got any black clothes. Yet, although I couldn't say why, I was convinced I should spend quite a lot of money on this suit which probably would look horrible. My sister couldn't understand it. "What on earth d'you want that for?" she asked. And I don't know what made me say it but I replied, "Oh, it'll come in handy for the odd funeral." '

Three months later Denise was driving home from a shopping trip in Shrewsbury when she suddenly became alarmed and stopped the car.

'I felt very strange,' she said. 'The pulling up feeling I'd had in my dream was back and very strong and there was death all around. I know it sounds crazy. Hysterical if you like. I can't explain it but, without doubt, death was very close. I looked over at Nathan but he was sleeping peacefully and I thought it was me who was going to die. It had been snowing and everything was very white and unnaturally sharp as if I was looking through binoculars, and all the time I was being pulled up.

'Death was so close I actually cried out loud, "Oh no, not me. I've got all the children to look after." I don't know whether that helped but gradually the feeling drained away and everything was normal again. I sat there a bit longer feeling shaky and wondering what had happened. Then I remembered the children would be coming home from school so I went back.

'Nathan seemed fine. There was nothing wrong with him at all. It was me I felt the warning was for. That night I put him in his cot as usual and he was quite happy. The next morning I went to get him up and he was dead.'

The doctors told Denise that her baby was a cot death victim. Very little is known about cot death beyond the fact that it is a silent killer which strikes apparently healthy babies without warning. It is more common in premature babies like Nathan than full-term children, they said, and they thought the fact that Nathan slept so much was probably significant, but that was all they could tell her.

It wasn't much comfort and, as the months went by, Denise didn't seem to get any better. She didn't care what happened to her, life didn't seem worth living, and she vaguely realized that she wasn't being fair to the rest of the family. In desperation she wrote to me.

At the time of the sitting, of course, I knew nothing about the whole sad story apart from the fact she'd lost a child. Then as I walked back into the sitting-room and I felt the baby in my arms I looked down and saw that it was a beautiful little fellow, with fairish hair curling into ringlets all over his head. He looked between five and a half and six months old and he was chuckling away. As I admired him a voice told me that Denise had one other child of her own and three of her second husband's children and that this baby, who was their first joint child, had gone to sleep and woken up on the other side.

Denise confirmed that this was right. Then a strong male voice with a Welsh accent interrupted. He said he was Denise's husband and he'd gone over very quickly with a heart attack.

'I still love her,' he told me, 'and for the love we had I have taken her son and made him mine. We couldn't live together but I still love her.' I thought he said his name was Ken but I misheard.

'Len,' Denise corrected.

Len kept going back over the failed marriage. It obviously worried him that he hadn't been able to make Denise understand how he felt for her when they lived together and he wanted to put it right now.

'It wasn't my wish to split up,' he insisted. 'I would have laid down my life for her but I couldn't communicate with her in the end. She always seemed beyond my reach. I thought, whatever she wants I'll agree to, but perhaps I was wrong. Maybe I should have worked harder at it. I shouldn't have let her go.'

He was also worried about the other children. Like many mothers in the same position Denise had sent all her love away with Nathan. She fed and cared for the other children in practical ways but emotionally she'd shut them out.

'Tell her to go home and give Emma Louise a big cuddle and the other three as well,' Len asked. But when I passed the message to Denise she began to cry.

'I can't, I can't,' she sobbed. 'All my love has gone with Nathan.'

This often happens and it's very sad for the children who're left because they don't understand what's happened. Their little brother or sister has mysteriously gone away and won't come back and mummy snaps at them and doesn't smile any more. You don't know what goes through little children's minds. Often they think they must be to blame. Their parents seem to be angry with them so they think the death must somehow be their fault.

'Denise, you must try,' I begged her. 'It's not fair on the other children. You must give them more attention,

21

particularly Emma Louise. She adored her little brother and she misses him terribly.'

Denise dried her eyes and promised that she would try, although she didn't know whether she would be successful.

The sitting went on and her mother, Hetty, came back to talk to her and mentioned the name Lilian.

'That's my real name,' Denise admitted with a smile, 'but I never liked it and everyone calls me Denise.'

As she spoke, a light almost like a torch beam suddenly appeared and started dancing about near her shoulder. I realized that someone else had joined us with a message. It was a man. He'd been over three years, he said, he'd passed with cancer and he belonged to Margaret.

'Margaret's a friend,' said Denise slowly. 'Oh, that must be her husband, Bill. He died three years ago of cancer.' She was puzzled, however, as to why Bill should turn up during the sitting because she hadn't known him very well during his lifetime. Why had he bothered to come? It was only afterwards when she met Margaret that it fell into place.

'Margaret said she wasn't a bit surprised,' Denise wrote to me later, 'because, although I didn't realize it at the time, the day of the sitting was the anniversary of the day he died.'

That special day Bill was obviously thinking of Margaret and when he spotted the communication lines open with one of her friends he didn't want to miss the chance of letting her know he was all right and he hadn't forgotten.

You often hear people say that grief brings couples together but sadly I've found this isn't always true. Sometimes parents become marooned in their sorrow, isolated from each other and unable to show their feelings.

The longer it goes on the higher the barrier between them grows and the more difficult it becomes to break it down.

I was reminded of this soon after Denise's visit when another young mother came to see me. Her name was Theresa and she was a pretty girl with dark curly hair and a look of hope in her eyes. It was only as the sitting progressed that I discovered the real tragedy her looks belied. It was nine years since she'd lost her son and in all those years she and her husband had never spoken of him, nor looked at his photograph. It was as if that child had never existed. Now, that's what I call a tragedy.

The sitting started in a light-hearted way. Two young voices came bubbling through. By the sound of them it was a boy and either a girl or a younger boy with a light childish voice. They were giggling and chattering to each other as well as to me, and they were messing about so much it was difficult to make out what they were saying.

'I've got two voices here,' I explained to Theresa. 'Did two children pass over?'

'Yes, but not both mine,' she said. 'One was my sister's.'

It turned out that they were both boys and, after sending their love to various members of the family, I asked them what had happened. There was much excited interrupting of each other but finally we got it straight. One had been ill and the other had had an accident.

As we talked, a sharp pain exploded across the back of my neck.

'I'm not sure which one it is, Theresa,' I said, 'but the back of my neck hurts.'

'That's my son,' she said quickly.

'Well, he was the one who was killed,' I said as the pain subsided. I asked him for his last impressions. 'I'm falling,' he said, 'and then there's a pain in my neck and nothing else.'

23

'Yes, that's right,' whispered Theresa. 'He fell from some scaffolding and broke his neck.'

As she spoke I had a fleeting impression of a vivid young face suddenly pressed against hers and her son's arms went round her neck in a quick hug. Theresa was very dark but her son was fair, almost blond, with bright unusually blue eyes. His name was Gary. It was nine years since he'd passed and he wanted to give his love to his father, Tony, and his brother Kevin.

'Mummy could look at me, you know, after it happened,' he explained, going back to the accident, 'because my face wasn't even marked.'

His father seemed to be particularly on his mind. 'I'm very proud of my dad,' he said, 'but he finds it hard to talk about me.'

Theresa agreed this was true, but Gary kept returning to it. 'My mum and dad didn't talk to each other for a long time.'

I hesitated. 'Should you be telling me this, Gary?' I asked.

He seemed to think he should.

'Well, what does he mean, Theresa?' I asked. 'Does he mean you didn't talk about him to each other?'

'Yes,' said Theresa. 'We still don't.'

The whole story came out. Since Gary's accident they hadn't mentioned his name, spoken of him, looked at his picture or displayed a photograph in the house. A stranger would never know they'd ever had another son apart from Kevin. It was one of the saddest things I'd ever heard. I didn't know whether to feel more sorry for Gary or for Theresa and her husband.

'Look, love, you're hurting Gary,' I explained gently. 'He's still your son. He still comes to your home and he thinks of himself as one of the family. But you're shutting him out. When small children go over they are brought

24

back by their relatives to visit their parents and they are hurt if it seems the parents don't want to know them any more. You can't just close the door and think if we don't talk about him it'll be as if it never happened. It doesn't work like that. You've borne your grief individually, you've never had a good cry on each other's shoulders, but it would help you so much if you could share it.'

'But it hurts to talk about him,' Theresa sobbed.

'Yes, but you're hurting Gary too, and I know you wouldn't have him hurt for the world. Get his picture out, no matter what Tony says. It will help. My son John Michael will be thirty-eight years old this year but every night before I go to bed I say "Goodnight, God bless you," and first thing in the morning when I come out of the bedroom I go to his picture and say "Morning, my love. How's all the crowd?" I miss him still, of course I do, and there are times when I say "If only . . ." but I can enjoy my life because I know he's all right and I'll see him again one day.'

I wasn't just saying this to cheer Theresa. It is quite true. To this day whenever I feel down and I get into one of my "If only . . ." moods, a great sense of peace and love will suddenly flood over me and I know that, although I can't see him, John Michael has come to reassure me that he's there.

I wasn't sure how much of this advice Theresa could take in in one go but I felt it was very important to try. I couldn't bear the thought of poor Gary going backwards and forwards for nine years to see his parents, only to find they'd shut him out.

I'm glad to say it obviously struck Theresa in the same light. Soon after the sitting I received a letter from her.

'When I got home from seeing you,' she wrote, 'for the first time in nine years, Tony and I were able to sit down and talk about Gary and get out his photographs . . .'

So, if I do nothing else this year, I know I've done something worthwhile . . .

I remember so well, the day I had proof that John Michael still lived, a load was lifted off my back.

If I had had £10,000 to give the medium who told me, it would not have been enough. There just is not enough money in the world to pay for that wonderful joy and truth. It's given through God's love so it is beyond price.

CHAPTER 2

I was standing in a house I'd never seen before. There was a bright, well-furnished living-room with a bay window at one end and a view of the garden at the other, but it was the fireplace that drew my attention.

On the wall beside the chimney breast was a large picture of a striking young girl with shoulder-length brown hair and wide expressive eyes with the hint of a smile in their depths. It was those eyes that held me. There was something oddly compelling about them. It was only a picture yet, no matter where you went in the room, when you glanced up those eyes seemed to be looking straight at you. You had the strangest feeling that when you turned your back, the expression on the girl's face changed and that if only you could spin round quickly enough, you'd catch it before it froze into its painted smile once more.

'It's me, isn't it, Doris? D'you like it?' said a voice beside my ear and I realized that Gail Kinchin was proudly showing me the portrait that now hung in her parents' living-room. The portrait that had been painted after her tragic death.

I gazed at it a moment longer, then the scene shifted and crumbled before my eyes, and I was back in my own flat with Gail's mother Josie sitting opposite me. But Gail was still there.

'It's true about my eyes,' she added. 'Mum says they follow her round and they do.'

Josie confirmed that ever since she'd hung the picture she'd noticed this. She had noticed other strange things as well. One evening when she moved Gail's photograph

27

away from the flower that stood in a vase beside it, the flower promptly wilted.

'It was the weirdest thing,' said Josie. 'I moved the photo on to the chair beside me and a couple of minutes later my husband said, "Look at that flower!" And it had drooped right over. Just out of interest I moved the photo back and after a minute or two the flower recovered.'

It was clear that Gail still took a lively interest in her family and wanted them to know that she wasn't far away. She had even appeared a couple of times.

'I haven't seen her,' said Josie sadly. 'I wish I had but on the day before the funeral her friend told me, "Gail's been to me." And I said, "What?" It sounded so peculiar, but she insisted she wasn't imagining things. "She's crying lots and lots of tears," she said, "because you are all remembering her but not the baby."

'And one night later her grandmother saw her. Apparently she asked, "Who's this woman who's having our dogs? You'd better tell her she'd better look after them properly." '

I was not surprised that Gail was so concerned for her family when I realized who she was and the horrifying circumstances of her death. The name had sounded vaguely familiar and, as the sitting progressed, I realized she was the girl who had been accidentally shot by the police a couple of years ago when her boyfriend used her as a human shield during a raid on his flat.

Many people will remember the case but know little of the events that led up to the nightmare. It was only when Josie told me the whole story after the sitting that I understood why Gail wanted to contact her mother so badly.

'Gail was a real tomboy,' said Josie. 'She was never bothered with the lads. She liked to come out in the evening with her stepfather and me, she was record mad

28

and she loved kids. She and her friend used to go baby-sitting and after a while Gail started baby-sitting for a couple who lived across the road. They had a little boy she was very fond of.'

The arrangement had been going on for some weeks when Josie began to feel uneasy. She discovered the couple weren't married and although she had nothing against David Pagett to start with her husband, Jim, had never liked him and she began to feel the same way.

'He was very smooth and a good talker and at first, when you had no reason to suspect otherwise, you believed what he said,' Josie went on, 'but after a while I realized it was all talk. He couldn't be trusted to tell the truth. The trouble was Gail, being so much younger, only sixteen, and more impressionable, was very vulnerable. She'd never had a proper boyfriend before, she had no experience of men and I suppose, in her eyes, he was wonderful.'

By the time Josie realized they were going out together secretly, it was too late. Gail was in love.

'He was twice her age and he really impressed her. He used to take her out for meals in nice restaurants and he bought her clothes. But there were also odd bruises beginning to appear on her arms. Well, of course, I didn't like it at all and I tackled Gail about it. We can both be a bit fiery. There was a row and I said, "If you don't stop seeing him you can pack your bags and go." It was just one of those things you say. I never dreamed she'd actually leave – but she did.'

David Pagett's common-law wife had walked out in disgust when she discovered the affair, leaving Pagett with their son.

'He wanted Gail to move in and look after the boy and she was quite happy to. She was very fond of them both,' said Josie. 'I couldn't stop her. I went to the police, I went

29

to the social services, but they said they couldn't do anything about it. Gail was over the age of consent and she needn't come home unless she wanted to.'

As the weeks went by it became clear that the relationship was going wrong. Neighbours told Josie of violent rows between the couple and when she saw Gail, the girl was usually bruised.

'I tried to persuade her to come home, but she never would. One day as I was going out I saw a car pull up opposite and Gail got out, crying and covered in bruises. "Why don't you come home, love?" I asked. "What's this hold he's got over you?" And she said, "You don't know what he's like, mum." And apparently on the night it happened Gail told her friend Marie that he had said, "If you go home I'll get your mum." And she really believed he would kill me if she left him.'

Despite his threats Pagett obviously still feared Josie's influence over her daughter because he suddenly moved his little family to a flat on the other side of Birmingham, well away from Gail's old home. But the contact was not broken. When Pagett was out Gail often phoned her mother and Josie, who had her own car, visited Gail whenever the coast was clear. One day, however, to her surprise, she found Pagett at home and apparently in a civil mood.

'He seemed really pleased with himself,' said Josie. ' "I think you ought to know she's pregnant," he told me. I'm quite sure he got her pregnant deliberately because he thought it would make me disown her. I must admit I was shocked but I was determined he wouldn't see it. "Good," I snapped, "because it won't be born in this hole." Later I told Gail I thought she had more sense but I wasn't really cross. How can you be angry about a new grandchild on the way?

'But I became more and more worried. Gail wasn't

going to ante-natal classes because Pagett didn't want anyone to see her bruises. One day his sister came round and said to me, "You've got to get that girl away from him. He'll kill her."

' "Gail, that baby will be born with something wrong with it," I used to plead, but still she wouldn't budge, although I knew she wasn't happy.

'Then one day she rang me and said she couldn't take any more. "Right," I said, "I'm coming to fetch you now."

' "But I can't leave, they've left me baby-sitting," she said.

"Timmy's all right, he's asleep, isn't he?" I said. "I'm getting my coat on and I'll be right over."

'I drove to the flat as fast as I could and when Gail opened the door she was shaking. She hurried to the car and I made the return journey even faster than the outward one. She was still shivering when we got indoors so I ran her a bath and as she climbed in I was shocked to see that you couldn't put a finger between the bruises that covered her body. She was black and blue all over.'

Josie hoped that now Gail was away from her boyfriend the worst was over and at first it looked as if she was right.

'He was very angry when he found out and he was on the phone every night arguing. We wouldn't let him speak to Gail and Jim, my husband, told him to keep away from the house or he'd break his neck. But Gail seemed to settle. We went out and bought everything for the baby, a cot, a bath and a carry cot, everything. She was delighted.

'Then Pagett started phoning during the day while we were at work and I'd come home to find Gail in tears. I spoke to the social worker at the hospital hoping for advice but she only said, "Why can't you compromise? Have her at home, but let her see him."

'I knew that would be a disaster but I certainly didn't want to keep Gail locked up. I encouraged her to go out with her other friends and she did. She seemed to enjoy herself.

'Then one night in June, Jim and I were going to Jim's son's and Gail and her friend were going to stay with the friend's sister. Jim and I dropped them off on our way out and thought no more about it. We must have come home just before midnight which was fairly usual. I went into the living-room to draw the curtains, Jim headed for the kitchen to put the kettle on, when the doorbell rang.

' "I'll go, love," Jim called and went out to answer it. I was just wondering who it could be at that time of night, when there was a great crash. Jim came dashing back, grabbed me and dragged me out into the garden.

' "Quick, he's got a gun!" he yelled.

'But Pagett was right behind us. I turned to see a double-barrelled shot-gun pointing straight at Jim. Without thinking, I lunged forward and wrenched the barrel upwards just as Pagett fired. There was a loud crack and the shot went through Gail's bedroom window. Furiously, Pagett swung round, knocked me down with the butt of the gun and aimed at Jim again, but this time Jim was ready. He leapt towards the garden fence which is four and a half feet high. Another shot rang out and Jim disappeared over the fence.

'There was silence. Had he been hit? Pagett seemed to think so. Was my Jim lying dead in our neighbour's garden?

'There was no time to find out. Blood was pouring from my head but Pagett dragged me up by my hair and marched me out to his car. "Right, you bastard!" he shouted. "Where's your daughter hiding?"

'I wouldn't tell him. I couldn't if I'd wanted to. My mouth was as dry as a desert. But he kept threatening to shoot me if I didn't answer. He had probably already killed Jim so I didn't doubt that he meant what he said. In the end I gave him the address of another friend of Gail's. I thought he might go there which would give me time to phone the police, but no. He pushed me into the car and took me with him.

' "It better not be the wrong flat, that's all," he snarled.

'Well, of course it was, but the girl who answered the door told him the truth. She didn't have much choice. I got another clout but I didn't mind because I thought at least the girl would have the sense to phone Gail and warn her that we were on the way.

'Well, she did, but unfortunately Gail had hysterics when she heard. Her friends told her to go and hide but she wouldn't.

' "He's got my mum! He's got my mum! He'll kill her," she kept sobbing and she refused to move.

'In the meantime Pagett was driving like a maniac and we got to the flat just as the other girl's boyfriend was arriving. Pagett called out "John!" all friendly, and when the girls opened the door to John, who they thought would be able to look after them, we were right behind him.

'Inside the flat Pagett covered us all with the gun.

' "Get over here," he ordered Gail, but she had seen my head was bleeding.

' "What have you done to my mum?"

'He hit her, knocked me in the ribs with the gun to prevent me going to her aid and threw her down the stairs. She was six months' pregnant. Then he dragged me down after her and pushed us both into the car. There wasn't much room because Gail was quite big by now, but she sat on my lap. Pagett jumped into the driver's seat, swung the car round and it was obvious he was heading back to his flat. He was driving like a lunatic and all the time he was hitting Gail in the face with his free hand. I was trying to protect her and wondering what on earth we could do. I thought if I grab the steering wheel she'll go straight through the windscreen.

'Then I looked back and saw a police car in the distance. I had no idea whether it was just a coincidence or whether they were looking for us, but Pagett saw it too.

' "I'm going to stop and you can drive," he said. Whether he thought they might be looking for a car with a man at the wheel and would be thrown off the scent if I was driving, or whether he simply wanted his hands free to shoot at them if they got too close, I didn't know, but I thought this was our chance of escape. I agreed and he stopped the car. Obediently I opened the door then I pushed Gail out as hard as I could and she ran into the street shouting for help.

' "He's got a gun! He's going to kill us!"

'Pagett was taken by surprise and, while he was off guard, I grabbed his hair and banged his head against the windscreen as hard as I could. I wanted to knock him out but it didn't even seem to hurt him. He twisted round in rage, threw me out of the car and leapt out after me with the gun in his hand.

'I was sure then that I was finished. He stood over me with the barrel of the gun inches from my head, his finger on the trigger. Then I heard Gail's voice.

' "Don't do it! Don't shoot! I'll do anything, anything you say, only please don't shoot!"

'To my surprise he hesitated, then lowered the gun and pushed Gail back into the car. The engine started and they raced away leaving me on the ground.

'I was really frantic then. I was terrified of what he

34

would do to Gail when he got her back to his flat. I jumped up and, as I stepped into the road, I saw a kid on a motor-bike coming along. The poor boy must have thought I was mad. I flagged him down, said "Follow that car!" just like they do in films, and climbed on the back. He wasn't at all happy about it but I don't think he dared disobey me.'

After a short distance Josie flagged down a passing car and they took her to the police station, then to the flat.

'The flat was surrounded by police when we got there and there was an ambulance standing by. "You'd better go in the ambulance," someone said and I thought they were worried about the wound on my head. But that obviously wasn't the idea at all. They locked me in. So that I wouldn't panic or get in the way, I suppose. For two hours I sat there chewing my nails in agony of fear and frustration. Then I heard movement outside.

' "The marksmen have arrived," said the ambulance driver cheerfully, thinking I'd be better for a progress report.

'I was horrified. "Oh, my God."

' "It's all right, they won't shoot," he reassured me but, even before he'd finished speaking, shots rang out.

'The ambulance doors opened and I burst out just in time to see Gail being carried from the flat on a stretcher. "Give me a gun and I'll kill the bastard!" I shouted as I ran to Gail. But I was crying and holding her hand and I knew I couldn't leave her.'

At the hospital, Josie was told that the baby was dead, Gail's chances of survival were slim, and that her husband, Jim, was alive but he might lose his leg. Pagett had wounded him in the thigh.

Gail died a month later. Pagett was sentenced to twelve years' imprisonment.

As Josie finished her terrible story you could have

heard a pin drop in the room. How she had kept sane these past two years I couldn't imagine. Sometimes I wonder what on earth is happening to the world, there seems to be so much violence. But at least knowing the background now helped to put the sitting into perspective. One thing that had puzzled me was the way Gail refused to talk about her boyfriend.

'Him!' she'd said emphatically, 'I don't even want to think about him.' She wouldn't even mention his name. I found that odd at the time but, after hearing Josie's story, the reason became clear. Gail loved her family very much and she was distressed at the misery David Pagett had brought them.

She had come through immediately I tuned in and I realized that she was quite a character. She was eager to communicate and very forthright.

'Isn't my mum smart?' she asked me, drawing attention to Josie's immaculate blue suit, shoes and handbag.

Gail wanted to reassure her mother she was all right. Then she said, 'I was so stupid, Doris. Can you forgive me, Mum? I'm very stubborn and the more they talk at me the more I go the other way. That was my biggest fault. My mother could see it wasn't right and she tried to take me out of it, but I wouldn't listen. Instead, my life was thrown away and he wasn't even free. I've found that out since. My mother wasn't even angered about the baby. She wanted the baby. Mum and Dad had bought me everything for my baby. Even the cot.'

Gail mentioned some family names and asked particularly to be remembered to a girl named Barbara who used to work with her.

Then she sighed and the power wavered. 'It's bloody hard work this, isn't it, Doris?'

'Yes, it is, love,' I agreed laughing. Gail clearly hadn't changed a bit. She'd never been a saint on the earth plane

36

and there was no reason to become saintly on the other side. But she was right. Communicating is difficult for spirit people, particularly the first time they try it.

'You see, I wanted to come home but he wouldn't let me,' she went on. 'He was a swine and I was the only one who couldn't see it, but I saw it that night and all I wanted to do was come home. Me and my baby. And if I had to come over why couldn't it have happened straight away? But they thought I was getting better, that was the awful part. Why couldn't I have come over with the baby? He went first and I lived on for nearly a month.'

Josie confirmed that this was right. There were more family details, then Gail told me that Josie had kept one of her rings.

Josie said this was true and spread out her fingers. She wore several rings on each hand and I wondered which one was Gail's.

'No, it's not one of those,' said Gail's voice loudly in my ear. 'She's not wearing it. There's another one and she's not got it on.'

It turned out that Josie had brought with her the cheap little 'engagement' ring Pagett had given Gail. She couldn't bring herself to wear it and on the way to see me she'd almost flung it in a rubbish bin, but at the last minute the thought struck her that it might help the communication and so she slipped it into her handbag.

Gail chattered on, describing the place where her mother worked and the health problems of one of her colleagues. Then she said, 'Give Eric a big hug for me. I miss him. I miss you all.'

I wondered who Eric could be, since Josie had said her husband's name was Jim, but it turned out that Eric and Jim were one and the same person.

'She's the only one who used to call him Eric,' Josie explained.

37

I kept hearing something about a motor-bike, too, but I couldn't make out what Gail was talking about. It was only afterwards when Josie mentioned flagging down a bike to help her follow Pagett's car that I realized Gail must have been trying to tell me something about that night.

She was very concerned about proving to her mother that she still visited the house and was interested in the family. She told me about that unusual picture on the wall, about a new baby recently born, and the birthday of her little nephew Adam. She even tried to tell me the name of the street where her mother lived but I couldn't catch it. It was just a mumble.

'Come on, Doris, think of trees,' she said in exasperation. But it was no use. 'Oak? Elm?' I tried. She laughed and shook her head.

Afterwards I discovered it was 'wood' – Brandwood. She also insisted that Josie had put something in her coffin with her but Josie denied this.

'It wouldn't have been a flower or anything, would it?' I suggested, but Josie said no. There was nothing. It was only a few weeks later that she remembered the promise she had made as Gail lay dying.

'She was unconscious and all wired up to drips and things,' said Josie. 'They said she wouldn't last much longer. I climbed on the bed beside her and took her in my arms and even though I knew she couldn't hear me I promised she wouldn't be parted from her baby. And she wasn't. When she died, I had the baby put in the coffin with her.'

It was two years since she'd passed but Gail was still worried about her mother. 'I come and see her at night,' she said, 'and I sit on the bed. She can't sleep. When she closes her eyes she sees that night all over again like a film.'

This really amazed Josie. 'Yes, that's right. When I try to sleep I can't remember nice things any more. It's just that night over and over again, every night. I see every detail in my mind just as if I'm watching a picture on a screen.'

Gail was getting tired now and her voice was fading away but, before she finished, her face, surrounded by a swinging curtain of dark hair, appeared beside her mother's and she said, 'Tell Mum I've got Daniel with me,' and in the last flash of power I had a glimpse of a beautiful toddler with bright auburn hair.

'She says she's got Daniel with her,' I told Josie, and at that she crumbled.

She hurried out of the room to compose herself but when she returned she looked a lot better.

'That's what I was waiting for, Doris,' she said. 'Only Gail and I knew that if the baby was a boy she was going to call him Daniel.'

Well, of course the baby was a boy, and though he was never born on earth, he was growing up with his mum in the spirit world and he was now a little toddler of two.

And Gail, true to her word, had named him Daniel.

CHAPTER 3

All my life I have been surrounded by children, earth children and spirit children, it makes no difference to me. The only sad thing about spirit children as far as I'm concerned is that, although I can see them, I can't cuddle them or spoil them with sweets. Apart from that they are children like other children.

A few years ago one or two parents started giving me snapshots of their little ones after they'd had a sitting with me. 'I'd like her to stay here with you and John Michael,' they'd say and naturally I would put up the pictures next to the only photograph that was ever taken of our son. Of course, as the months went on other parents would notice the pictures and that would prompt further snaps, until today I have so many photographs I've had to mount them on a special cork board and the way things are going I shall need another board very soon.

I know each of them by name, I try to remember their birthdays and, probably because I have no grandchildren of my own, I like to think of them as my spirit grandchildren. Call me daft if you like, I don't care. They are individuals to me, they have been to my flat to talk and, if they have a message for their parents, they know they can come back and mention it to me whenever they like and I will pass it on.

I try to give them fresh flowers every week, at Christmas I put a tiny tinsel Christmas tree on the shelf for them and when I'm going away I tell them, 'I won't be seeing you for a few days. I'm going to Manchester (or wherever) so I won't see you unless you'd like to come with me.'

And this book is for them, that's why it's called *Innocent Voices In My Ear*. Oh, I know some of them get into bad ways and do silly things that they regret afterwards, but underneath they're still innocent children. There's little Robert who had a tumour on the brain, two-year-old Martin Vosper who was killed by falling scaffolding, baby Oliver Thomas who was shaken so violently he died of brain damage, there's Lilian who made a mistake trying to frighten her parents, there's Careen who took her own life, her sister Charmain who died in a road accident, there's Paul who was killed in a motor-cycle crash and Sandy and Mark and Jonathan and, well, I could go on and on. The important thing is that they're all innocent children growing up strong and happy in the spirit world.

What strikes you forcibly when you look at my kids, and visitors often remark on it, is how beautiful they are. Every single one of them is the sort of child you'd notice in a crowd.

'It's always the best ones who die young,' these visitors often add, and unconsciously I think they have hit on the truth.

Time and time again I hear bereaved parents saying the same things. If they've lost a baby it was no ordinary baby. It never cried, it was no trouble, it would go to anyone, it was unusually forward. Older children are always described as being particularly bright, full of life and somehow extra-lovable. The teenagers are always the kind, unselfish ones who attract friends wherever they go. No one pretends these children were angels, they all had their bad moments, but every parent will say that the child who died was special and somehow unlike the other children in the family.

Now, of course I realize that in these circumstances parents are naturally biased, but often their view is confirmed by people outside the family and it's more than coincidence to hear the identical characteristics attributed to children who have nothing else in common except an early death.

Every time I look at my kids I'm reminded of this and I've come to the conclusion that they are God's special children. They are old souls who don't need to spend much time on earth. They have their useful purpose to fulfil and when they've done their job they have to return to the spirit world. I like to think that the parents of these children, and I'm one of them, have been specially chosen for the task and that we should be thankful that we were allowed to have them, if only for a little while.

I mustn't give the impression that my sitting-room is open *only* to spirit children. There are photographs of living children dotted about all over the place, too, and I've known some pretty special earth children over the years.

As a child, I dreamed of a nursing career but, after my father died, my mother couldn't afford to let me stay on at school and my education wasn't good enough for medicine. Instead, I worked for a time as a ward maid in a large hospital but it wasn't the same. Mother wanted me home and I decided that if I couldn't be a nurse I wanted to be a children's nanny.

Unfortunately, even that seemed impossible. It was a responsible position and you needed experience. How a girl of fourteen going on fifteen gained the necessary experience I had no idea. Neither had Mother but, in her practical way, she told me to put such notions out of my head and get on with the work I *could* do. I was a strong healthy girl, so I was sent to various houses in Grantham to act as a general dogsbody.

In her heart of hearts, though, Mother must have felt this wasn't good enough because, after only a few months, she was not only prepared to listen to an alternative, she actually allowed it.

One day the relative of a neighbour of ours, Mrs Anthony, came to see her. Mrs Anthony had just accepted the position of housekeeper in a household in Bournemouth and she was looking for a maid to take with her.

'Now, your Doris is just the sort of girl I'm looking for,' she told Mother. 'She's wasted here. In Bournemouth she would be working in a properly run household, she'd wear a uniform and she'd learn how to conduct herself. She'd become a properly trained maid. With that experience behind her she could go anywhere.'

Mother was impressed, but *Bournemouth*? It seemed like the other side of the world. She didn't think she could let me go so far away. After all I was only fifteen.

Here Mrs Anthony played her trump card. 'But Doris is a sensible girl, very grown up for her age,' she said. 'And, besides, I would be with her. I would take care of her.'

The next thing I knew I was off to Bournemouth. I was very excited. There were two new uniforms in my case, a print dress for the mornings and a black dress with a little white apron and cap for the afternoons. I wasn't quite sure why you had to change twice in one day but Mrs Anthony assured me that it was the right thing to do.

'They do things properly in Bournemouth,' she said. 'It's a very genteel place.'

I took that to mean posh and was even more excited.

As the steam train chugged away the miles to the south coast I tried very hard not to wriggle in my seat. Mrs Anthony had said I was very grown up for my age and I was determined not to let her down.

'Now, you just behave yourself for Mrs Anthony, our Doris,' Mother had said as I left, 'or she'll send you home.'

43

I didn't want to go home. I was going to live by the sea in Bournemouth in a grand house owned by posh people and in a year or two I was bound to work my way up to the position of nanny. Such things happened, I was sure of it.

I don't know what I'd been expecting – some sort of stately home perhaps – but at the first sight of the house my hopes came crashing down. It was a dark gloomy place and the sea could have been fifty miles away for all you could see of it. Across the road was a forest of brooding pine trees and the pungent scent seemed to fill your nostrils wherever you went. At night, as I lay in my tiny attic bedroom, I could hear the wind tearing through the tree tops and the branches creaking, and when the gales blew in from the sea I was sure I'd wake up to find a fallen pine completely blocking the street.

One day in my new job was enough to convince me that my dreams of working my way up to nanny were hopeless. The master and mistress, a colonel and his lady home from India, seemed pretty old to me and, besides that, the mistress spent all her time in bed. She was an invalid, Mrs Anthony explained. I don't know what was wrong with her but she had a private nurse living in and it was quite obvious that there would be no babies.

I did have a small charge to look after, however – the family parrot. I'd never seen a parrot before, outside picture books that is, and when they introduced me to Christopher I was charmed. He was a magnificent bird with brilliant turquoise feathers splashed with yellow and green. All day long he sat on a perch in the mistress' bedroom, grumbling to himself or preening for visitors, and to look at, he was wonderful.

It was when they explained my duties regarding Christopher that I became apprehensive. Christopher did not spend the night upstairs. At bedtime I was to carry him down to the conservatory and say 'Do your duty, Christopher' before leaving him for the night amongst the potted palms. The next morning I had to carry him back upstairs to his mistress.

It sounded simple enough. But that first night as I approached the perch I noticed what a malicious glint he had in his hard little eyes and how wicked and sharp that cruel curved beak looked. Gingerly, I put out my hand and lifted the perch. There was a loud screech and, quick as a flash, Christopher twisted round to peck my fingers.

Frightened, I dropped the perch.

There was a gentle murmur from across the room. 'It's all right, he won't hurt you. Be firm with him.'

I gritted my teeth and tried again. The same thing happened.

'Now, do hurry up, dear,' said the mistress, sighing. 'He can't stay here all night.'

I scowled at the parrot and the parrot scowled back. It was no use. I had to get him to the conservatory even if I was bitten to death in the process. I took a deep breath, seized the perch, and raced for the door before I could change my mind. All the way down the back stairs (servants weren't allowed to use the front ones) he squawked, flapped and nipped at my hand in protest, but we reached the conservatory intact.

'Right, do your duty, Christopher!' I hissed from a safe distance and banged the door on him.

It was the beginning of a twice-daily battle. I was scared to death of that parrot and I can only assume the parrot was scared to death of going up and down stairs.

My other duties were easier but not much fun. I got up at six o'clock and cleaned all the grates and lit all the fires before the rest of the household rose. Then I was on call for cleaning and polishing and helping Cook with the vegetables, and at tea time I took a tray up to the mistress.

All the time I was learning how to behave properly and trying to carry out the instructions of Mrs Anthony.

I didn't always succeed. One afternoon I was hurrying down the back stairs with the tea tray when the heel came off my shoe. I slipped, the tray flew out of my hands and the china tea things went crashing to the bottom and smashed to pieces on the hall floor.

The silence that followed was awe-inspiring but not long-lasting. Mrs Anthony came running down the passage.

'Doris, whatever have you done?' Then she saw the broken china. 'Oh, you clumsy girl.'

I came limping down the rest of the stairs. 'The heel came off my shoe,' I explained, holding out the culprit, but Mrs Anthony was already on her knees collecting pieces of china.

'Come on, get this cleared up before the mistress wonders what's going on.'

But Mrs Anthony wasn't really cross and I soon discovered why. A little later she called me to her.

'Well, Doris, I must say goodbye,' she said briskly.

My mouth fell open. 'Why, are you going out?'

'No, I'm taking up a new position.'

'A *new* position?' I gasped. 'But what about this one? What about me?'

'You?' She looked surprised. 'Well, you're doing very nicely, dear. As long as you don't have too many accidents like this afternoon's I'm sure the mistress will be well satisfied with you. Just try to remember the things I've taught you.' And with that she went off to pack her things, leaving me speechless.

It didn't stop there. Soon after Mrs Anthony's departure, the cook stopped coming, so I had to cook dinner as well. Luckily, the private nurse was sympathetic.

'You ought to get out more, Doris,' she said, and when

I explained that I'd like to but I had nowhere to go, she mentioned a girls' club nearby.

The discovery of the club transformed my stay in Bournemouth. It was a noisy, friendly place, full of girls my own age, and we made our own entertainment with a round of fancy dress parties, concerts and amateur dramatics.

It was through the club that I moved on to my next job. The woman who ran the place was concerned when she found out about my life. She knew I had to work very hard in that depleted household and she said, 'I don't think it's good for Doris to be there. There's nobody young for her to talk to.' So concerned was she that she helped me find another place.

My dreams of working up to nanny flooded back but, once again, I was out of luck. There was less work in my new job but no chance of children. The mistress was an old lady who was stone deaf and the house was run by her much younger companion, an arty type, tall and very thin with a fluting voice and long, trailing chiffon scarves.

The companion was kind but rather eccentric. She played the piano and she liked to pretend the house belonged to her. In the evenings after she'd got the old lady to bed she used to say to me: 'Go to bed, Doris. I'll bring your supper up.' And she would bring me supper on a tray in bed, purely so that she could have the house to herself.

I didn't mind because, if I wasn't going out, I was happy to read in bed, and if I *was* going out the companion didn't mind because she had the house to herself anyway. We got along quite well and, being arty, she took an interest in the theatrical projects of the club. She even helped me make my fancy dress costumes.

After that uneasy start I found I was enjoying Bournemouth very much and I was quite settled when the letter

47

from Mother came. Poor Mother, she could never make up her mind what to do with me. She would send me away to a distant job with what she considered to be good prospects only to find she was lonely without me and wanted me back again. This happened several times and it happened in Bournemouth. I was needed at home, she wrote, she enclosed the fare and I was to come back as soon as I could.

Reluctantly I said goodbye to my new friends and headed north. I wasn't very happy. It seemed I was back where I started when Mrs Anthony had called on Mother. I was no nearer achieving my ambitions. Or so I thought.

Oddly enough as it turned out, I was closer than I'd ever been.

Mother had found me a job at a place called Harrowby Hall. I'm not quite sure what it was, possibly some sort of government training scheme, but there were men from all over the country staying there and this meant an enormous amount of cooking. I was to help the cook as kitchen maid. The potato peeling, vegetable chopping and washing up seemed endless, but people often dropped in for a chat and the hours passed quite quickly.

A local man called Commander Pesani was a frequent caller and one day I heard him talking to the housekeeper.

'So we're desperate for somebody who loves children to come and help out,' he was saying.

The housekeeper nodded sympathetically, then she caught sight of me. 'It's a pity we can't do without Doris,' she said. 'She adores children.'

'Yes, I do,' I added wistfully and, as I walked away, I felt the Commander's eyes on my back.

Later that day as I was taking some rubbish out to the bins I was surprised to see that Commander Pesani hadn't left. He walked quickly across the courtyard.

'Do you really love children?'

'Oh yes, more than anything.'

'And do you think you would like to help out in our nursery?'

I nodded.

'Well, look, come and see Mrs Pesani next week and we'll see what can be arranged.' Quickly, he handed me his card and then hurried away as if afraid the house-keeper would catch him.

And that's how my happy days at The Red House in Melton Mowbray began. The Red House was a large red brick building set in beautiful grounds and when I went to see Mrs Pesani she explained that they were looking for a nurserymaid to assist their nanny. There were three children, Vivienne (five), John (four) and baby Patrick, and they wanted someone to live in, in a room close to the night nursery. It sounded marvellous to me and I was sure I could get Mother to agree. After all, compared with Bournemouth, Melton Mowbray was just down the road.

Once again I was fitted out with a smart uniform, a brown dress trimmed in cream with a cream apron, and I set off eagerly to my new life.

Nanny was rather forbidding at first: a thin, prim woman in a smart uniform with a veil down the back of her hat. She was very strict, she told me, and didn't stand any nonsense.

'And I won't allow spoiling in my nursery,' she added sternly, obviously suspecting a weakness in that direction. Rightly, as it turned out.

The children were lovely. Vivienne was a pretty girl with dark, almost black, hair and eyes, John was slim and sensitive-looking with soft wavy hair, while Patrick was a fat, good-tempered baby, a lazy child who would sooner laugh than cry.

The two boys slept in the night nursery, Nanny slept in

the room next door, Vivienne in a room on the same landing, and my room was just down the corridor. The day nursery was downstairs and had its own little kitchen and the children's toys – and they had just about every toy imaginable – were kept in an outhouse in the grounds.

The children visited their parents once a week for lunch on Sundays and they said goodnight to them at bedtime. They also saw their mother on Nanny's day off when she helped me bathe them. Apart from that they spent their time with Nanny and me.

My duties were fairly simple. After Christopher the parrot, I reckoned I could cope with most things. I cleaned the nursery, made the beds and mended clothes. I also cooked light meals. Food in the nursery was very plain. The children always had to eat their bread and butter before they were allowed anything more exotic and they only had fancy cakes on birthdays. There was a lot of Marmite on toast and boiled eggs with soldiers and sometimes if they'd had a light tea they were allowed milk and a plain biscuit which was a great treat. Their teeth were absolutely perfect and they had beautiful skins as a result of this diet.

As Nanny had instinctively known, I was a spoiler. If the baby was crying I couldn't resist going to see what was wrong with him. 'What's the matter, darling?' I'd ask, despite Nanny's warnings that he only did it to get attention. And sometimes when the children came out all warm and pink from their baths I'd let them come down to the day nursery in their dressing gowns and give them a biscuit. Of course if Nanny found out I got my head in a sling.

'Dose, will you *not* do that,' she'd say, folding her lips into a thin line.

They all called me Dose. I managed to get through my chores each day so that I had a lot of time left for playing with the children. I used to crawl around the floor with them like a big kid myself. I would get down on all fours so they could ride on my back or we would play hospitals and they would bandage me until I looked like the Invisible Man. They were also very fond of playing shops and I let them take the food out of the pantry and arrange it on the table in front of whoever was shopkeeper. Then we set up a little bell for the customer to ring as he came through the 'door' to make his purchase.

John took this game very seriously as I discovered later when I took him to the children's harvest festival service at the church.

John had never been to a proper church service before and he watched in fascination as the vicar, followed by the choir boys, walked in procession towards the altar. His eyes grew rounder and rounder and when the vicar climbed up into the pulpit his mouth dropped open. Silence fell over the congregation. The vicar took a deep breath and was just about to start the service when a clear piping voice which carried beautifully through the old stone building said, 'Oh, Dosey, isn't the vicar *rude*! He's got up there with his feeder on!'

Heads turned, there were stifled giggles, and the vicar didn't look too amused. Blushing scarlet, I shushed John and with a sour little smile the vicar opened the service. But John hadn't finished with the vicar yet.

The children's harvest festival was a pretty affair. The church was filled with flowers, and small children clutching baskets of fruit and vegetables packed the aisles. The highlight of the service came when the children filed to the altar to present their offerings to the vicar.

I explained all this to Vivienne and John, adding, 'And afterwards the offerings are taken to the hospital for the sick people to enjoy.'

They seemed to understand and, when the moment

51

came, Vivienne, being the eldest, went first. She used to go to dancing classes and, inspired by her last lesson, she handed over her basket with a charming little curtsey. Everyone smiled and there were murmurs of 'Dear little girl!' I swelled with pride. That was *my* little girl they were talking about. Then came John. He strode towards the vicar, thrust out his basket and then stood there with his legs apart, hands behind his back like a miniature version of his father. The vicar looked a bit puzzled and said something to him but John didn't move.

'John!' I called softly. 'John!'

He didn't budge.

'John. Come back to Dose, John!'

'But he hasn't given me any shillings for it yet,' John wailed for all to hear.

As he knew very well from our games of shop, when a customer was given a basket of food, the shopkeeper was given a handful of 'shillings' in return.

They were well-behaved children generally but, like all children, they loved a joke. Nanny was a bit strict and they weren't sure how she would react to their fun, but the minute her back was turned they were up to their pranks with me.

There was a little table with matching chairs in the nursery kitchen and the seats came out of the chairs for easy cleaning. One of the children's favourite tricks was to remove the seats from my chair and then call me for 'tea'.

'Dose, tea's ready!' they'd call and I would come in and say:

'Where am I to sit?'

Bursting with laughter they'd pull out a chair, spluttering, 'Sit here, Dose, sit here!'

And of course, pretending not to notice the missing seat, I'd sit down and my bottom would go right through.

52

They found this so funny they'd roll about on the floor laughing and laughing. But one day this harmless game almost got us into trouble. I went straight through the chair in the normal way, but this time, being rather plump and perhaps sitting down more heavily than usual, I got stuck. Try as I would, I couldn't get out and when I stood up the chair came with me.

The children found this hysterically funny.

'Come on, you've got to help,' I told them. 'Push, push Dose's bottom.'

Well, they tried but they were laughing so much they didn't do any good and I found I was laughing, too. It seemed to get funnier and funnier and in the end we made so much noise Mrs Pesani came in to see what was going on.

She stood in the doorway, looking from the hysterical children rolling on the floor to me with my behind stuck through the chair, and for one awful moment I thought she was going to explode with anger.

Then her lips started to twitch and she began to laugh.

'You look as if you need some help, Dose.'

I breathed a sigh of relief. It was all right, she wouldn't tell Nanny. I would be in trouble if she did that.

No, the children were rarely naughty but they often got themselves into trouble with Nanny for thoughtless behaviour, particularly if it involved getting dirty.

One afternoon they were going to a party and we'd got them washed and changed and ready to go and Nanny sent them down to wait in the garden while she prepared herself.

I was racing round collecting up the discarded clothes and tidying the nursery before we left, because Nanny couldn't bear to walk out on a disorderly nursery, when something made me go to the window. It was too quiet, I suppose, and I was wondering what they were getting up to. I don't know what I'd expected to see: Vivienne sitting on the grass in her party dress perhaps, or John making mud pies. But the reality was worse than I'd imagined.

There was John with a rusty old kettle in his hand, which he'd obviously filled with pebbles from the drive, standing on tiptoe pouring a stream of little stones on to baby Patrick's head.

Patrick, cheerful as ever, didn't seem to mind. He just sat in his pram smiling away as the pebbles piled up on his clean new bonnet, which by now would be filthy, to say nothing of the condition of John's hands and trousers.

Horrified, I threw open the window.

'John, what *do* you think you're doing?'

Startled, he looked up at me and then down at his brother as if noticing him for the first time. Then he patted him on the head, scattering pebbles all over the pram.

'I'm sorry, but I thought you were the tea-pot, darling!' he said.

How could I be cross? I rushed downstairs with a new bonnet for Patrick and a damp cloth to wipe John's hands, but I couldn't scold him.

John was probably the most imaginative of the three and it was difficult to keep up with him at times. He had a topsy-turvy way of looking at things which was quite logical, as long as you understood his logic.

The Pesanis rented a seaside house in Clacton for a month in the summer and one year, after a glorious holiday on the shore, John, Vivienne and I were driving home with the luggage. It was quite late at night, the sky was dark and the moon was hazy with mist the way it is when it's going to rain.

The children were quiet in the back and I was just thinking they must be asleep when John spoke.

'Look, Viv,' he said, 'there's God in bed.'

Vivienne peered out of the window.

'Don't be stupid,' she said scornfully, 'I can't see God in bed.'

'Dosey, you can see God in bed, can't you?' he appealed to me.

I looked out but, much as I would have liked to, I couldn't see a thing that in any way resembled God in bed.

'No, I'm afraid I can't, John,' I admitted.

Impatiently, John craned his head out of the window and looked up at the moon.

'You are stupid,' he said in disgust. 'Can't you see his bedside light?'

Most children are psychic until the ages of eleven or twelve when the world intrudes, and I looked for signs of it in my young charges. At the time, of course, I didn't know the word to describe the quality I was looking for, and I didn't realize how common it was. I only remembered that when I was about Vivienne's and John's age I had several playmates nobody else could see and I half expected Vivienne and John to have some.

If they did, they never mentioned them to me and never gave any sign that there was more going on in the nursery than Nanny and I were aware of. At the time I decided that this was further proof of my own 'peculiarity'. It was years later that I realized Vivienne and John had no need of spirit friends because they had each other and were never lonely. Invisible friends tend to turn up to play with solitary children, particularly children who have lost a brother or sister.

I was alone a lot as a child and my mother had almost died as a result of a fallopian pregnancy, so I did have a spirit brother or sister growing up on the other side. Our adopted son Terry was in a similar position.

He was an 'only' child to us because we'd lost John Michael and all my subsequent pregnancies ended in miscarriage. As a small boy Terry spent a lot of time on his own, except he wasn't alone. Often when he was playing in his room I'd hear all kinds of thumps and bumps through the wall, sounding for all the world like two boisterous boys having a game. Over the top of it would come Terry's voice:

'Give that to me, John Michael. You played with that yesterday.'

In the summer he spent long hours on the lawn with the toy sword John had made for his 'sword fighting'. He was quite alone, yet if you watched him for a moment or two you realized he wasn't alone. He was aiming blows and receiving blows and concentrating on a fixed spot, just as if he was fighting another boy who could not be seen by us.

I was always very careful not to make a fuss about this or behave as if I thought it was in any way unusual. I knew what I had gone through as a child, forever nagged and hounded for being 'strange', and I was determined Terry shouldn't suffer in the same way. After all there's nothing odd about it, it's perfectly natural.

I was reminded of this when a neighbour in Grantham mentioned that she was having similar problems with her small daughter.

'My mother-in-law says I must do something about Claire,' she sighed. 'She says it's not natural.'

'What's the matter with Claire? She looks perfectly well to me,' I said, for Claire was a picture of glowing health, an apparently happy, well-balanced little girl.

'Yes, but she's got this friend called Roger,' said her mother.

'Oh, and where does Roger live?'

'That's just it. Roger doesn't live anywhere. He's an invisible Roger.'

It all became clear. 'Oh, one of those.'

She looked put out. 'What d'you mean, one of those?'

'One of the spirit children,' I explained. 'Have you ever lost a baby?'

'No,' she said. 'Never.'

'Well, did you ever have a miscarriage?'

She thought for a moment. 'Yes, I did, at four months.'

'Don't you think it's possible that this could be her brother and she can see him and you can't?' I asked.

She stared at me for a moment as if unable to make up her mind whether I was serious or not.

'Well, you must admit it's pretty far-fetched.' Then she stopped. 'Yet, you know, he seems so real to Claire, I almost think she can see him.'

'Anyway, the child is happy,' I said. 'She's obviously in good health. It's not doing her any harm, so does it matter?'

'Yes, you're quite right,' she said. 'I'll tell my mother-in-law to mind her own business.'

And she did. Before they knew it they were accepting Roger as part of the family even though they couldn't see him. When they were going out in the car, Claire would be strapped in her seat and then she'd say, 'Make room for Roger,' and even her daddy would stand back to let Roger climb in beside her. There were practical advantages, too. Before Roger had come along Claire had been afraid to go upstairs in the dark on her own, but now Roger held her hand and she went upstairs quite happily.

I happened to be there one evening at bedtime when this was going on.

'I'd better come up with you, Claire,' said her mother.

'No,' said Claire, 'I'm a big girl now, I can go up on my own.'

'But I'll have to switch out the light when you're in bed,' said her mother. 'You can't reach.'

'It's all right, Roger will do it,' said Claire confidently.

Her mother turned to me in exasperation.

'You see what I mean?'

'Well, never mind, let her be,' I said. 'You can go up and turn it off when she's asleep.'

So we stood at the bottom of the stairs and watched Claire go up. She went into her bedroom, chatting to Roger. She climbed into bed and lay down. And as we stood watching at the foot of the stairs, there was a loud click, and the light went off.

The sequel to this story came years later. On a return visit to Grantham I happened to bump into Claire, now grown up with children of her own.

We chatted for a while then I said:

'Claire, do you remember anything about when you were a little girl?'

She seemed to know what I was getting at.

'About Roger, you mean?'

'Oh, you remember Roger, do you?' I asked.

'Oh yes,' said Claire. 'He was real, you know. I wasn't making him up like everybody thought. It was lovely to have him around. Whenever I was scared I used to say, "Hold my hand, Roger", and he would take my hand and I felt better right away.'

'When did you stop seeing him?'

'I think it must have been when I was about eleven or twelve,' said Claire. 'It wasn't a sudden break. My life became busier and then one day I realized I hadn't seen Roger for a while. I've not seen him since.'

So the world intruded on Claire and Roger when she was twelve years old. But she will see him again one day. When she finally makes the trip to the other side, Roger will be waiting for her, along with her other friends and relatives.

CHAPTER 4

It was a miserable day. Outside the window the clouds were piled up, grey on grey as far as the eye could see, and the wind whistled through the tower blocks. There were bright flowers on the window-sill and a line of cheerful get-well cards on the table, but today they couldn't lift my spirits.

I was in hospital *again* and it was really getting beyond a joke.

'Surely I've had more than my fair share of ill health,' I grumbled to the spirit world. 'I mean, this is quite ridiculous. I'm either working or ill.'

There was no answer. So they can't even be bothered to reply, I thought crossly.

It was adhesions, or so they said, that had landed me in hospital this time. I needed an operation because of all the other operations I'd had. It sounds crazy, I know, but they assured me it was true. Scar tissue had built up inside my body from past operations and had attached itself to my liver, causing severe pain. In a tricky, time-consuming operation, the surgeon would have to patiently snip it all away and I wasn't looking forward to it one bit.

'Sometimes,' I said out loud to the spirit world, 'I think you've forgotten me.'

There was complete silence from the other side but an unmistakably earth-bound knocking at the door startled me out of my thoughts.

'Come in,' I sighed.

'Hello, Doris,' said my lovely young nurse. 'Here's some more mail for you.'

And she dropped a large envelope on the bed. If the

spirit world had forgotten me it was clear my many friends on this side had not. I was touched by the constant stream of cards, flowers and telephone messages that poured into the hospital, even Michael Aspel sent good wishes over the air during his radio show.

Today, however, in my self-pitying mood even this display of kindness couldn't cheer me. I couldn't be bothered to open another envelope. I haven't got the energy, I was telling myself dramatically, when I noticed that the address was written in the large rounded hand of a child.

Instantly I melted. I hadn't sunk so low that I could disappoint a child, had I?

I ripped open the envelope and pulled out a large red poster, covered with home-made get-well cards and illustrated poems by Katy Beckinsale, eight-year-old daughter of the actor, the late Richard Beckinsale, and her friend Amber.

'To Dear Doris, We hope you will get better,
There's not a lot to say,
We know you can get better,
Tomorrow or today.

Love Katy.'

That was the main card, beautifully coloured in red and green. Next to it on a frilly-edged sheet patterned by a small pair of scissors and decorated with red hearts, Amber had written her poem.

'Oh dear Doris, PLEASE
Call upon my Nanny so fair, her beautiful blue eyes
and fleecy white hair,
also my grandad so brave, I hope up in Heaven he
doesn't look so grave,

61

PLEASE call upon my horses so fair their manes and
    tails is as soft as human hair,
Also my Aunty Lidia who I have never seen,
But I have heard her face is like a moon beam,
And so is yours.

                    With love,
                 Amber XXXXXXXXXX'

Next to it, Katy, who had obviously read my first book,
had stuck her poem, lavishly illustrated in pink, lavender
and purple.

'Your baby doth lieth in Heaven, his violet eyes look
    down each day,
And in your head of love and tenderness, his heavenly
    voice seems to say,
Mother I wish thee well, and Father and Terry as well,
    Mother please don't be sad, I have only received my
    PROMOTION.'

And as I read these words the tears poured down my
face. The spirit world had not forgotten me, but it took
an eight-year-old child to remind me of the truth.

I first met Katy when her mother Judy came to me for
a sitting. She had seen me on the Russell Harty Show and
wrote to Russell asking if he could put her in touch with
me.

I was a great fan of poor Richard's. I used to laugh and
laugh at his television shows, but I knew nothing at all
about his private life and I was very surprised to find he
had a daughter of Katy's age. Surely he wasn't old
enough?

He assured me he was and there were other surprises
as well. Far from being a jolly, jokey type, he was in fact
very sensitive and concerned. During his lifetime he said

he used to think he was a natural pessimist. He was very sorry to leave his wife, the actress Judy Loe, behind and I could see why. Judy was a beautiful girl and very brave. She smiled and laughed, yet deep down in her eyes the loss was there, even though several years had gone by since Richard passed.

Richard was a very good communicator and he came through easily but he was very sad at first.

'I was so frightened,' he said. 'There was always this great fear, not only the night I passed but before. I thought I was a natural doomsday boy, a real pessimist, but I realize now I must have known.'

The night he fell ill, Judy was in hospital. They wanted another child and she would need an operation to make it possible.

'I was very frightened that night,' said Richard. 'Then I started getting pains in my left arm and in my chest. I rang some friends and they said feel your pulse, but I didn't know what it should have been.'

Later that night he had a heart attack. He was very sad as he talked of those last hours and Judy confirmed that the facts were correct. What's more, later on when she was sorting out his things, she came across several poems and writings that seemed to show that he knew he wouldn't have long to live. She was so moved when she read them that she collected them together and had them published. One short piece seemed to say it all:

Baby girl widow please take care of my children.
Baby girl widow will make my dreams come true.

When he wrote those words nobody suspected, least of all Richard, that there was something wrong with his heart.

As the sitting went on, however, Richard cheered up. He sent his love to his Judy Sunshine as he called her.

'Judy was my life,' he said. 'Judy and Kate. My only regret is that I couldn't talk to Judy about my fear. I couldn't make her understand.'

Then he mentioned a girl called Sammy, his daughter by his first wife.

'But, my dear, you're not old enough!' I said in surprise, and he laughed.

'Oh yes, I am. But I was very young when I married and it didn't work.'

He wanted particularly to thank Judy.

'Judy, bless her heart, took my daughter into her heart as well as into our home,' he said, 'and Katy is her sister. I'm only sorry I only had two years to know my daughter Samantha properly.'

As he spoke I suddenly saw him quite clearly beside Judy. I'd always had a mental picture of Richard as he was in *Rising Damp* but he looked different now. His face had filled out, his dark hair was much shorter and those deep shadows had gone from under his eyes.

He sent his love to Ronnie Barker, 'my dearest friend' he called him. He mentioned Katy's birthday and he wanted Judy to be happy.

'Walk in sunshine, you and Katy,' he told her. 'I hope one day you will meet someone who can be a loving companion to you and a father to Katy. I'll always be Katy's father but I wouldn't want you to go through the rest of your lives alone.'

He also talked about his mother, Margaret, and, when she got home, Judy must have told her, because soon afterwards Margaret rang me. She introduced herself and we were chatting when suddenly Richard cut in.

'You don't say Margaret, you say "'Ow's our Maggie

then?" ' he told me and when I passed this on, Margaret started to cry.

'That's it,' she said. 'Every time he came home he called out "Ow's our Maggie then?". He never called me anything else.'

Richard stayed very close to his family, particularly to Katy, whom he adored. She was very like him, with the same dark brown eyes that look straight through you and the same perception.

I've noticed before that when there are small children involved, parents who've passed come back frequently to see them and give them a helping hand when necessary. Children of these parents often remark in later years that they always had the feeling their mum or dad was close when they were in trouble, that although they couldn't see their parent, they could feel their presence. This isn't the result of a fertile imagination. It's a real experience.

Parents do come back when their children need them and it makes no difference how humble or exalted that parent was on earth. First and foremost he or she is a parent.

I was reminded of this recently when a sitting with a young girl called Annie suddenly took the most unexpected turn. I'd been introduced to Lee Everett, the healer wife of comedian Kenny Everett, and one afternoon when she came to visit me she brought a friend called Annie.

Afterwards, as they were leaving, I glanced at Annie and suddenly I could see her differently. Instead of the pretty, modern young girl I had seen before I could see great turmoil and confusion.

'My word, you want some sorting out,' I couldn't help saying aloud.

Her jaw dropped and she stared at me in surprise, but Lee said, 'You can say that again, Doris. She does.'

65

Poor Annie was in a hell of a muddle. She'd got involved in a business project, she'd given up her flat, her job and just about everything she possessed in an effort to get it off the ground, but nothing seemed to be happening and she was drifting from one day to the next not knowing what to do.

She was a nice, kind-hearted girl and I hated to see her in such a state.

'Look, love, I don't know if it will help but would you like a sitting?' I asked. 'Perhaps the spirit people will be able to suggest something.'

Now, as I've said before, I'm not a fortune teller but occasionally the spirit people can see round corners and when one of their loved ones has reached an all-time low they will often let slip just a little of the future to cheer that unfortunate person and help them live through the present. I couldn't promise they'd do it for Annie, but I thought it was worth a try.

The sitting started off in the ordinary way. Annie's brother came through and various members of her family, but in the background I kept hearing a voice say:

'Ask Yoko, ask Yoko.'

Yoko, I thought, that's strange. I only know of one Yoko, Yoko Ono, the Japanese woman who was married to John Lennon. Obviously it was a more common name than I imagined.

Then came the name John Lennard.

'Oh, that's the lawyer who's involved in the business project,' said Annie.

Then another voice interrupted. 'My name is John Lennon.'

I thought I was getting mixed up with John Lennard who was alive and working with Annie, but the new voice was very firm.

'No, I'm John Lennon, I'm over this side,' he insisted.

'She doesn't know me, but my best friend was talking to her on the phone last night. Elton John from New York.'

I repeated this and Annie said, 'Yes. I was talking to Elton last night.'

It turned out that she used to work in the music business and knew Elton John very well, although she'd never met John Lennon.

Nevertheless, John Lennon seemed to know all about Annie's project.

'Why don't they ask Yoko for backing?' he said. 'After all, they named the project after me.'

Annie agreed that this was true. He mentioned a few more details about the business which were confidential, and then he went back to Elton.

'I loved that boy,' he said. 'He's written a song about me you know. It's called Johnny. He played my song all over the world.'

I don't know much about pop music but Annie seemed to think this was pretty accurate. Nevertheless I still wasn't convinced that I was talking to John Lennon. For one thing it didn't sound like him to me. This man had an American accent and I expected John Lennon to sound Liverpudlian.

'Can you give me any proof it's you?' I asked.

'Yoko and I had matching briefs with our initials on,' he said, 'and she has kept four pairs of my solid gold spectacles.'

Then he started talking about a picture with flowers round it and lots of candles, but neither Annie nor I could understand what he meant. It didn't make sense to us.

'D'you mean that Yoko keeps a picture of you with flowers and candles by it?' I asked.

No, he said, that wasn't what he meant at all. He tried to explain again but I couldn't catch it.

'It's no good. I'm sorry, love, clear the vibration and let's try something else.'

It was only later that we solved the puzzle. Apparently, on the anniversary of his death the fans went round Central Park with a flower-decked portrait of John Lennon and they all lit candles.

Next, he showed me the place where he was killed. Instantly a typical New York scene appeared in my mind. Tall buildings and the trees of Central Park nearby. He owned the whole block, he explained.

'And you've been there,' he said.

'Oh no, I don't think so,' I assured him.

'Yes, you have,' he insisted. 'You did a radio programme there.'

And suddenly the picture changed and I saw an image of John and I standing in a magnificent plant-filled hallway waiting for the lift to take us up to the apartment where Lord Fitzgerald and his wife Peggy broadcast their late-night radio show to the wide-awake New Yorkers.

'Oh yes,' I said slowly. 'That was the last time we were in America. So that was your building was it?'

But John Lennon was off again. He seemed a strange boy. He sounded cocky and rather arrogant, I'm afraid, but he was also concerned about helping people. He went back to Annie's project.

'There's plenty of money. I'd like Yoko to back you as long as you devote part of your time to peace.'

I asked him what he was doing on the other side.

'I'm still composing,' he said. 'And I've met two Brians, one who killed himself with drugs and the other who drowned himself in a swimming pool.'

Annie said he must be referring to Brian Epstein, the Beatles' early manager who died of a drug overdose, and Brian Jones of the Rolling Stones who was found dead in his swimming pool.

'What about the man who shot you?' I asked. 'Do you bear him any bitterness?'

John said he didn't. 'After all, he wasn't right in the head, was he?' Then he laughed. 'And if I had to come over I did it the right way, didn't I, in a blaze of publicity!'

He seemed to have a black sense of humour but underneath it he was a caring person.

'There were a lot of things left undone that I should have done,' he said, and his two sons were particularly on his mind.

'I left Yoko you know,' he said, 'but I realized my true happiness lay with my family and I went back.'

He worried that his eldest boy Julian felt unfairly treated.

'He's gone blond now,' he said, 'but the trouble is he thinks he ought to have a lot more and Yoko thinks she's doing the right thing by waiting till he's older.'

And finally he talked about Sean, the younger son. It was clear that Sean had a special place in his heart and he still spent a lot of time close to him.

'I've shown myself to Sean,' he said. 'Sean has seen me.'

Small children are psychic, so it's quite likely that Sean has seen his daddy and he will certainly continue to feel his presence as he grows up.

It's very strange the way so many pop musicians go over young. I know there is a lot of drinking and drug-taking in that profession which would account for some of the deaths, but a surprising number of these young people go over through no fault of their own. John Lennon was murdered, other singers have been killed in plane crashes, electrocuted by their guitars, or like Marc Bolan, been involved in fatal car accidents.

I have done quite a few sittings for the grieving wives, girlfriends and mothers who are left behind in these tragic cases and, from talking to the mothers, I realize that no matter what sort of wild image the young man may have presented to the rest of the world, no matter what sort of bad habits he may have been led into, to his mother he is still her innocent child. Beneath the permissive exterior lies the little boy she always knew.

I realized this when Marc Bolan's mother, Mrs Phyllis Feld, came for a sitting. It was several years since Marc had been killed but I still had a vague recollection of him. Wasn't he the boy with all those long curls down his back and the eye make-up? Being a Jim Reeves fan myself, Marc Bolan wasn't really my cup of tea so I'd never followed his career, but if you'd asked me what he was like I would probably have said that by the look of him he was one of those couldn't-care-less, rebellious types. Which just shows how wrong you can be. When he came back to talk to his mother, I discovered he was a gentle, kind-hearted young man. He had made mistakes, he knew it and he was ready to admit it.

Mrs Feld had written to me asking for a sitting and I booked her for the only day I happened to have free, but it turned out to be a lucky choice.

As soon as I started working Marc came through singing *Happy Birthday*.

'Why is he singing that?' I asked his mother.

'It's his birthday today,' she explained.

'Twenty-nine,' said Marc.

'Is he twenty-nine today?' I asked.

'No,' said Phyllis, 'but he was twenty-nine when he was killed.'

He then went on to mention his little boy, Rolan, and gave his age, and then he talked of Gloria.

'That's Rolan's mother,' said Phyllis.

'My mum's lovely,' Marc went on. 'She has never blamed Gloria for what happened.'

70

Apparently Gloria was driving the car the night the accident happened. The Mini went out of control, hit a tree and Marc was killed.

'Gloria was all right,' Marc explained. 'She wasn't unconscious or anything. She kept saying, "Wake up! Wake up, Marc!" But I'd already gone. I think a tyre burst.'

Then, for some reason, he started singing again. This time it was a jolly song called *Tie a Yellow Ribbon Round the Old Oak Tree*, which I found an odd choice. I mean, I'm fond of the song but from the little I knew of Marc's work I didn't think this was his sort of music at all. When he finished the chorus, he muttered something about a girl coming from America on his birthday and tying a ribbon round a tree.

It was double Dutch to Phyllis and me. We couldn't make head nor tail of it.

'We don't know what you mean, love.'

He repeated the message several times but it was no use.

'Let's come back to it later,' I suggested. 'We're not getting anywhere at the moment.'

But a few days later the meaning became clearer. There was a story in the paper about Marc Bolan and it mentioned that his fans still make a pilgrimage every year to the tree where he died. It didn't specifically mention the American girl but since he had a lot of American fans the chances are that an American girl was amongst them.

Marc went on to talk about another Mark. 'But it's his real name,' he said, 'spelt M-A-R-K.' It was only then that I realized Marc didn't spell his own name the same way.

'He has a cousin called Mark,' said Phyllis.

He mentioned other family names and birthdays. Then he gave the name Grace.

Phyllis shook her head. 'I don't know anyone called Grace.'

'No, Mum doesn't know her,' said Marc, 'but tell her I've met Elvis Presley and his mother Grace over here.'

Phyllis didn't think this was unlikely. 'Oh yes, he adored Elvis Presley,' she said. 'He would have wanted to meet him.'

Marc added that his mother was soon going to Los Angeles (which was correct) and Elvis wanted her to phone someone called Prissy and give his love to Lisa.

'Elvis' wife was called Priscilla,' said Phyllis, 'and his daughter is Lisa.'

Then Marc talked about his career. He mentioned several personal financial details which his mother confirmed and he said he was worried about her.

'My mum shouldn't be working,' he said. 'I worked hard and made a lot of money, but I was ripped off. I thought a lot about my music but I was no good as a businessman.

'Fame and money came too quickly. I couldn't handle it. I wouldn't listen to my dad. I thought I was a big star but Dad always said "be careful".'

Phyllis nodded sadly. 'Yes, that's quite true. His dad did worry about him.'

And finally, like John Lennon, Marc's thoughts went back to his son. He was very proud of little Rolan.

'I was writing a song for Rolan just before it happened, you know,' he told me. 'A new song.'

Perhaps one day Rolan will write a song for his dad. Marc would like that.

CHAPTER 5

It was Halloween night in America. All across the country excited children were scurrying from door to door shouting 'Trick or Treat!', adults dressed as witches and ghosts were hurrying to fancy dress parties and John and I, rather bemused by the eerie celebrations, were on our way to visit friends in Connecticut.

It was a cold night, the sort of night when the wind sighs in the trees, the dead leaves rustle in the gutter and normal objects cast strange, unnatural shadows. A night when even grown-ups hurry to switch on the lights.

Normally such things make me smile. I can understand the tingle of pleasant fear people enjoy listening to ghost stories or playing creepy games, but I can't share it. Ghosts, ghoulies and things that go bump in the night hold no terrors for me. If I see a ghost I simply wish him good day and ask how he is. But this particular Halloween I began to think the atmosphere was affecting me. The nearer we drew to the beautiful old mill house where our friends, the Wiehls, lived, the stranger I felt.

The car pulled into a lush shrub-lined drive, now a mass of heaving black shapes, and I began to feel distinctly weird. There was a hollow, drained sensation in my stomach that grew worse as we approached the house and by the time the car stopped I was feeling definitely ill.

I jumped out, thinking the fresh air would do me good, and then stopped dead. Whatever it was, I'd walked right into it. I was standing beneath a Victorian-style lamp-post from which swung a macabre Halloween pumpkin and the bad vibrations were all around. I wanted to scream and shout and throw things, but somehow I couldn't move.

'Why, Doris, what's the matter? Is something wrong?' It was Pam Wiehl, come to welcome us.

'Oh, no, no,' I stammered, forcing down the urge to scream. 'Let's go inside. I just feel a little, well, odd.'

It's such a beautiful place, I thought, glancing back at the lamp which glimmered on a breathtaking swimming pool. What on earth's going on?

Later, I found out. Pam's nineteen-year-old daughter, Sandy, had leapt up from the breakfast table one morning, rushed up to the roof and thrown herself off into the pool, which was empty at the time. Pam, hearing the crash, had raced outside and seen her daughter broken and dead at the bottom of the pool.

She told me later that she'd stood under the lamp, torn in two, paralysed with indecision. She didn't know whether to rush to her daughter or rush to phone an ambulance and, being pulled in two directions at once, she couldn't move at all. She stood there in agony, and when she opened her mouth to scream, no sound came out.

Strange as it may seem the sheer horror of that moment lived on. So powerful was the emotion Pam felt that morning, the air was still charged with it and any sensitive person would pick it up.

We had been meaning to visit the USA for a long time and our kind American friends pinned us down to autumn 1982. It's amazing how things snowball. On our last trip to New York we met a couple who'd lost their son, Greg, in a car crash. They came to me for a sitting and, as soon as I tuned in, four young people, all nineteen years of age, came bursting in to talk to us. One of them was Greg, and the others were called Sandy, Jamie and Chris.

They had all known each other on earth, they explained, and were still friends on the other side.

It turned out that the grieving but enterprising parents had formed themselves into a bereavement circle so that they could exchange help and comfort. Once Greg's parents had been to me for a sitting they were eager to persuade me to visit the rest of the circle and do the same for them.

'Next time you come to the States, come and stay with us and we'll introduce you to everyone,' they said. 'They'd be so pleased to meet you.'

I felt as if I knew Greg's family home already. During the sitting he had shown me a room which I took to be his parents' sitting-room. I saw a large window and on the wall beside it was a picture of Greg in casual clothes.

His parents, Pat and John, shook their heads blankly.

'No, that's not our living-room.'

'They don't recognize it, Greg,' I told him.

'Yes, they do.' He showed me the scene again but this time from further back so that I could see a red couch facing me. I described it to his parents.

'It's where **you** watch telly,' I added.

'Oh, our den!' they cried. 'Yes, it's exactly like that.'

Greg went on to talk of his passing. It was early morning just before dawn and a misty rain was falling. I had the impression of a wide open area, and a curve in the road, then a confusion of lights and a bang. Greg said he was killed instantly, his back and neck were broken and his chest was crushed. He was annoyed because his parents didn't receive all his belongings.

'They took my watch and I wanted Dad to have it. I'd just cashed my pay cheque but that was missing, too.'

'Yes, there was only one dollar in his wallet when we received it,' said Pat.

Most of all, Greg was sorry for the way he'd sometimes

treated his parents. 'I really socked it to them when I was growing up. But now I realize how much they loved me. Dad was disappointed because I didn't go to college, but I needed time to find myself. I think I was almost there, but then that stupid accident happened.'

Some weeks later, Greg's mother phoned to ask me yet again if John and I would be able to visit them. Within seconds of hearing Pat's voice, Greg was at my side.

'There's been a beautiful wedding,' he told me, 'and I went along. It was terrific!'

His mother gasped. 'Well, that's amazing,' she cried. 'Greg's sister, Debra, got married last week.'

'Did she marry Jean Marc?' I asked, remembering that during the original sitting Greg had mentioned Debra and a young man called Jean Marc. 'They're more than friends!' he told me.

'Why, yes,' said Pat. 'That's right, she did.'

This information made her more determined than ever that we should visit them.

'Sandy's parents are particularly anxious to meet you. After all, you did mention Sandy during the sitting.'

Well, of course, John and I would have loved to go but what with long-standing engagements and spells in hospital it was the end of 1982 before we could manage it. Yet once we arrived we were glad of our timing.

Connecticut in the fall was breathtaking. Never had we seen such colours. The air was crisp and sparkling and we drove down wide, open roads ablaze with fiery trees. Mile upon mile we saw nothing but brilliant trees each vying to outshine the one beside it. There were scarlets and coppers, acid yellows and lime greens, each one setting off the next until our eyes ached from gazing at them. John and I drove for miles without saying a word, so entranced were we with the scenery.

'What a pity you won't see it at its best,' people kept

76

saying to us and our jaws dropped. How could it possibly look lovelier than it did already?

'Why are the colours so much brighter than at home?' I asked John.

'Maybe it's the soil,' he suggested.

Whatever the reason, we were very thankful to have seen it.

As with all my trips abroad, word soon got round and television shows, public meetings and church services were added to my schedule. I ended up visiting New York and Baltimore as well as Connecticut but, unfortunately, on these tours the messages tend to blend into one another in my memory and afterwards I can only remember a few of the more striking ones.

I particularly remember the church service in Connecticut. Quite a few children came back to talk to their parents but after a while I kept hearing an insistent male voice. He wanted to talk to his wife.

I searched round the crowded hall looking for her and eventually I saw a light hovering around an intimidating, rather wealthy-looking lady. I could tell immediately that she didn't think much of this at all. In fact she told me later that she hadn't wanted to come and after what happened I can't say I blame her.

'I've got a message for that lady there,' I said, waving in her direction.

'Me!' cried the lady, aghast.

'Yes, I've got a man here and I think it's your husband.' The lady turned pale.

'Tell her to stop being so selfish,' said the crusty male voice. 'Tell her to stop hanging on to things.'

I passed this on as tactfully as I could. I do try to censor or at least modify certain messages especially in public where they could cause embarrassment. But on this occasion he wouldn't let up until he'd made his point.

'She's got two big houses,' he said, 'and now she's bought an apartment. What does she want three homes for at her age? She's hanging on to my clothes when she could give them away to be put to good use, and she's hanging on to me. Tell her to stop.'

This tirade quite took my breath away.

'He says you're hanging on to his clothes and you're hanging on to him,' I explained gently. 'He doesn't like it. He wants you to get rid of the things you don't need and start living.'

The woman looked as if she was going to choke. I must have frightened the life out of her, but fortunately her husband had said what he wanted to say and was willing to let other people take their turn so I was able to move on.

I was worried the lady might be offended, but once she'd had a chance to think about it I believe she felt calmer. She came up to see me afterwards.

'Well, I don't know what to say.'

'I'm afraid your husband was rather frank, dear,' I apologized, 'but he felt it was important you should understand these things.'

'Oh yes, it was typical of him,' she said.

Deep inside, I think it was a relief for her to be able to relax and let go at last. She was hanging on to her husband's things in a desperate attempt to hang on to her husband. Now she knew that she hadn't really lost him, that he was still close, she could relax.

In Baltimore it was a television show called *People Are Talking* that best stands out in my memory.

I was working with a combination of a live audience and unseen viewers who were telephoning the studio. There were two presenters, a man and a woman, and they seemed a bit uneasy with me. They didn't know what to expect and when the recipients of messages occasionally broke down in tears, overcome by emotion, they were rather alarmed.

I explained, as I usually do, that tears are a release and I'm very rarely asked to stop relaying the message, but the presenters were doubtful at first, although by the end of the show I think they'd changed their minds.

'Are you all right?' they kept asking members of the audience. 'Do you want her to stop?'

And time and time again they received the same answer. 'No, no, I'm crying because I'm happy.'

A few minutes into the show a young boy's voice came through. His name was Mitchell and he'd been killed in a motor-cycle accident.

'I went very quickly,' he said. 'My neck was broken.'

'Yes,' sobbed his mother who was in the middle of the audience. One of the presenters rushed over and put an arm round her shoulders but the woman didn't seem to notice.

'Mum said don't go,' Mitchell continued, 'but I went. I'm so sorry. It wouldn't have happened if I'd listened to her.'

'That's so true,' said his mother. 'He wouldn't listen to me. I didn't want him to go.'

But Mitchell didn't want her to be sad. He was an intelligent lad and he was determined to prove to his mother that he still spent a lot of time with her.

'She's been out with Betty,' he said.

'That's my friend,' his mother explained.

'And tell her I was with her when they went to the store and Mum bought a blouse. She paid for it and got as far as the door, then she said, "No, I don't think it's me," and she took it back again. That's typical of Mum. Always changing her mind!'

By this time, the mother's tears had dried up altogether

79

and her eyes were like saucers. She stared at me as if she suspected I'd been following her round the shop.

'That's exactly what happened,' she whispered.

The light moved on shortly after this and I was flitting from person to person when suddenly I got the name Jamie, followed by the name Griffin and the show came to a standstill. Nothing. Nobody could identify either of the names. There was complete silence.

Now I'll be the first to admit that I make mistakes and sometimes I mishear things, but these two names were quite distinct, not the confused blur you sometimes get when several voices are trying to communicate at once.

'Doesn't anyone know Jamie or Griffin?' I asked again.

Still nothing.

'They don't know you, dear,' I told the boy, but I was puzzled. It was so clear there must be a link with the programme somewhere. Perhaps the name was for one of the callers on the phone lines.

As it turned out I was right, except the person concerned hadn't even dialled the number at the time the message came through.

Unknown to me the mother of an eighteen-year-old boy named Jamie Griffin had been watching television when she suddenly heard me mention her son's name. Jamie had gone missing and the police suspected the worst, but Mrs Griffin refused to believe it. Her son was still alive, she was convinced. She believed he had probably lost his memory and was wandering around somewhere, confused and unaware of who he was.

When she heard me on the television she was seized with the idea that I might be able to tell her where she could find her son and she immediately phoned the police officer in charge of the case to ask if I would be allowed to help. The police had no objections, so they contacted the television station and, almost before I realized what

80

was happening, it was agreed that I would do a sitting before the cameras for Mr and Mrs Griffin.

As it turned out it was a very difficult project. As soon as the Griffins arrived I found that, like the police, I feared the worst. I kept hearing a young voice, a boy. I couldn't swear it was Jamie, and I wouldn't want to, because as I've said before I can make mistakes, but whoever it was I was getting details of a crime that had taken place.

The sitting started and immediately I was approaching a river bank. Then I stopped abruptly. I couldn't seem to move any farther. In my ear the name was being whispered but it sounded too implausible. I queried it but was given the same name again.

'The name of the river begins with a P,' I said, 'and it sounds like Powder River but that's ridiculous. There's also a waterfall nearby and that's called Powder Falls. I know it sounds ridiculous but that's what they say.'

'I think you must mean Gunpowder River and Gunpowder Falls,' said Mr Griffin.

Apparently the police thought these places figured in the case. Then I got the impression of a body which had been moved twice and I described a location. I was going up a narrow path in wild countryside.

'I've come to a place where the track forks and I can go right or left,' I told them. 'I'm going left and I can see an overhanging rock and a gorge below me.'

The parents shook their heads but Mrs Griffin looked alarmed.

'I don't care what anyone says, my son's alive,' she insisted. 'If you tell me different I won't believe it.'

The poor woman was obviously in a dreadful state.

'I can't tell you anything definite, dear,' I explained gently. 'All I can do is pass on what they tell me from the other side. Now, whoever it is I'm talking to, is giving me a name, a surname.' I mentioned it.

Again the parents looked blank, but I discovered afterwards that my information was correct. The officer in charge of the case phoned me later.

'That name you gave was my undercover name. No one apart from my chief and me know that name. Not even my wife.'

He went on to say that he, too, believed the body had been moved and they'd found a shallow grave in the location I'd described, but it was empty. He also knew the place where the path forked.

Mrs Griffin, by this time, had had enough. She must have known instinctively that there was no chance now of my telling her that her son was suffering from amnesia.

The person who was talking to me from the other side gave me the nickname of Jamie's grandfather and grandmother.

'A guess. A lucky guess,' said Mrs Griffin wildly.

He also mentioned Atlantic City.

'That's where my car was found,' said Mr Griffin. 'Jamie borrowed it to go to a Unity meeting at the church and he never came back. They found the car abandoned afterwards.'

Then came the name Michael.

'That's the boy who was with him,' said Mrs Griffin.

'They're telling me there was a row,' I explained. 'The boys were on their way to meet a man but there was a row.'

'Yes, but I kept telling you he's got amnesia,' hissed Mrs Griffin.

I stopped. It wasn't fair to continue. This lady had only called on me because she wanted me to prove her theory. She didn't want to know the truth. If I couldn't support her theory then she wouldn't listen. She wasn't ready yet to have an open mind and it wasn't right to force things on her that she wasn't ready to accept.

Of course, if the police found the body of her son, then that would be different. She would have to face brutal reality, but I could offer her no such tangible 'evidence' and it would be wrong to distress her unnecessarily. I thought back to the time years ago when John was missing, presumed dead after parachuting into Arnhem, and I was told by a medium that he was definitely in the spirit world. I had been devastated. What's more, the woman turned out to be wrong.

'I'm sorry, but the power's fading,' I said. 'I'm very tired. I think we'll have to call it a day.'

The cameras stopped, chatter broke out over the set, and people started walking about again. It was as if a spell had been broken.

Mr Griffin stared at me for a long time, then he came and sobbed on my shoulder. Mrs Griffin was quite composed. She patted her hair in case it had fallen out of shape, smoothed her clothes and stood up.

'My son is alive,' she told everyone who approached to offer her sympathy. 'I don't care what *anyone* says. I know he's alive.'

Of the two, I thought it was Mrs Griffin who was most in need of help.

I was all for leaving the case there but afterwards, when the officer in charge rang, he persuaded me to change my mind. I had come up with enough correct information to convince them that I might be of some practical use.

In particular, he was interested in the place I'd described where the path forked and a huge rock overhung the gorge.

'I know exactly where that is,' he said. 'If we took you to that spot, d'you think you might get any more information? We think it could be very important.'

'Well, I might,' I said. 'But I can't promise. Sometimes it works, sometimes it doesn't.'

In the end he convinced me I should try and we made arrangements to meet with the family and go together. But it wasn't to be. Somehow the press got to hear of the plan and contacted the police to see if they could go along as well. The police said no, but that didn't put them off.

'Doris, the police can't stop us. It's a free country, we can go where we like. But it's up to you. If you say you don't mind if we're there, they can't do anything about it.'

It was a terrible dilemma. If I said no, I suspected they'd write nasty things about me, but if I said yes, the police would be upset and so, very likely, would be the family.

I remembered the last time in New York when reporters had led me to believe that the family of a missing boy had agreed to media coverage of my investigations at the scene of the disappearance. The whole thing had turned into a circus and the mother, who it turned out had not been consulted, was almost hysterical. That had been a bitter lesson but I learned it well. I was determined it would never happen again.

What on earth could I do? The problem churned over and over in my mind. In the end it was John who came up with the obvious solution.

'Don't go,' he said. 'It's as simple as that. If you don't go, the press can't accuse you of being awkward and the parents can't accuse you of turning the case into a circus.'

So I didn't go. To those closely involved I explained the truth. To everyone else I had a bout of diplomatic ill health.

Yet, I still haven't finished with the case. The police were so convinced that I could help them, that they sent detailed maps of the area to my home in London so that I could work on them when I returned.

And I must say that one look at those maps was enough to make me very glad I didn't make the trip. The countryside is so very steep and rugged I reckon the journey would have finished me off!

As always, though, my most important work during that visit was the work I did in private. Amongst the pretty white clapboard houses of that north-eastern corner of America there was a lot of grief and tragedy and so many disturbed children. I couldn't understand why these children from beautiful homes with parents who clearly adored them were so mixed up. The ones who hadn't passed in tragic circumstances were receiving psychiatric help. What was the cause of all this confusion?

I asked Ramanov about it one night and he said he thought that the affluence was partly to blame. The parents worked terribly hard, some of them starting at half-past five in the morning and going on till late in the evening. The result was that they could afford a luxurious life-style but they expected their children to achieve the same success. Some children could cope with this but others couldn't and felt under pressure.

At the same time many parents seemed unusually protective of their children. One man kept telling me that he was trying to get his son to go back to school because it would be so much better for him. Yet that son was twenty-five years old, old enough to be a husband and father.

'When they are grown, you have to let children go,' said Ramanov. 'You have to let them be responsible for themselves because that is what they are here for. How else can they do the work they've been sent to do?'

We enjoyed our visit, but staying in the homes of bereaved parents was a heartrending experience. The children were so close that I kept bumping into them, and seeing them in their family setting brought home just how great a loss their parents had suffered.

In the home of Mark Ernst in New York, for instance, I went to the downstairs powder room and found Mark waiting for me in the corridor.

'Come down here and look at this, Doris,' he said and he led me through a door I hadn't noticed before, down another flight of steps to the basement.

'This is where a lot of my things were kept,' he explained, indicating the typical family jumble, 'but it got flooded one year.'

I'd first met Mark's parents months before when they came for a sitting at my flat in London. They were polite but rather wary of me at first and determined not to give anything away, so when they walked in I said:

'Oh, my dear, you've lost a child.' They denied it. I was convinced they had and that it was a son but, since they didn't want to mention it, I decided to let the sitting take its course and see what happened.

Mark's grandmother and great uncle and various other people came back, but eventually Mark wouldn't keep silent any longer.

He had been found dead in bed, he told me.

'Dad, forgive me,' he said. 'It wasn't me. I was killed. I didn't do it. Honest to God, I didn't do it.'

He was twenty-one and he was already over when they found him, he told me. But he was very concerned because people were saying he had committed suicide.

'They said I took an overdose, but I didn't,' he insisted. 'I was killed. I went to bed but to sleep.' There had been drink and medically prescribed drugs involved but Mark assured me that suicide wasn't in his mind. Unknowingly he had swallowed a combination that proved lethal. But

86

it wasn't suicide. He loved his family and he wouldn't have wanted them to suffer.

'I know what they're doing,' he said. 'My brother Etan has got a new set of wheels. Tell him to be careful.'

'Has Etan got a new car?' I asked.

'No, a new motor-cycle,' said his father.

'Oh, that's what he means,' I laughed and explained what Mark had said.

By the end of the sitting the Ernsts were no longer wary.

'When you come to New York you must promise that you'll stay with us.' They insisted and we promised.

Well, of course, we took them at their word and we had a wonderful time. They looked after us as if we were VIPs. They had a beautiful house and we hadn't been there five minutes when Mark turned up.

One day I noticed his mother looking through a large folder and instantly Mark was at my side.

'That's mine,' he said. 'It's special.'

Sure enough, when I mentioned what he'd said, his mother opened the folder to show me a collection of Mark's old school essays that she'd treasured ever since he was a boy.

At poor Sandy Wiehl's home in Connecticut the vibrations were even stronger but, as I said before, it was in the garden by the pool that you could feel them most.

Her poor parents had been in a terrible state over the tragedy but when I did a sitting and spoke to Sandy I realized that, like Mark, she hadn't intended to kill herself.

She showed me what had happened and I had a swift impression of falling and suddenly halfway to the ground there came the thought: 'Oh no, there's no water in the pool.'

'I forgot the pool had been emptied,' Sandy told me.

It was a desperate gesture, intended to show how unhappy she was, but it had gone terribly wrong. The poor girl was ill, mentally ill.

'If I'd have been in my right mind I wouldn't have done it,' she explained. 'I had every opportunity but I went into depressions. One minute I was on top of the world, the next down on the floor in the flick of an eyelid.

'Nobody could do anything about it. And I was stupid, Doris. I did stupid things, things I knew I shouldn't be doing, just to be like all the other kids. But then afterwards I felt guilty and that made me more depressed. I was so mixed up.'

She was much better now, she said, and she wanted her mum and dad to know that she was very sorry for what had happened.

'What I did to my folks!' she sighed, lost for words to describe her behaviour. 'You see I thought I was grown up, but I wasn't really grown up at all. I must have been such a pain. I moped about the place and sometimes I lost my temper. I shouted at people. I understand now but at the time I was out of my mind.'

She gave her love to her family and talked a lot about Flip. I thought this must be some kind of fish but her parents roared with laughter.

'No, it's her brother Flip. A nickname for Philip.'

I had to laugh. 'I thought it was short for Flipper. I wondered if she had a pet dolphin or something!'

Flip apparently had seen Sandy since she passed but he thought he must have dreamed it. Sandy wanted him to know that it was real. She had also been around when her sister Kim, and Kim's friend Jenny May, had been discussing her in Kim's bedroom.

'They were trying on my clothes and talking about me and I shouted, "I'm here, damn you! I'm here!" but they couldn't hear me. It was so frustrating.'

Then she began speaking in French. She was quite fluent and I couldn't understand a word.

'I'm not showing off, Doris,' she said in English, after I was suitably baffled. 'I just wanted to show you what I was capable of and how much I might have achieved if I hadn't been ill.'

'Yes, she was very good at French,' her mother agreed.

Finally Sandy described a large wooden chopping board that stood on the worktop, or counter as the Wiehls called it, in the kitchen.

'One day I will knock on that board and then Mum will know I'm there,' she said. 'They're teaching me how to do it.'

I think Pam and John found this a little hard to believe but when we went into the kitchen I spotted the chopping board in exactly the position Sandy had described. Everything was quiet, however, and there was no sign of Sandy. It could take her years to learn how to knock, I supposed. I couldn't even guess how long such a skill would take to acquire.

But Sandy was obviously a fast learner. One day when we were gathered in the kitchen, but well away from the work top, we heard a loud rapping noise.

Pam opened the kitchen door. The hall was empty. She went to the window. There was no one there.

The knocking sounded again, hollow and insistent, and this time it came unmistakably from the chopping board.

'It's me,' cried Sandy. 'Have you forgotten?'

Pam looked at the chopping board in wonder. 'Well, I never would have thought it possible,' she murmured.

'You might as well get used to it,' I laughed. 'Now she's learned to do that, she'll be knocking all over the place, I expect.'

Quiet, beautiful Connecticut soon became the centre of a burst of activity – or at least that's the way it seemed to us. The bereavement circle was large and we visited home after home.

The Wiehls particularly wanted us to meet Dave and Skip Warren because their daughter, like Sandy, had taken her own life and there could be no doubt that she intended to. Betsy, who was twenty-one, worked in an animal clinic and one day she'd injected herself with a massive dose of animal poison, normally used to putting animals to sleep.

'You can't be right in the head to do a thing like that,' Betsy said when we started the sitting. 'It was a stupid thing to do but I'm happy now. I'm better off out of it.'

Her marriage had failed and she was very depressed.

'I couldn't seem to form relationships,' she said. 'I did try and I worked at it, but things always seemed to go wrong. I used to drink vodka, too. I started drinking in high school and it got worse and worse.'

She envied her sister Susanne because she had a baby, but these days she was mainly sorry about her mother. Skip had had several cancer operations and was coping very bravely, but Betsy felt that she hadn't offered her the support she should have done.

'I was so wrapped up in my own misery, Doris, I had no time for anyone else. If only I'd been kinder to my mother.'

Skip agreed that this was true. 'Yes, that's right. She had no time for my problems.'

Finally, Betsy was worried about her father.

'He feels guilty, Doris,' she said. 'When I started drinking he used to drink with me and now he blames himself. It wasn't his fault though. Please tell him to stop drinking so much. It's no answer.'

David had been pretty sceptical when the sitting started and, though he seemed impressed afterwards, I wasn't sure whether he would be affected by his daughter's words. But a couple of weeks later Skip rang me.

'And how's David?' I asked.

'Oh, he's being so good, Doris,' she said happily. 'He's cut down on his drinking and he's really trying. I'm so proud of him.'

As I said earlier, guilt is one of the emotions that haunts bereaved parents and it is quite extraordinary how they will go over and over the cause of death until they can find something to feel guilty about. It is no good outsiders getting impatient and accusing them of being ridiculous or of looking for something to make them unhappy. They can't help it and it seems to be a normal, if sad, reaction. I went through it myself when I lost John Michael and I've seen it in just about every bereaved parent I've ever met. It is cruel to tell them to 'pull themselves together'. They need understanding, love and gentle reassurance.

You wouldn't think, for example, that parents could blame themselves for their son's cancer, but the Kreegers did. They, too, were members of the bereavement circle. Their son, Scott, developed a cancerous mole at the age of twenty-one. It was a senseless tragedy for which no one was to blame. Yet Scott's mother blamed herself for giving him the wrong diet as a boy, and Scott's father blamed himself for passing on genes that were clearly faulty.

Scott, of course, blamed neither.

As soon as I walked in the room for the sitting I could tell that his father didn't hold with any of this nonsense, he'd only agreed to it to please his wife. Waves of disbelief and doubt were pouring out of him into the room, making it very difficult to concentrate.

Oh dear, I thought, we'll have to try and sort this out

91

first or we'll never get anywhere. 'Could you tell me something about him?' I asked the spirit world.

'He's an attorney,' came the reply.

I smiled at Mr Kreeger.

'Mr Kreeger, I know you don't think much of this sort of thing,' I told him. 'But I'm getting the message through that you're an attorney. Is that right?'

His face changed and I could see that he was shaken. 'Well, yes, yes, I am,' he floundered. 'But the Wiehls could have told you that.'

I didn't remember them doing so but he was right. They could have done.

Nevertheless the sceptical waves faltered and receded and I felt I'd be able to work more comfortably.

'Well, never mind,' I said. 'Let's see if we can find Scott and get him to convince you.'

I tuned in again and Scott didn't take much finding. He appeared in the room, between his parents, a very good-looking boy with striking colouring. Dark, almost black, hair, pale skin and deep blue eyes.

'What a handsome boy!' I couldn't help saying aloud.

'Yes,' sniffed his mother, 'he was.'

'No,' I corrected. 'He is.'

Scott sent his love to his parents, his sister Lisa and his girlfriend April. He had been very fond of April, he told me. He was a gentle artistic boy and he had been deeply involved in some sort of artistic project.

'Was it a hobby, love?' I asked him.

'No. It was my work.'

He tried to tell me what he did but I couldn't make head nor tail of it.

'I did it with Lisa,' he said. 'I did the designing and cutting out and we took it in turns to paint.'

Whatever could it be?

'Does this make sense to you?' I asked his parents.

'Oh yes,' they said. 'That's absolutely right.'

Well, that was the main thing. As long as they were happy it didn't matter if I didn't understand the evidence.

'There's a single red rose,' Scott continued.

At this his parents shook their heads. 'No, he didn't do any roses.'

'Well, did you give him a single red rose, when he was ill or at his funeral?' I suggested.

Again they shook their heads.

'Sorry, Scott,' I said. 'They can't place the rose.'

He was most insistent that the rose fitted in.

'Yes, but they can't accept it, love,' I explained. 'Maybe they'll think of it later.'

But Scott did not want to change the subject. He was absorbed by his work.

'Ask them to let you have a piece of my work as a memento of today.'

'Oh no, I couldn't do that.'

'Yes, you can,' he said. 'I want you to have something.'

'But I can't say that,' I protested. It would look as if I was taking advantage of his parents in the worst possible way.

'What can't you say, Doris?' asked Scott's mother.

'Well,' I hesitated. 'It seems a dreadful cheek, but . . .' and I told them what Scott had said. To my relief they didn't seem offended.

'What a good idea,' said Mrs Kreeger. 'We'd love you to have something to remember Scott by and what better keepsake than a piece of his work?'

'But what did he do?' I asked, wondering what I was letting myself in for. Supposing he carved life-size elephants or something?

Scott laughed at this.

'No, nothing like that, Doris,' he said and tried once again to explain but all I could hear was a 'sk, sk' sound.

93

Sketching perhaps? I wondered. But no. He wouldn't need to cut that out and paint it.

'It was scrimshaw,' said his mother. 'It's a dying craft. An old sailors' craft.'

Apparently, if I understand it correctly, patterns are cut into ivory, painted, and then sealed.

'Some of Scott's work has gone to the museum as an example of scrimshaw,' she continued, 'but there are quite a few pieces left.'

The sitting went on, with Scott giving names of various members of the family and family friends, then he talked about a holiday he'd enjoyed with his father.

'We went to New Zealand,' he said. 'We had a marvellous time, didn't we, pal?'

And at those words his father broke down and went and stood by the window, staring out over the garden. Apparently father and son had been very close and they always called each other 'pal'. That one little word had done more than anything else I'd said to convince Mr Kreeger that Scott was still near.

The sequel to this story came a few days later. Lisa brought it. I found a beautiful pendant on a red ribbon. The medallion was a piece of creamy ivory into which had been cut an exquisite red rose, every petal precise and perfect. Accompanying the gift was a note from the Kreegers.

'When we looked through Scott's things we came across this single red rose,' they wrote. 'This must have been the rose you were talking about and we're sure Scott would have wanted you to have it.'

I deliberated long and hard about what to do with that rose. If I wore it as a pendant it would only be seen on special occasions and would spend the rest of the time hidden away in my dressing-table drawer. Really, it deserved to be on permanent display.

94

In the end I made up my mind. Now it hangs beside the picture of Scott on my board of spirit children.

One of the nicest things that struck me about all these American children I spoke to was their thoughtfulness towards the people who were left behind, and this was demonstrated once again, just before I returned to England.

I was talking to Lisa Ernst, Mark's sister, on the telephone towards the end of our trip when Mark suddenly joined us.

'Ask her about Malcolm,' he said.

'Do you know anyone called Malcolm, Lisa?' I asked obediently.

'Oh, yes, he was a friend of Mark's,' she said. 'He's English, like you, but he's in hospital at the moment. They don't know what's wrong with him.'

Poor boy, I thought. It's bad enough to be in hospital at the best of times, but to be in hospital in a strange country thousands of miles from home, far from your family, must be awful.

'D'you think he'd like to hear another English voice?' I asked Lisa.

'Oh, I'm sure he would.'

I jotted down the number of the hospital and when I next had a spare moment I rang Malcolm. The boy was in a terrible state. Apparently he was suffering from some mystery virus, or so they thought, and he'd lost the use of his legs. He was lying there all alone with no family to visit him and the doctors didn't know what to do for the best.

At the sound of my voice he was so overcome he burst into tears.

'Oh, Doris,' he said. 'At a time like this the person you really want is your mother. But if I can't have my mother, you're the next best thing!'

95

We had a long talk, during which I told him about John's work as a healer.

'We're just about to go back to England,' I said, 'so I'm afraid John won't be able to do anything for you in hospital, but would you like him to put you on his absent healing list?'

John works with this list every night. He writes down the names and addresses of people who're sick, together with details of their ailments, and every night he sits down quietly and sends out healing thoughts to them.

'Well, it can't do any harm, can it?' said Malcolm. 'And the doctors don't seem to know what to do with me.'

So Malcolm went on the list.

A week later we were told he was on the mend, and the last we heard he was walking again and due to come out of hospital any day.

Whether it had anything to do with John I don't know. But I think we can safely say that Malcolm was given a helping hand from his friend on the other side.

CHAPTER 6

How does that old saying go? Be it ever so humble, there's no place like home? Well, I must admit that after all my travels I've found it to be absolutely true. John and I had a wonderful time in America and we stayed in some magnificent houses with servants to wait on us and vast, manicured grounds.

Yet when we walked through the door of our little flat we both looked at each other and sighed with relief. Home! There was a pile of washing from our trip. Les and George had painted the flat right through and had the curtains cleaned. It was like a new flat. The view from the window was not of gently rolling lawns but the block of flats opposite. Yet it was our place and coming back to it was like swapping an elegant but tight dress for a battered old dressing-gown.

As always, our first priority was sleep. I can never sleep on planes and we'd been up all night on the flight back, but once the jet lag receded I was able to unpack and sort through my memories and mementoes of the trip.

There was a new pile of photographs for my spirit children board. I spread them out on the table in front of me. Scott, Greg, and Mark, Sandy and Betsy. I paused and put Sandy and Betsy side by side, studying their fresh young faces for signs of despair. But there was nothing to see. The torment that ruined their lives could not be captured by the camera.

'You can't be right in the head to do a thing like that,' Betsy had said.

'If I'd have been in my right mind I wouldn't have done it,' Sandy had cried.

97

Two poor sick girls, whose sickness couldn't be seen and therefore couldn't be understood by ordinary people.

I think there is probably much more mental illness around, unrecognized and untreated, than people realize. I wonder why it is that we can accept the fact that a body will fall ill with colds, flu or worse, quite frequently through a lifetime, but we can't accept that a mind could suffer similarly.

Perhaps people like little Paul, the boy who took his clothes off when he was being ignored, are the lucky ones. Paul was mentally retarded and it was fairly obvious, so people could see and understand his condition and they treated him sympathetically. No one expected too much from Paul, and when he achieved something they were pleasantly surprised. Paul never felt a failure and his parents, Jean and Steve, adored him.

At the sitting, Paul's grandpa, Joseph, spoke first.

'Paul couldn't talk on earth because he had a convulsion when he was a baby,' Joseph told me. 'And Jean and Steve are worried because he was unconscious when he passed and they couldn't say goodbye.'

I passed this on and Jean and Paul agreed that it was true.

'Well, you mustn't worry about it,' I assured them. 'Because Paul didn't know anything about it and there was no need to say goodbye. He hasn't gone. He's with you still.'

Paul was grinning away while I said this and to prove I was right he piped up:

'Yes, and Sarah's got the pennies out of my money box.'

'Yes!' cried Jean. 'Sarah's Paul's sister. That's the only thing she asked for. Two or three days after he died she said, "Paul won't need his pocket money now, Mum, so can I have it?" '

'She's got my teddy in bed with her, too,' Paul added.

Jean and Steve exchanged looks. This too was true and an expression of joy began to spread across Jean's face. But Paul was still chattering away. On the other side he had found his voice and he liked using it. He said his daddy had put a rose in a vase beside his photograph and he liked that. He thought the month of February was important.

'Yes,' said Jean. 'He died on the fourteenth and it would have been his fifth birthday on the twenty-fourth.'

But Paul was off again. 'Look at this. It's our house.' Suddenly I was walking through a front door and upstairs. 'See there's a new stair carpet,' he said as we climbed and when we got to the top we turned right and went into the bathroom. I was confronted by mirrors.

'This is the best room,' said Paul.

Quickly I explained where I was to his mummy and daddy.

'As I got into the bathroom there are mirrors facing me,' I explained.

'That's right,' said Jean. 'The whole wall's covered in mirror tiles.'

'Well, one day,' I told her, 'you will walk in there and see Paul's face reflected in the mirrors facing the door. You'll just see his face smiling at you. Don't be afraid when it happens. Just say "Hello son" and talk to him.'

Jean and Steve looked pretty amazed at this information but Paul seemed so sure he would do this one day, probably with his grandpa's help, that I had to mention it and I'm convinced that sooner or later it will happen. It must have been pretty hard for his parents to swallow at that time, however, but Jean did agree that the bathroom was special to Paul.

'He spent every night of his life in that bathroom,' she explained. 'He loved a bath and he loved to watch himself splashing about, in the mirrors. It was one of his favourite games. We all used to enjoy it because it made Paul so happy.'

'I liked going out in the car, too,' Paul interrupted. 'It was a new car and I used to look at everything out of the windows.'

'Yes, he did,' said Jean, then she turned to her husband. 'You see, I told you he knew we'd got a new car. He was much brighter than people thought. I was sure he could tell the difference between the new car and our old one.'

The sitting went on, more relatives came back to have a word with the young couple and that was when, my attention being diverted from him, Paul stripped off his clothes.

As it turned out, it was the best thing he could have done. Steve had been sitting there listening to what was going on with an incredulous expression on his face. He had come to the sitting sceptical, what he had heard had amazed him, but he still couldn't quite believe – until Paul took off his clothes in a gesture both typical and unique. There was no way I could have guessed such an unusual habit.

After the sitting, Jean and Steve lingered to talk to me about their son. He was such a happy boy, they explained, and they missed him so badly. It didn't matter a scrap to them that he was retarded. They loved him as much as it is possible to love a child. Any ill-informed person who said that they were better off without him was cruelly mistaken. Paul might have been damaged but he had his own special part to play in the family.

A few days later they wrote to me, thanking me for the sitting and with the letter was a tiny brooch in the shape of a butterfly.

'Please wear this brooch in memory of Paul,' Jean wrote. 'We think of him as our little butterfly.'

As I read the letter tears came into my eyes. What a

perfect description of their little boy. Vivid and beautiful, brightening everything he touched and then gone in a flash – just like a butterfly.

There was no question that Paul was a wanted child and Jean and Steve coped well, but other parents aren't so lucky. Some children are so badly handicapped that, although their parents love them, they can't care for them at home. Sadly, there are also other children whose parents reject them almost at birth for the same reason. Yet, in a way, there is no need to be too sorry for these little ones because often they are quite happy in their own little worlds.

You hear a lot of horror stories about the things that go on in mental hospitals. I couldn't say whether or not they are true, all I do know is that when I spent some time working in a mental hospital after I finally qualified as a nurse in my forties, I saw only love, devotion and extraordinary patience.

I'm not saying that the nurses were all saints; far from it. It was just that those kids, no matter how damaged, were so wonderful in their own special ways, that you couldn't help loving them.

To be frank, there were some really horrifying cases in the hospital. Or at least they were horrifying at first sight. But it was amazing how quickly you got used to them.

I remember the day, not long after I'd started work at the hospital, that I was sent down to help out at the new infirmary. They were short of staff and, despite my inexperience, they thought I might be useful.

The sister was standing beside a cot as I walked in and she was holding a baby in her arms.

I hurried over to her in that brisk nurse's walk that I'd recently acquired. Fast and efficient but with no suggestion of panic.

'Hello, my name is Nurse Stokes,' I said. 'I've been sent down to help you out, Sister.'

She glanced up at me and her eyes held mine for a moment or two as she silently weighed me up. Then she smiled.

'Oh good. Well here, hold this. This is Nigel.' She handed me the baby.

By this time everyone knows how I feel about babies and I took the little scrap with pleasure. I should have noticed and been warned that something was wrong by the way Sister didn't move off after passing the boy to me but remained where she was, watching my face. But I wasn't warned. I hardly even registered it.

I was instantly enthralled, the way I always am when I've got a baby in my arms, and I looked down at little Nigel. The most beautiful little face looked back at me and a pair of baby blue eyes stared into mine. My face was folding instinctively into a smile, when I noticed something with a cloth over it next to Nigel's head.

Curiously, I lifted the cloth, and my stomach seemed to fall away. There was another head underneath, with little indentations where the features should have been.

Nigel was one of nature's mistakes.

I bit my lip hard, so as not to pass out and, as the room swung back into focus, I glanced up at Sister. She was watching me gravely.

I took a deep breath.

'What a dear little face,' I said as calmly as I could.

Sister smiled. 'Yes, isn't it? Right, carry on then, nurse,' and she bustled away obviously satisfied that I could cope.

There were more horrors in store. Later that morning one of the other nurses came over.

'You're the new nurse, aren't you?' she said quickly.

'Well, you'll be going in to see the new baby. Take a grip of yourself. I nearly fainted when I went in.'

Before I could question her she was gone. Uneasily, I finished mixing the feed I was preparing. What on earth could be worse than poor Nigel?

I didn't have long to find out.

'Ah, Nurse Stokes,' said Sister, coming alongside me suddenly. 'Leave that for a moment, would you. You'd better come and see the new baby.

This time I was prepared. Grimly, I followed her up the ward to a special room where a single cot stood alone. I steeled myself firmly as I approached it. The warning was a great help and this time I had no fear of fainting, although the poor little mite was a dreadful sight.

She was premature, she had spina bifida and something else had clearly gone wrong, because her head went up into a sharp point and she seemed to have no flesh on her bones. The skin hung in folds from her pathetic, wasted limbs.

I swallowed hard but I had a good grip on myself as I'd been advised.

Nevertheless, I think I went home that night in a state of shock. It seemed so cruel that those poor misshapen children should have been born. Wouldn't it have been better for them to pass over at birth then linger in this way?

I couldn't understand it. I still don't understand it, although now I know there must be a reason and that those innocents must have a part to play, no matter how obscure it seems to us. All I can say with certainty is that they are not unloved and I believe they are not unhappy.

Within days I found I didn't notice Nigel's deformity. I didn't even see it. When I looked at him all I saw was that lovely face. To me he was a beautiful baby.

It was the same with the new baby in the special room.

Before the week was over us nurses were falling out about whose voice she recognized and who she liked best. Of course, looking back I don't suppose she recognized any of us, but we liked to think she did.

Some of the sick children on the ward did know us. There was Geraldine who'd been in a car crash. She wasn't marked at all but she couldn't see and she couldn't sit up. Yet she was a cheerful little thing and she knew your voice.

Every morning I used to tickle her and say 'Who's a pretty girl then, Geraldine?' And she'd gurgle away with pleasure.

Then there was Anthony. He was about four or five but he had water on the brain which left him with a great swollen head and a tiny undersized body. Nevertheless, he knew when he was wet or cold or hungry and when you talked to him he'd smile up at you.

You soon got to love them, those poor little children and, despite everything, the ward was a happy place.

Not all the children were as severely handicapped as Nigel, Geraldine and Anthony. Often they were capable of far more than anyone believed possible. That's what made working with them so rewarding.

You weren't supposed to have favourites but you couldn't help it and one of mine was a spastic girl called Patsy Kelly. She couldn't walk and she had to have her hands tied up in an apron because for some reason she kept putting them down her throat and making herself sick. Despite this, she was a lovable character.

'Who's a bad 'un?' I used to pretend to scold. 'I'll give it to you. Who's a bad 'un?' and she used to rock herself in delight and laugh till the tears rolled down her cheeks. She may not have known what the words meant but she recognized them and understood that they were spoken with love.

One day we were getting the children ready for a walk in the gardens. It was quite a laborious procedure because they all had to be taken to the lavatory before going out. We used to round them up and change them one by one and sit them in the corridor to wait until everyone was ready.

This particular morning I thought I'd finished when I discovered that little Sharon had had another mishap and her knickers were soaking wet.

I whisked her up, took her back and laid her on the changing table again.

'Who's a bad 'un!' I was saying to her as I worked. 'I'll give it to you! You wet these knickers and I'll have your guts for garters!'

Sharon thought this was a tremendous joke. She was giggling and I was laughing and I suppose my voice must have been louder than I realized because outside in the corridor, Patsy Kelly, who couldn't walk, suddenly got to her feet and, beaming all over her face and rocking like a boat, she tottered towards the door from which she could hear those familiar words.

'Who's a bad 'un!'

The incredible event was the talk of the hospital for weeks and Sister never got over it. Such things didn't happen after all . . .

One day Sharon, as well, shook me rigid. She was a pretty girl of five with brown curly hair and blue eyes. She had been in the hospital all her life. We were the only family she'd ever known. She had never spoken and we all assumed she couldn't.

Then came the time when she caught German measles along with several other children. This was serious, as it could lead to an epidemic in the hospital from which some of the patients might not recover. Great precautions were taken which involved a lot of extra work for the nurses.

105

Sheets were wrung out in carbolic and hung in lines across the ward. The doorknobs were covered in carbolic and the nurses had to wear rubber gloves.

Inside the isolation area the children just lay in their beds with nothing to do. I felt sorry for them. It seemed boring to me to have to lie there all day so, when I was on duty, I used to sing to them to liven things up.

I'm absolutely tone deaf and not by any stretch of the imagination a singer, but nevertheless I enjoy singing and those children, who after all knew no better, seemed to enjoy listening to me. I used to go from cot to cot singing each child a different song and for some reason I chose a jolly little tune called *He Wore a Tulip*, for Sharon.

'He wore a tulip, a bright yellow tulip and she wore a red red rose,' I used to sing and her eyes would widen and she'd listen to this with rapt attention. After a few days she began coming to the end of her cot when I started to sing and she'd pull herself up and look right into my eyes and if I stopped singing she rubbed my face until I started again.

She never tired of this game and for me it became a routine. Then one day I started off in the same old way:

'He wore a tulip, a bright yellow tulip and she wore a . . .'

'Wed wed wose,' interrupted a strange little voice.

I stopped dead and stared at Sharon. Surely that wasn't her? She couldn't speak.

'He wore a tulip,' I began again cautiously. I was probably imagining things but I might as well put it to the test. 'A bright yellow tulip and she wore a . . .' I paused.

'Wed, wed wose,' Sharon finished.

If the bottle of baby lotion in my pocket had suddenly offered an opinion on the weather I couldn't have been more surprised.

'There's a clever girl, Sharon!' I cried and I tried it

again. Each time I sang the song, Sharon finished it for me.

'Sister, come and listen to this,' I called when her head appeared round the carbolic sheet. 'Sharon's just spoken.'

'No!' said Sister, coming over to the cot. 'She's never spoken in five years.'

'Well, listen.' I launched into another rendering of *He Wore a Tulip*. At the appropriate place I waited and, sure enough, in chimed Sharon:

'Wed wed wose . . .'

That song became Sharon's party piece. She had never spoken, and she never did speak, but you sing *He Wore a Tulip* and she always came in at the end.

It wasn't just the nurses who found the children surprising, sometimes they amazed their parents as well. There were some parents who never visited, some who came every week, and some who could only get to the hospital every now and then.

It was the irregular visitors who got the most surprises. I remember one little girl called Sylvia who was in a shocking state when she was brought to us. I don't know what happened to her mother, but her father had to go away to work and he'd left Sylvia in the care of an elderly relative who could hardly look after herself let alone a backward child as well.

By the time the social workers heard about Sylvia she was a mess. I'll never forget the day they brought her in. I'd never seen a child in such a state.

She was filthy, her hair was so matted and unwashed it looked like an ancient dog blanket, and she was thin and under-nourished. We could only guess at her former life-style from her behaviour with us.

The first thing to do with her was to give her a bath, but she was obviously a complete stranger to washing. She was terrified of water. She screamed and kicked and

107

yelled and it took two of us to get her in the bath and even then she wouldn't sit down. We had to wash her standing up.

Finally after a good half hour's struggle, a thin, bedraggled little creature emerged from the bathroom, rather sorry for itself and resembling a drowned rat, but clean.

'Come on, love,' I said taking her hand. 'Let's get you something to eat.' That was when we discovered more about her former life. Faced with the meal table Sylvia was totally at a loss. She'd never sat at a table before and she'd never eaten proper food or, if she had, it was so long ago she couldn't remember it. The old lady had existed on bread soaked in sweet tea and so had Sylvia.

In those first few weeks life with Sylvia was hard work. She had been happy enough with the old lady and she couldn't understand why she should change. But gradually she settled down and, as a proper diet, regular washing and plenty of sleep began to take effect, we realized that she was a very beautiful child.

Her hair, which had been lank and lacklustre, grew thick and glossily black, her skin which had been pale and delicate turned creamy pink with health and suddenly you noticed that her eyes were enormous and the deepest shade of blue I'd ever seen.

The months passed and then came the news that Sylvia's father was coming to visit her. I'd grown very fond of Sylvia by this time and I wanted her to make a good impression so I went to the store and found her a pretty blue dress the colour of her eyes. Then on the great day I rushed down to the city before going on duty and bought a length of blue ribbon to match the dress.

Back at the hospital I brushed Sylvia's hair until you could practically see your face in it, dressed her in the new dress and tied the ribbon into a bow. She looked wonderful.

'Who's a beauty then?' I said taking a step back to admire her. 'Don't you look nice? Good enough to eat.' She dimpled with pleasure.

Hand in hand we went downstairs and I tapped on the nursing officer's door.

'I've got Sylvia here for visiting,' I said, putting my head round the door.

'Right. I'll be there in a minute, nurse,' said the nursing officer, collecting up the papers on her desk and, thinking she meant she'd be following us, I walked on with Sylvia to the visitors' room.

There was a man standing in the hall as we passed but I didn't give him a second glance. I assumed he had an appointment with someone.

Anyway, when we reached the visitors' room it was empty. Oh no, I thought, don't say he's not going to come. But I didn't want Sylvia to sense my disappointment so I sat her on my knee and started telling her a story.

A few moments later we heard voices in the hall.

'Where's Sylvia?' asked the nursing officer in surprise.

'I don't know,' answered an unknown male voice. 'I haven't seen her.'

'But Nurse Stokes has only just brought her down,' said the nursing officer with a hint of impatience creeping into her voice. 'Didn't she take her into the visitors' room?'

As she spoke, we could hear footsteps crossing the hall, the door opened, and the nursing officer and the man we'd passed in the corridor appeared in the doorway.

'Why, yes. Here she is,' said the nursing officer.

The man's mouth just fell open as he took in his daughter. She looked so beautiful he hadn't recognized her.

The sequel to that story is that Sylvia turned out to be a talented artist. Years after I left the hospital she sent me a beautiful picture which I still treasure and to this day she paints the most fantastic oil paintings.

It is amazing how much the children do remember. There was a blind girl called Geraldine, for instance, who came to us when she was very small. At first, she was a bright little thing who chattered away and helped us look after the tots. The only problem with her was that she kept hitting herself in the eyes. Whether it was in frustration because she couldn't see, we didn't know, but to prevent her harming herself she had to have her hands fastened behind her back all the time.

It used to break my heart to see her like that and I used to think, poor little girl your arms must ache. So when I undressed her ready for bed I used to untie her arms and stretch them over her head and to the sides. To distract her from hitting her eyes during these exercise sessions I used to say to her:

'Tomorrow I'm going to bring you a parcel and what will be in it?'

Geraldine would say, 'An apple!'

I'd say, 'And an . . .'

'Orange!'

'And a piece of . . .'

'Chocolate cake!' Geraldine would cry.

She began to look forward to our parcel sessions at bedtime and all the time she was making good progress. Eventually she was judged to have improved so much she was allowed home.

We never did find out what happened or what went wrong but somehow Geraldine deteriorated and she was sent back to us. She never spoke again.

The years went by, I left the hospital and long afterwards I went back for a visit. As I walked through the grounds I noticed a group of patients sitting in a circle on the grass and a scattering of the nursery children skipping round them.

The children spotted me first and came running up shouting, 'Nurse Stokes! Nurse Stokes!'

I was busy saying, 'Hello, love, hello, love,' to each one individually when suddenly I heard one of the adult patients say:

'Would you look at her!'

I glanced up to see Geraldine, in the adult wing now, coming towards me. She was blind, but her sense of hearing was so acute she knew exactly where I was. She came straight over, put her head on my chest and started to cry. And I thought, they do remember, they do.

Afterwards I made my way from the gardens into the hospital and arrived at one of my old wards just on bath time to see one of my other favourites, Jenny Lee.

'Hello, Jenny,' I said going up to her.

'Hello,' said Jenny impassively as if she'd never seen me before in her life.

'I've brought you a pat of chocolate!' I whispered.

She beamed all over her face and took it eagerly.

'You took me to the pictures, didn't you, Nurse Stokes?' she said as plain and distinct as anything, 'to see my sister.'

I was amazed. It must have been three years ago or more since I'd taken her to the hospital cinema to see her sister, Frances Lee, in a film. Yet, despite the fact that I wasn't in uniform and she didn't know I was coming, Jenny remembered both me and the occasion.

Sometimes, of course, it was heartbreaking. We knew that many of the children had short life expectancies but knowing that didn't make you stop loving them and didn't make it any easier when they passed. Although I wasn't working as a medium while I was nursing I couldn't

111

switch off my psychic powers, and therefore I always knew when a child didn't have long to go. Yet knowing in advance was probably harder to face than not knowing, because I felt so helpless.

When Patsy Kelly's time was close I was frustrated to find that I'd been sent to work on a different ward, the adult ward, so I had hardly any time to be with Patsy. That was probably why I was transferred. Yet it's amazing what can happen.

One afternoon I was asked to take a message to the sister of the nursery ward, whose office happened to be close to the room where Patsy lay unconscious with a nurse at her side twenty-four hours a day.

I obediently delivered the message but afterwards, instead of going straight back to my work, I couldn't resist looking in to see how Patsy was.

To my surprise the nurse on duty seemed to be expecting me. 'Stokes, an amazing thing just happened!' she said excitedly. 'When you were talking to Sister just now I'll swear Patsy could hear your voice. She's been unconscious all this time yet as soon as you started talking she opened her eyes, grinned all over her face and tried to sit up.'

I looked down at Patsy, now as silent and unmoving as she had been the last time I peeped in, and it seemed very hard to believe.

'Hello, Patsy,' I whispered. 'How's my bad 'un then?' There wasn't a flicker and in the distance I could hear the murmur of spirit voices come to take her home. My eyes filled with tears.

'It won't be long now, nurse,' I said, my voice wobbling and I turned and hurried away. It wouldn't do to be caught sobbing on duty.

A few hours later Patsy passed over. She was fourteen years old.

Later I went to visit her in the chapel and when I saw how lovely she looked I knew that it was selfish of me to wish her back. I would miss her infectious laughter on the ward but she was happier now with her relatives on the other side.

'Well, you're at peace now, Patsy,' I said aloud as I left her for the last time.

But, unlikely as it might sound, there was more fun and laughter than tears. After tea when I was on duty I organized hilarious games of hokey-cokey in the ward and during the day when the weather was fine, we played 'Here We Come Gathering Nuts in May' on the field outside.

The children varied enormously in intelligence but this didn't cause any problems. We put the brightest next to the most handicapped and they helped each other. It was wonderful to see how patient the children were with each other and how they looked after the least able. A child who was blind need never fear the teasing you might expect from normal playmates. There was always someone there to see they came to no harm.

Some of the children, particularly the epileptics, were extremely intelligent. We used to keep a record of the number of fits each child suffered and if they went for two years without a fit we used to have a party.

They took great interest in the recording of fits and they knew how long they had to go before their party. Those who achieved the two years were ecstatic. They came rushing into the ward, their faces alight with pleasure, shouting:

'I'm out of the fit book, nurse. I'm out of the fit book.'

Others were so clever you wondered why they were in the hospital at all. One woman had been there as long as anyone could remember, so long, in fact, that I couldn't find anyone who knew why she'd been admitted in the first place.

Perhaps years ago she'd had an illegitimate baby at a time when women who got into trouble were sometimes hidden away so as not to bring shame on the family. Anyway, whatever the reason, this woman was so settled in the hospital she wanted no other way of life and it would have been cruel to push her into the outside world.

She was happy and she ran the private ward. It was unofficial, of course, but she knew how it worked far better than any of the nurses and whenever a new nurse arrived she would take her under her wing and show her how everything was done.

Other patients weren't so obviously intelligent but they were very talented in other ways. I've still got an exquisite work basket made for me by one of the patients and there were two girls who could knit beautifully. No matter how intricate the pattern it presented no problems to them. It reached the stage where if any of us nurses got into a muddle with our knitting we'd take it to them. They could look at it, spot what was wrong, pull it apart and put it right, in minutes.

Of course there were plenty of other patients who gave no trouble but who were harmlessly eccentric. One of them was a little girl called Emily. Emily was a sweet, gentle girl who had an obsession with hats and handbags. She was devoted to her collection and I used to beg all the hats and handbags I could get hold of to help her increase it. Emily gave offence to no one and she said very little. All she wanted to do was put a hat on her head, a handbag over her arm, and walk up and down the corridor. After about ten minutes she's go back to the ward, change her hat and handbag and repeat the process.

She would cheerfully play this solitary game all day long and nobody could persuade her to do anything else.

Emily's obsession was unusually deep, but all the children, even the most handicapped, were very attached to their few possessions. They all had to have something that was theirs, even if it was only a carrier bag with a postcard in it. They would take these possessions everywhere with them, even to bed.

Entertaining people with such mixed abilities could have been difficult, but the hospital had an enlightened attitude. Facilities were provided and the patients benefited from them in different ways, according to their capabilities.

On Good Friday, for instance, there was a religious service followed by a film about the crucifixion. Some patients enjoyed it in the normal way, others had no idea what was going on but liked to hear the singing and watch the moving pictures.

The vicar had to be ready for anything. One year the religious service seemed to be dragging on longer than usual and the children were shuffling a bit, wondering when the film was going to start.

Unfortunately the vicar didn't seem to be aware of the restlessness of his flock and he launched into another lengthy prayer. He didn't get far. Two lines into the prayer a little boy near the front of the hall piped up:

'Oh bloody 'ell, our men!'

There was a stunned silence. Then the vicar said, very quickly:

'In the name of the Father, the Son and the Holy Ghost, Amen,' missing out the whole of the middle section of the prayer and brought the service to a swift end.

There was no point in scolding the boy. He didn't understand what it was all about. All he knew was that when he said 'Our men' the picture would start.

There were quite a few mongols at the hospital and

they were delightful, so cheerful and affectionate. They used to wash our cups out for us and rub our feet after a long day on the ward. They loved music and had regular dancing lessons. Once a month the older ones had a proper dance with a band from outside.

This was the highlight of their days. The girls used to make long evening dresses to wear and the nurses would make up their faces for them. They thought it was marvellous. Out on the dance floor they'd bow and curtsey to each other and then swing round the room beaming at the nurses as they sailed past as if to say, 'Look at us!'

There were usually few nurses in attendance but we took part in the fun and, if we were asked to dance, we danced. The boys would have been very offended if we refused.

Many of these older ones were allowed out into the town on their own and, like small children, they were innocently determined to enjoy themselves and were quite uninhibited.

Often John and I would be quietly shopping in a crowded store when suddenly a great yell would ring out, startling shoppers.

'Yoohoo! Yoohoo! Nurse Stokes! Mr Stokes! Yoohoo!'

Heads would turn and John and I would look up to find we were being greeted from the other side of the store by a merry bunch of waving patients who were quite unaware of the disturbance they were causing.

These patients became highly independent and this was encouraged. A large house was bought for them just up the road from the hospital and the rooms were beautifully fitted out, two beds to a room, with matching bedspreads and curtains and good quality carpets on the floor.

There was one nurse and a sister on duty but the patients more or less took care of themselves. In the early

116

days the staff used to walk them backwards and forwards to the main hospital for school or classes or to work in the laundry, but after a while they put in a petition asking for the right to make the journey unaccompanied.

They went down to the town without an escort, they said, so why couldn't they be trusted to go to the hospital on their own?

Initiative was rewarded and they got their permission.

In the evenings they ran their own club and this was an entirely private affair. Strictly no admittance to nurses without an invitation. It was all very innocent. They spent the evenings concocting weird meals and dancing to the music on the radio. John and I were invited one evening and they cooked us a feast of bacon and onions. It arrived swimming in grease but we had to eat it. We wouldn't have hurt their feelings for the world.

They all stood round, bursting with pride as they watched us eat, saying:

'Isn't it good? Isn't it good?'

And, smiling through the grease, we assured them it was delicious.

I don't want to give the impression that working with the mentally handicapped is all joy and fun, because it isn't. It's exhausting, demanding and very hard work. There are difficult patients and some can turn violent. I should know because I had to give up nursing after being injured by one. But I would like to stress that in my experience mental hospitals are not all gloom and misery.

Of course, patients have their off days. Don't we all? But most of the people I worked with were content and secure, happy to stay in a protected work where no one expected more from them than they were capable of achieving.

CHAPTER 7

'Oh, eh, hello Doris. I hope you don't mind. I've brought my friend with me.' There is a slight pinkening of the cheeks and the eyes fall to study my shoes. 'Well, you see I was a bit scared to come on my own.'

This is the nervous sitter. I know her well.

'That's all right, love. I don't mind a bit,' I say. 'Come on in.' And I take her inside, knowing that after a few minutes she'll be quite relaxed.

It's amazing how many people are frightened when they arrive for their first sitting. They think I'm going to fall into some terrifying trance, or draw the curtains and condemn them to darkness and supernatural shadows.

In fact, we merely settle ourselves into armchairs and have a chat, in broad daylight unless, of course, it's winter when I might have to turn on the electric light.

Afterwards the sitters unanimously agree that there is nothing remotely scarey about the process. Yet people who have never experienced it still frequently ask:

'But what *happens* at a sitting?'

So for all those who are still curious I thought it might be interesting to record a sitting in full, as it happened.

Below is a transcript of a sitting I did with Susan Otter and her husband in early 1982, omitting only some personal details that are private to the couple and some irrelevant conversation.

DORIS: I think by the size of his light that Simon hasn't been over a year yet, has he?
SUSAN: March.

118

DORIS: Now he's talking about someone called Bill. Do you know a Bill?

SUSAN: No.

DORIS: That's funny. I thought he said Bill. It can't be right then. It's not Bert, is it?

SUSAN: Yes, that's my father.

DORIS: That's it. He said you'd been talking to someone about him but I thought he said Bill. Oh, he's saying 'No I didn't, I said Bert. I speak English, don't I?' He's a cheeky young thing.

SUSAN: Yes, he was.

DORIS: Now he says there's been a birthday since he went over.

SUSAN: Yes, in May. He would have been nine.

DORIS: He said they all cried and I had some flowers and me Grandad Bert said why couldn't it have been me?

SUSAN: Yes, he did say that.

DORIS: He says: but I'm all right, Mummy. It was very quick. He went out and never came home.

SUSAN: No.

DORIS: And I never saw me daddy. I saw him the night before.

SUSAN: Yes.

DORIS: I feel as if I was thrown. As if something hit him very quickly and he was falling into unconsciousness.

SUSAN: Yes, the disease hit him very quickly.

DORIS: And he never came round again. The back of his head hurt.

SUSAN: It did. It was a brain disease.

DORIS: That's the only indication he can give me. Call me Granny Doris, love, all the other kids do. I've got two grannies already, he's saying. Well, I'm an extra one, darling. But he said it happened within twenty-four hours, love. Incredible. From being a

119

healthy little boy he got very hot and he felt sick and I fell asleep then.

SUSAN: Yes.

DORIS: He said you took a sweater out and you kissed it and put it back. Didn't you, love?

SUSAN: Yes, I did.

DORIS: You see, he was there then when you did that and he saw you. He hasn't gone away. He's round the house still.

SUSAN: Yes, I know, I can feel it.

DORIS: Now, who's Philip he's talking about.

SUSAN: That's his dad.

DORIS: That's what I've been waiting for. I said to him, I know he's your daddy but what's his name?

DORIS: Right, so that's your daddy. Now, are you going to let anyone else speak? No, no he's not going to let anyone else talk ... I can see him so plainly ... He's talking about the police for some reason.

SUSAN: They came to take statements for the inquest reports because he'd only been in hospital twenty-four hours.

DORIS: I see, because he was saying, the police came, you know. I was very important ... I expect you were, darling. Now, who's Anne ... A ... A no it's not, it's Alan.

SUSAN: My brother-in-law.

DORIS: He says Alan was in our house, Granny Doris. He came back so I did a bit of good.

SUSAN: Yes, we hadn't seen him for years.

DORIS: Now, who's Rose ... R ... R it's an R ... sound. Hold it, hold hold it, don't get yourself fussed, lovey. Well, I am listening, Simon, honestly I am, but you keep bobbing about, first to your mummy, then to your daddy ... Richard it is! Richard!

SUSAN: Yes, next door.

DORIS: He said, Richard, will you listen. I used to play with Richard, he was my best friend when we weren't falling out!

SUSAN: Yes!

DORIS: He used to say I'm not friends with you any more, but do you know, Richard cried and he brought me a little bunch of flowers.

SUSAN: Yes, he did.

DORIS: 'Cos they stand and watch. He says there were so many people there. Margaret was there. Who's Margaret?

SUSAN: Richard's mummy.

DORIS: He says yes, they all cried. Richard was my best friend and we used to take it in turns on my bike. So you only had one bike between you, did you?

SUSAN: Yes, in our garden.

DORIS: And Margaret cried and do you know what she said to my mummy? She said, It could so easily have been me.

SUSAN: Yes, that's what she said.

DORIS: Now, there's somebody called George on the spirit side . . . I think he belongs with your father, love.

SUSAN: Oh, his brother George.

DORIS: George is here when he can get a word in with young Simon. He's telling me there was a great hoo-hah and they still haven't been able to find a satisfactory answer as to why it happened, but he says it doesn't really matter, now, does it. Simon's here, he's happy, he's full of joy . . . Who's Betty?

SUSAN: Aunty Betty.

DORIS: Betty loves me, he says she's got a picture of me and she puts roses by it.

SUSAN: Yes, she does.

DORIS: She puts them down and says those are for you

121

Simon . . . Now, George is saying he knows what the problem is. You are worried because you felt you couldn't say goodbye to him. And you blame yourself, love, we all do it, believe me. There's not a parent comes into my house, including me, that doesn't ask themself was there anything I could have done? Should I have noticed anything? Should I have insisted on having another doctor? Should I have done this, should I have done that? We all go through it, love. But there was nothing you could have done . . . He was one of God's special children . . . Now, March the seventeenth is important.

SUSAN: March sixteenth was the day he died.

DORIS: Why they are telling you this is that when March sixteenth comes round you're not to say it's a year since our Simon died. You must give him some flowers and say happy anniversary, love. Because it'll be the anniversary of the first year of his new life . . . Who's Tony? It's a T sound. Tony, Terry, Tommy . . . No, you've missed it Simon. Now hold it. What are you showing me? He's taken his shirt off and here, on his shoulder blade he's got a little mole.

SUSAN: Yes.

DORIS: I said you're not going to strip off, are you? And he said no only my shirt to show Mummy that it's me . . . Now there's a J . . . Jamey . . . no, Jenny.

SUSAN: That's his friend's mum.

DORIS: What about a caravan, love? I've just been talking about a caravan but you know a caravan too?

SUSAN: Yes, his grandpa's caravan. He lives in a caravan. We've just been there.

DORIS: Well, he went with you . . . You see, for a child like Simon who was eight when he went over, to suddenly find himself having to live somewhere else

122

with people he didn't know before was a great shock, so they let him come back and see you and join in with what you're doing. And he says we went to the caravan, you know. We did. And I, I-I-I-I . . . He stutters when he gets excited.

SUSAN: Yes, he did.

DORIS: He's getting so excited his tongue trips over itself. At the caravan there's four steps, you know, and we've been going there since Mummy had to lift me down but now I'm a big boy and I walk up and down them myself.

SUSAN: Yes, we've been going there since he was very small.

DORIS: And he says he still goes and cuddles his teddy.

SUSAN: No, we put the teddy in with him.

DORIS: Oh, I see you've got your teddy with you . . . I thought you meant you came and played with it . . . And you've got that other . . . elephant, is it? Funny-looking thing. I don't know what you call that? Your Wopple?

SUSAN: Womble.

DORIS: Now he's saying something about a guitar. I thought he said his daddy promised him a guitar when he's a big boy.

SUSAN: He always loved guitars. He had a little wooden one. Mark's got it now.

DORIS: I was going to have a proper one when I was a big boy, he's saying.

SUSAN: Yes, he used to talk about playing in a pop group.

DORIS: There's Mark his brother, then there's someone called Michael and someone called Nicolas.

SUSAN: His friends.

DORIS: Yes . . . and . . . Wait a minute, darling, wait a minute. Simon, love, off you go again, I can't keep

123

up with you. Tell me again. Yes, you had your teddy with you, yes and you had your womble. Now, what are you telling me? He's putting my hand over, like that. So you put something in his hand. Did you say a photograph?

SUSAN: Yes, I put a photo of the two boys in his hand.

DORIS: That's it, because he folded my fingers over and said it's a picture . . . And he twists his hair round. All the time he's talking to me he's twisting his hair . . . Do you drive for a living, Philip?

PHILIP: No, but I drive a long way to work.

DORIS: Oh, 'cos he said I drive with Daddy, you know. A long way we go. So that's what made me ask if you drive for a living. Oh, he's saying no, Daddy's got a big machine, he's ever so clever.

PHILIP: Yes, I work in a factory.

DORIS: Now . . . slowly, slowly, Simon. He won't let George do it. He will do it himself. Now, you know your sitting-room. It used to be two rooms.

SUSAN: The house where he was born was like that.

DORIS: And then the wall came down. Now, where you live now I'm facing a glass door and there's a picture on the right of him and a picture on the left, too.

SUSAN: There used to be a picture on the right but I took it down and now there's just the one on the left.

DORIS: Had he just had a watch?

SUSAN: Yes, just before Christmas.

DORIS: It's a proper watch, he says. Mark's got that now. He's talking about Christopher.

SUSAN: Christopher sat next to him at school.

DORIS: And there's a little chair that he used to take out in the garden.

SUSAN: Yes, a fold-up one.

DORIS: He says I used to go and sit out in the garden

with Mummy and I had my own little chair ... Oh, you didn't! Now, just a minute, let the grown-ups show me a picture, darling ... You've got me a bit lost now because you get very excited. Now, there are kitchen units and they look like pale olive green.

SUSAN: That's Lynne, next door but one.

DORIS: That's where he's taking me and there's a chopping board or a tray or something, on these units. He said I knocked it down.

SUSAN: Yes, he did.

DORIS: He's done it since he's been over to let you know he's there.

SUSAN: She blames it on Gary.

DORIS: No, it's Simon. He says it makes ever such a bang. And then he's talking about a dog.

SUSAN: Poppy.

DORIS: The dog can see me but they can't see me. That puzzles him ... You know when he was born, the cord wasn't round his neck, was it?

SUSAN: It was round Mark's.

DORIS: Oh, that was Mark, was it. He says the cord was round his neck and he nearly died, but then he didn't and it was me ... Now he said he had a money box and that's been opened and d'you know how much was in it? There was nearly £4.

SUSAN: Yes, he was saving for his Lego fire station.

DORIS: I only wanted two more pounds then I could have had it.

SUSAN: Yes, he could.

DORIS: £6 it was. You see they don't forget. He's still your child even though you can't see him ... Oh, he's disappeared now. I don't know where he's gone ... It's all right, he's back. No, I'm here, he said and I asked where he'd been and he said I've been to fetch Elsie.

125

SUSAN: Elsie lived over the road. She's only just gone.

DORIS: Did she have a stroke? Because Simon says she had a head thing too.

SUSAN: Yes, she did.

DORIS: Elsie says to tell you that your little boy is more beautiful than ever. She used to see him every day. He used to go down to post a letter because there's a letter box at the end of the road.

SUSAN: Yes, there is.

DORIS: Now they're talking about someone called David.

SUSAN: Yes, he lives next door.

DORIS: Then there's Mark and Lesley and Geoffrey.

SUSAN: His cousins, but he didn't know them.

DORIS: He does now ... And he used to love pink blancmange I heard him say ... Now, who's Maisie? Think of your mum. Is there a Maisie or Mabel connected with her?

PHILIP: Yes, Auntie Mabel.

DORIS: Somebody called Arthur.

SUSAN: That's my side.

DORIS: And somebody's got a van, I thought he said.

SUSAN: We've just got a funny little car. A Panda.

DORIS: It's not a van, love, it's a Panda. Oh, I thought it was a van, he says. It's not like the other cars we had.

SUSAN: No, it's not. It's square, like a little box van.

DORIS: Now, that's Irene or Eileen living. I have to give you both because they sound alike to me.

SUSAN: Irene.

DORIS: Then there's Kathleen.

SUSAN: Katy. It should be Kathleen but we call her Katy.

DORIS: His birthday's just gone, there's another one in August and one in October.

SUSAN: Yes, mine.

126

DORIS: Now, what is it you're telling me? Just before you went to the spirit world you had a new red sweater?

SUSAN: Yes, he had a new red sweater. He was buried in his favourite red shirt.

DORIS: You can ask me about it, he's saying, I don't mind because I'm here. They've told me about it. It's only like a garden in memory of Simon. There's a tree there, and roses planted.

SUSAN: Yes.

DORIS: When Mummy and Daddy go there I try to tell them please don't cry because it's only my garden. I'm not there. Can you tell me where you come from? All I've got written down in my book is 'child' . . . I thought he said Chester.

SUSAN: Winchester.

DORIS: December the ninth, I think he said. No? Could it have been September, November. No, I'm guessing at it. Let it go Simon, love. I think you've done extremely well. Do you think I look like my daddy, he's asking. Yes I do, love, and your mummy too. He's got your eyes, Susan, that's for sure . . . Well, I've got to get washed and changed now, love. You've done extremely well.

I know it was a terrible blow to you, love, losing him so quickly. But at least it was over in a few hours. He didn't suffer. Not like some of these parents whose children have leukaemia and they have to watch them suffer for years . . .

Anyway, I'll make you some more tea . . .

Well, as you can see, there is nothing eerie about a sitting. It's just a three-way conversation filled with trivial little bits of family information. Not much in themselves, but important to the people concerned because they are things that only the loved one could

127

have known, described in the language that he used to use.

There is such a difference in the way sitters arrive and the way they leave. Particularly the parents who've lost children. They walk in droopy and desolate, hope almost gone. And you should see the way they go out. Heads held high, the spring back in their step because suddenly they can face the future.

CHAPTER 8

It was cold, very cold, and all around me the world was exploding. Smoke blurred my vision, there were voices shouting, great flashes lit up the sky and crashes like thunder shook the ground under my feet.

Half-deafened and confused, I stumbled about, then there was a tremendous bang and everything went blank. I had a last vague impression of pulling something over me, of covering myself and then there was silence.

So began one of the strangest cases I have ever worked on. I have no real explanation for it even today. Yet it happened and I faithfully recorded every detail. It puzzles me still.

The above scene was shown to me as the last impression of Philip Alan Williams, a young soldier missing, presumed dead in the Falklands War. His parents had attended a memorial service for him in their local church and they were invited to the official memorial service at St Paul's Cathedral. But still they grieved and in desperation they wrote to me.

I had a very busy schedule but they sounded so unhappy I went against my normal family rule and agreed to see them on Sunday afternoon. Usually I try to leave weekends free unless I have church work to do because the older I get the more rest I seem to need. Psychic contact seems to be very physically draining.

Anyway, the Williams's arrived and I was glad I'd broken my weekend rule. We had a marvellous sitting. Philip Alan came through and gave a mass of information about his family, along with quite a few private, personal details that no one, apart from his closest friends and family, could have known. He described the place where he was last seen, the people he was with and the terrifying events going on – all with great accuracy as we discovered afterwards.

Yet unknown to us, as his parents were speeding down the motorway to London, halfway across the world in the Falklands Philip was walking into a house in Goose Green. He was cold, half starved and exhausted. He was given a meal and put to bed by the kind family and, at the time of our sitting, he was not on the other side, but in a deep, exhausted sleep.

So how did it happen? I've got no definite answer. My only theory is that the part of us that lives on after death, the spirit, is naturally present within us when we're alive and in some circumstances it can leave the body during deep sleep, travel about and return to the body before the sleeper wakes. These travels are sometimes remembered afterwards as a dream.

I realize this might sound far-fetched but it would explain the many cases you hear about where a person 'dreams' of going to visit a close relative or friend and finds them ill, only to discover the next day that that person really is ill.

I believe that in Philip's case he was anxious about his parents, knowing that they must have feared the worst, and when he slept, his 'spirit' restlessly came in search of them to give them reassurance.

The psychic 'pull' must have been very strong when you consider that the three of us, his mother, father and me, were sitting there concentrating all our energies on contacting Philip, willing him to come and talk to us. The power generated must have shone out like a beacon on the astral plane and guided him straight to my living-room even though it was half a world away.

I cannot prove this theory of course but one little

remark after the event makes me think I'm right. During the sitting Philip mentioned something about his father having bought a new car. Now, he would not have known about this in the normal way because his father didn't get it until after Philip had sailed for the Falklands. Yet the person I was talking to mentioned the car. Very puzzling. Then when Philip finally arrived home from his ordeal his father proudly showed him the car but Philip didn't seem surprised.

'It's funny, Dad,' he said, 'but while I was away I had a funny dream. I can't remember it all but I remember I dreamed you'd got a new car – and you have.'

To me, that proves Philip was able to reach out to his parents from thousands of miles away even though he dismissed the experience as a dream.

That's my theory anyway but I'll put down the whole story and you can make up your own mind whether you agree with me.

The Williams's arrived, as arranged, having driven hundreds of miles for a one-hour sitting. The poor things must have been worn out so we put the kettle on to make them some tea, but even as I was crossing the hall I heard the name Goose Green.

Anyone who followed the Falklands War will know that Goose Green figured very heavily in all the reports about it, so I could be accused of guessing. Nevertheless, I heard the words so clearly and distinctly I was sure they were significant.

'Your son didn't go missing at Goose Green, did he?' I asked the parents.

They shook their heads. 'No. He wasn't involved in that, Doris,' they said firmly.

I was puzzled. I knew this wasn't a mistake because it was too clear, but if they said the boy hadn't been to Goose Green, then he hadn't.

It was only the next day we learned that even as we were talking Philip had turned up in Goose Green.

Anyway we sat down in the living-room, tea-cups within reach and I was about to tune in, when an odd feeling began to nag at me. There was something not quite right here.

'Are you quite sure your son's been killed?' I asked them.

'Oh, yes,' they said. 'We were invited to the memorial service at St Paul's and everything.'

'He couldn't have been taken prisoner?' I queried.

'No,' they said firmly. 'We were told there were no prisoners.'

I bit my lip. It was quite wrong of me to go on like this. I could be planting cruel seeds of hope in their minds when there was no sense in hoping. The Army were quite sure Philip was dead and they should know. The parents seemed to have accepted the fact and that was the best thing for them. It would be very wrong to unsettle them now. And yet . . .

Firmly I stamped on this rebel instinct and tuned in. I was instantly reassured. A young, male voice came straight in and gave the name Philip Alan. Called Alan for his Dad.

'Yes, that's Philip,' said his mother.

He gave his father's name, his sister's name and the name of a great friend of his.

'They've had a letter from Jimmy,' he said. 'And Stewart came to see them and they talked about me.'

His parents were astonished.

'Yes, that's true.'

Then he told me about himself. He chuckled and said he was a handsome lad, he had fair hair and he was trying to grow a moustache.

132

'Oh, I don't know about the moustache,' said his mother.

But Philip, if Philip it was, was adamant that he was trying to grow one.

He mentioned more family names and friends and asked to be remembered to various people, but he seemed unusually confused about which side some of his family were on. Occasionally a person making his first communication gets a little mixed up but in Philip this confusion was very strong. He would talk of people he'd met as if they were on the other side. Yet his parents would assure me that while these names were correct the people concerned were very much still with us.

Albert and Kitty were a typical example. He said something about meeting Albert and Kitty.

'But he couldn't have done,' said his father in dismay. 'Albert and Kitty are still alive. I was only talking to them the other day.'

'Philip, love, d'you mean you met Albert and Kitty or your father met Albert and Kitty?' I asked. He mumbled something about his father meeting them.

'Well, you must make it clear what side they're on, darling, or we'll get in a right mess. I thought you meant they were with you on that side.'

There was a strange scrambling of the vibration and a strong sense of confusion. Philip couldn't seem to understand what I meant. Abruptly he changed the subject.

'I didn't want to go you know,' he said. 'When I joined I never thought there'd be a war. On the way out we were laughing and joking but underneath we were scared . . .' I can't print the word he used but let's just say that Philip's language was just as rich as it always had been.

His mother nodded sadly. 'No, he didn't want to go,' she said. 'That's quite true.'

But he hadn't finished. He wanted them to know that,

although he had been frightened at the beginning, he hadn't been a coward.

'At least me mum and dad can be proud of me. I found me guts in the end. When it came to it you don't have time to think, you just go straight in.'

Then another voice interrupted, a young woman's voice.

'I'm Barbara,' she said. 'You mustn't worry about Philip. We're looking after him. He's all right.'

'That's his aunt,' said Mrs Williams.

Barbara said she was only in her thirties when she passed. She had been ill for some time but at the end it was very quick.

'I just went to sleep and woke up over here,' she said.

But Philip wasn't going to let Barbara take up much time. In the background I could hear organ music and Philip wanted to talk about his memorial service.

'They played *The Lord is My Shepherd* and lots of people came,' he said.

'I gave our Gareth a watch before I went away and he's still got it.'

He was also concerned about the pay still outstanding for the time he was in the Falklands. He wanted his father to chase it up.

'I earned the bugger,' he said, 'so you might as well have it.'

But Barbara was back. 'Don't you worry,' she said again. 'He'll be all right.'

Then yet another voice came in.

'I'm Elizabeth,' she said.

'That's his grandmother,' said Mrs Williams.

And she too was anxious to reassure them. 'Don't worry, we're looking after him.'

Listening to the tape afterwards I was struck by this constant reassurance. Relatives often like to let parents

134

know that they are caring for the lost child who is now happy and well on the other side, but I have never heard it stressed so often during one sitting.

'Don't worry. He's all right. We're looking after him.' I heard it again and again. At the time I supposed that Mrs Williams must be particularly worried about Philip because his body had never been found and she didn't know he had died. Afterwards of course I realized that Philip's aunt and grandmother were not merely reassuring us but trying to tell us what was happening. They certainly were looking after Philip and he *was* all right. There was no need to worry.

Philip was not going to let his grandmother have any more of a say than his aunt. Back he came again as soon as Elizabeth finished speaking. He mentioned the new car, then he said, 'Dad's been talking to Joe Bailey. He works with him.'

Mr Williams nearly fell off his chair.

'Joe Bailey. Yes, that's right. I have,' he said. But then he remembered what he most wanted to know.

'Can he tell us what happened and where?' he asked.

'Can you give me your last impressions, Philip?' I asked. Again there was that strange scrambled sensation. A feeling of confusion and bewilderment. Then came the nightmare battle scene and a name.

'Temple something,' I said. 'Tem, tum . . .'

'Tumbledown,' said his father. 'That's right.'

Philip was getting agitated. 'There were all these explosions and then boof! That was it.' It sounded as if he had probably stepped on a landmine or been caught as one exploded.

'Chalky White was there and Anderson . . .' he added.

'Yes,' cried Mrs Williams. 'We had a letter from Sergeant White's widow, and Anderson *was* there too.'

'I was in the Guards,' said Philip.

His parents confirmed that he was indeed in the Scots Guards.

'How old are you, love?' I asked.

'Almost nineteen,' he replied.

Again this was correct. Yet suddenly that peculiar feeling was back, something was not right. What on earth was it?

'Well, I don't know,' I said aloud. 'If it's not Philip I'm talking to, how does he know all these things? It must be him.'

His parents were quite convinced of it. The way he talked. The occasional swear words he used and the information he gave were absolutely in character.

Yet the very next morning the news came through that Philip was alive. He was safe and well after living rough for several weeks. When he arrived home he was dressed in Chalky White's clothes, his own having been in an appalling state after weeks in the wild. He had also grown a moustache.

There had been a terrific explosion, he said, and he didn't remember any more until he found himself wandering alone in the bleak Falklands countryside. Thinking he was behind the Argentine lines and would therefore be taken prisoner if he was caught, he laid low until, at last, the bitter winter weather forced him to seek help.

His parents were overjoyed and when they phoned to tell me the good news I was delighted for them. But I was also mystified. If Philip was alive then who had I been talking to during the sitting? Could it have been one of the other young men who was killed that day? But no, the details were too personal to Philip. Could it have been Barbara? Again I had to dismiss the possibility. Barbara had turned up later in the sitting and was definitely a new voice. What's more Barbara's voice was unmistakably feminine while the person I'd thought was Philip was unmistakably a young man.

The only conclusion I could come to was that somehow I had been talking to Philip, even though Philip was not dead.

So how did it happen? Well, as I've said, I've got my theory but I wouldn't insist it was right or force it on anyone else. I'll leave you to make up your own mind.

Philip Alan Williams however wasn't my only contact with the Falklands War. Soon after my sitting with his parents another set of distraught parents telephoned me. Marion and Don Pryce had lost their son, a Fleet Air Arm electrician, when his ship the *Atlantic Conveyor* had been hit by an Exocet missile.

Soon after the disaster, the Pryces' daughter, who was a nurse, accidentally knocked a book on the floor when she was looking for something else at the hospital where she worked. Irritably she picked it up and saw that it was called *Voices in my Ear*. Something about the cheerful yellow cover attracted her interest and although she was in a hurry she turned the book over and read the little introduction on the back.

It was enough to convince her that the book might contain something that would help ease the terrible sense of loss the whole family was suffering, so she took the book home. It was passed rapidly to every member of the family and when they'd finished it they went out and got the sequel, *More Voices*. At the end of that Marion phoned me.

I was still feeling bewildered over the Philip Williams case but I couldn't refuse the Pryces'. Something in Marion's voice told me I had to see her. The Pryces were a very close family, it turned out, and all five of them arrived on my doorstep. Mother, father, and three pretty daughters. It was a pleasure to see such a lovely family and, though our small sitting-room looked rather over-crowded, I enjoyed it immensely.

I'd always wanted a big family myself and though it wasn't to be I still enjoy the company of other people's families.

We chatted for a few moments then I felt the presence of a young man. He was a tall, slim lad with thick hair and the sort of friendly, open face that immediately attracts people and invites their trust. As he hovered close to me I felt compelled to touch my hair with my fingers.

Marion gasped. 'That's our son! That's what he used to do. He used to touch his hair just like that!'

'I'm Don,' said the boy. 'And there are two Dons over here now. Me and my grandad.'

At that an elderly male voice interrupted.

'Yes, he was named after me, not his father. We used to be called the Three Dons.'

I asked the youngest Don what had happened to him. Immediately I could smell fire. I could see flames licking around and I could hear a lot of shouting.

'I was helping some of the others to get overboard,' said Don, 'and I think my life jacket caught fire. When I jumped into the sea it went down.'

He was drowned very quickly, but at least he didn't suffer for hours in the icy cold waters of the South Atlantic.

But Don didn't want to dwell on the war. He changed the subject and talked instead of his friend Danny and his girlfriend Sarah.

'I think I would have married Sarah,' he said, 'if it hadn't been for the war. Just before I went, you know, Mum took me out to buy me some new things. She bought me some underpants.'

'Yes, that's true, I did,' said Marion.

He went on to give more family names and he said that

138

his sister had some pictures on the wall over the fireplace which he had given her, that his parents had a crucifix on their bedroom wall and that he'd given his youngest sister a soft toy. He also mentioned Mr Bond, his scoutmaster.

'Oh yes, he was a very keen scout,' said Don senior.

Then the grandfather came back.

'I died of cancer of the lungs,' he said, 'but there's no need to be sad. It was a happy release to go.'

'Is Don happy with you all over there?' I asked.

Don's voice came back. 'Not yet,' he said sadly, 'I miss you still.'

The power was fading but with a last effort he muttered something about 'Flowers and a message of love'.

There was a pause. 'Roses,' he added.

This didn't mean much to his family.

'Did you give him roses by his picture or at the memorial service?' I suggested.

But no, the Pryces couldn't think of anything that seemed likely. However the day of the sitting was 4 August. Afterwards they discovered that on 30 July their next-door neighbour had dropped a wreath made of silk roses from his helicopter into the sea around the Falklands with a message of love for Don and all those who had lost their lives there.

I never thought I'd live long enough to see Britain involved in another war or that I'd one day work for parents and wives who were suffering the way we suffered in World War II.

I know from bitter experience about the tragedy of war. There were the weeks of heartache when I was informed my husband was missing, presumed dead at Arnhem. Then the anxious months when I discovered that he'd been found but he was a prisoner of war and seriously injured.

Long before that I lost the boyfriend I hoped to marry

when his plane was shot down. I'd met John Stewart at a dance. He was a rear gunner in the Air Force, a tall fair-haired boy from Scotland.

He was kind and thoughtful and he was the first person to buy me an Easter egg. It was a big one with roses on it and I was thrilled. It was typical of John.

We had been going out together for eighteen months when we decided to make it permanent. He was stationed in Huntingdon at the time and I was in Wales and he wrote to ask me if I would meet him at Grantham so that we could visit my mother. Afterwards he said we could travel up to Scotland to meet his parents and buy an engagement ring.

I thought this was a wonderful idea and I dashed off to apply for a forty-eight-hour pass. Yet as I handed over my request a voice seemed to say in my head.

'You're not going to go.'

This sobered me up a bit. Oh, I suppose they'll turn me down, I thought. I was convinced that if I wasn't going it was because something my end would prevent it.

The pass was granted, however, and I forgot all about those warning words. Then on the Thursday before we were due to leave a bulky packet arrived for me. It contained the letters I'd written to John, with a note to say that he had been killed.

The terrible thing about war is how quickly it can flare up. In the case of the Falklands conflict it was over very quickly too, yet for hundreds of people those few weeks changed their lives for ever and they will never be completely happy again. They will carry sadness in their hearts – for as long as they live.

Violence isn't confined to war. It seems to spill over into everyday life and I get an increasing number of cases these days involving ordinary people who've met violent senseless deaths.

I've asked Ramanov about this and he says it's because we don't love each other enough. That until we learn to love each other more and not to expect more from people than they're capable of giving, then these things will happen.

I expect that's true but I still don't understand what makes one person lash out at another. I mean what makes a man beat the woman he's supposed to love so savagely that he smashes her bones? It doesn't make sense. All I can do is try to comfort the other victims, the ones who are left to grieve when the violence goes too far.

The case of Shirley X (I won't give her full name because she doesn't want her children to know the whole story) is a particularly horrifying example. Her mother came to see me because she was desperate to know more about what had happened to her daughter.

Shirley came through quickly enough but she was full of regrets. She couldn't settle until she'd told her mother how sorry she was for the mess she'd made.

'I threw my life away at thirty-three,' she said, and as she came close my whole body seemed to ache and there was a burning pain in my stomach.

'I suffered very badly,' she said. 'I couldn't have taken much more. I tried so hard to stay but it was no use.'

'Shirley, can you give me your last impression, love?' I asked. She said she went under and then I felt a falling sensation as if I'd been thrown. It was difficult to make out what was happening.

'I wasn't killed outright,' Shirley explained. 'I suffered.'

At first I couldn't see her, but I could feel that her hair swung down round her shoulders. Then she appeared by her mother and I realized she was a strikingly beautiful girl, with film star looks.

'Now, how can I describe your hair, Shirley?' I asked. 'You're not blonde and you're not auburn.'

141

'You could say sandy, I suppose,' she replied, but she was being modest. Her hair was a lovely natural golden colour.

'We used to call it honey blonde,' said her mother.

She mentioned the names of her ex-husband and her two children who lived with him. She talked of her grandad and dozens of other relatives and friends.

Then she mentioned a man's name.

'That was the person who was supposed to be her friend who lived in the same block of flats,' said her mother.

'Hah hah,' said Shirley when she heard this. 'Friend!'

She sighed. 'I didn't want to say because I didn't want to upset Mum, but it was him. He threw me and belted me and I hadn't got a lot left to make me look nice after the divorce but all I had was taken. My jewellery, rings and watches, everything was taken.'

'Yes,' said her mother, 'he stole them.'

'And now he's walking free,' Shirley added bitterly. 'You see, my mum and dad helped me so much over my husband and I'd been a real trial to my parents. I've got to be honest about myself, and then I made another big mistake and I was too bloody proud to go and say I've made a mistake, can you get me out of it. It cost me my life. Can you understand why I couldn't go to them when I should? I'm very proud, an arrogant young bitch and I couldn't face telling them.'

'That's the way she speaks,' I added hastily, in case her mother thought I was being insulting.

'Oh yes, that's all right. I know.'

Shirley went on to tell me she promoted things for a living.

'Yes, she did a lot of demonstrations,' said her mother.

'I made a very good living but I was so stupid, I always fell for the takers, not the givers. He was very cruel to me. He was evil, yet he had a fascination for me.'

142

She was worried about her sister who had had a nervous breakdown over the tragedy, and she was full of remorse.

'I lived in a slum and it was a slum, Doris,' she said. 'I came from a good home, a good clean home yet I just couldn't . . . I don't know. I'm so sorry for all the heartache I caused my parents, but my kids will be all right. As far as they're concerned I just died and that was it, but please God they never find out about the rats and the state my body was in.'

Her mother explained that Shirley had been dead for three months when she finally got the police to break into the flat and her body was a mass of fractures and broken bones.

'My ex-husband was upset when he heard,' said Shirley. 'There was no real bad feeling between us, we were just not compatible. He wanted a home bird and I was never a home bird. That was the main problem. Now he's got a wife who's content to stay at home.'

In the end her life was so unpleasant Shirley said she was glad to have gone to the other side.

'I was scared stiff of him,' she said. 'He wouldn't let me out of the flat. Before the last beating he fractured my femur and I never did get to the hospital. I was glad to be out of it.'

Afterwards her mother told me that they tried everything to get Shirley away from this man but she would never come. They even paid for a taxi and sent it to the door but it returned empty. Letters and phone calls went unanswered and when they tried to visit her this man wouldn't let them in. She was ill, he would say, the place was a mess and Shirley didn't want to see them.

Eventually they were able to convince the police that this wasn't merely a family dispute, that they felt there was serious cause for alarm, but by then it was too late. Shirley had been dead for three months, this man had pawned her jewellery and withdrawn the money from her building society account. He spent a short time in a mental hospital but there wasn't enough evidence to convict him of murder.

I came across another dreadful case like this quite by chance. I'd been asked to take part in a radio phone-in on Capital Radio.

It was the sort of show where listeners ring the studio and I try to get a few details for them over the phone line. This is more difficult than working with the sitter close to you but sometimes you get very good results.

The phone was going non stop and the programme was flowing with the usual loving messages, when a male caller was put through to me. At once I heard the name Susan, which turned out to be the name of his daughter, then there was a terrible pressure round my neck. I was choking for breath. Shocked, I realized that this girl had been strangled. But how could I say that over the air?

'This girl should not have died,' I croaked, my throat still dry from the unpleasant experience. 'She went over very quickly. It shouldn't have happened. Do you understand what I mean?'

The man assured me he did. There were a few more family details and then I was urged to move on to the next caller. Reluctantly I had to leave the bereaved father but I hoped he would contact me privately.

He did. Soon after the show I got a phone call asking if I could possibly see Mr and Mrs Chalkley, whose daughter, Susan, had spoken to them through me on the phone-in.

Apparently the case had been in the papers while I was away in Australia. Susan had been strangled by her lover who then set fire to the house in an effort to get rid of the body, even though Susan's small daughter was still inside.

Susan couldn't rest because she was so angry about

this and because she was upset by the things that people were saying about her. She didn't mind for herself but she couldn't bear to see what it was doing to her parents.

'It was the first time, Mum, I don't care what anyone says, it was the first time. Believe me,' she cried.

'I was living apart from my husband and I was going to get a divorce and then this had to happen. I know my parents worry that I suffered a lot but I didn't. I was unconscious almost immediately.'

The gossip that always surrounds such cases was still on her mind. 'I know what people have said but I didn't keep a bad house,' Susan sobbed. 'It was the first time, before God, on my baby's life, that I'd ever gone to bed with somebody.

'I don't know what I was thinking of. I was lonely and fed up and look what happened. But I wouldn't want them to think badly of me. We were brought up decently.'

She mentioned a few family names and remembered her grandmother and her two sisters' birthdays.

'I was the middle one of the family,' she explained. Yet she was still sad.

'There's been so much aggravation since it happened over my baby,' she said and her mother nodded. 'He didn't want to know about our Mandy before, so what the hell does he want to start now for? Now I've gone and my sister and my family have stepped in and said they want her, he's suddenly said he wants her.'

I paused for breath. Susan was getting very cross, and it was difficult to keep up with her.

'Presumably she's talking about her husband,' I said.

'Yes,' said Mrs Chalkley. 'That's right, but Mandy is very happy and well looked after by her father.'

Susan calmed down at this.

'Oh, she's beautiful, my little girl,' she told me. 'She's got big eyes and a fringe across her forehead . . .' Her voice changed again. 'You see it was in the bedroom. Then there was the bathroom and Mandy was in the room next to the bathroom. The bastard set a fire, you know. Thank goodness the bathroom was in between my bedroom and where Amanda was. The bastard . . . You see I used to go out, I won't pretend I didn't, but I didn't bring men home to sleep with me.'

She was starting to upset herself again, so to change the subject I asked her for some more details about her family.

She mentioned the boy who used to run errands for her, she talked of Whitley Bay where she'd spent many happy holidays as a child and then she spat another name.

'Dickinson.'

'That's the name of the man who did it,' said her father.

Finally as the power faded, she made a last effort to help her mother.

'Mum, you're going to stop taking those tablets now, aren't you?'

Mrs Chalkley crumbled. 'I've already tried to stop but I can't,' she sobbed. 'I go down so much.'

'Oh, tell her she must,' Susan begged me.

'They're not doing you any good, love,' I said. 'Susan does so want you to stop. She tells me you still feel guilty inside but it's not your fault. You think if you'd taken a bit more interest, maybe she wouldn't have got married when she did, or maybe the marriage would have worked. But there was nothing you could have done. She is a very strong-willed girl and she'd made up her mind.'

Susan, of course, had not changed a bit. She hadn't become a little angel now she was on the other side. She was still strong-willed and she was still angry about what had happened to her.

This is often the case. Possibly after years on the other side people learn saintly forgiveness and tolerance, but those who feel rushed over before their time remain angry for quite a while.

Stephen Peace, for example, was only nineteen when he was killed in a motor-cycle accident. He was a very good rider and had passed an advanced motor-cycling test, yet his skills couldn't help him escape a fatal accident. He was very sad because it happened at an exciting moment in his life.

'Julie and I were going to get engaged,' he said. 'On Julie's seventeenth birthday. I loved her very much, as she loved me, and I still love her.'

Everything was going well for him when one day he rode down Market Street he said, near his home.

'I was riding down the road when this woman pulled out in front of me. She did a U-turn without looking. I tried to avoid her, I turned the bike hard, but it was no use. I went into her sideways.

'And do you know,' he added furiously, 'that bloody bitch got away with it!'

He was anxious about Julie.

'She can't forget me,' he said. 'But I want her to be happy. I want her to go out with other people. She's so pretty. Her hair comes down to her shoulders and it flicks up at the ends. She always wears T-shirts. Even in the winter.'

Fred and Pat Peace, Stephen's parents, agreed that all he said was true and, hearing them, Stephen seemed to calm down. I've noticed that the one thing that helps these angry people is to get their grievance off their chests.

'Oh well,' he finished. 'Mum always said "That bloody bike, it's a bloody death-trap." If only I'd listened to her.'

CHAPTER 9

Early one spring morning in 1982, Waiter 25 clocked silently into the Pizza Inc Restaurant in Swallow Street, London.

He punched his number into the special clocking-in device on the till, which automatically recorded it, along with the date and the time. It was 20 March and the time was 6.54 a.m.

But when the owners, Richard and Barbara Possner, arrived an hour later at 8.00, the place was deserted, the doors were still locked and bolted just as they were left the night before, the burglar alarms were undisturbed and the till was switched off because the Possners possess the only key to switch it on.

Of Waiter 25 there was no sign. But then that didn't surprise them. They don't have a Waiter 25.

'The thing is, Doris,' said Richard Possner when he telephoned me several weeks later, 'it's just not possible. I mean, without the till key you can't record anything on the till. It just won't work. There is only one key, which Barbara and I keep for security reasons, and it was with us that morning in our flat.

'What's more, forgetting the key for a moment, we know someone must have been in the restaurant at 6.54 a.m. but how did he get in and out without setting off the alarms or breaking any of the locks?'

It was a mystery all right but this incident alone hadn't driven them to seek help. It was only when strange things were happening with such regularity that the staff were getting uneasy that the Possners realized something would have to be done.

148

There was the burglar alarm, for instance. The bell was situated inside the restaurant high up on a wall where no one could reach it without a ladder. So, when during a routine test the Possners discovered it wasn't working, they called in a specialist.

'When he opened up the bell he found a stone wedged inside it, breaking the circuit,' said Barbara. 'He said in all his experience he'd never seen anything so clever and he was used to dealing with the work of professional criminals. But even if a criminal had thought up the idea, how would he have got in to tamper with the bell? Richard and I keep the keys to the restaurant and you couldn't help noticing a man on a ladder messing about with the alarm.'

Then there was the clock. On the wall they had mounted a handsome station clock powered by an electric battery so that it didn't need winding. It was a lovely clock. Everyone admired it, but within days of coming to the restaurant it went wrong. No matter what anyone did, it would not go past twelve midnight. At midnight it stopped dead. In the end the Possners had to get rid of it.

But they couldn't get rid of everything. They needed the gas oven, for instance. Yet after a while even this became faulty. For no apparent reason the gas kept blowing out and nothing could be cooked. The engineers were called in and although they solved the problem, they deepened the mystery.

'They said they couldn't understand it at all,' said Richard. 'They said a hidden screw deep inside the oven had come unscrewed, but it wouldn't have done so on its own. Yet unless you were an expert on these particular ovens you wouldn't even know the screw was there, let alone know what it was for. You certainly couldn't see it by looking through the oven door.'

When they opened the freezer and found all the meat

149

defrosting because the switch had apparently turned itself off, they weren't even surprised so hardened had they become to the peculiarities of the restaurant.

The 'ghost', they told each other, had a weakness for gadgets. They began to feel they understood how his mind worked.

Well, they shouldn't have said that. Not aloud anyway. Because then he changed his tactics. One afternoon Richard walked into the restaurant and noticed a strong smell of gas. Several people complained about it and everyone could smell it.

Naturally assuming they had a leak, Richard telephoned the gas board. The emergency engineers arrived almost immediately. One sniff was enough to confirm that there was indeed a very bad smell of gas. Yet when they set up their instruments they could find no trace of a leak. After an exhaustive search of the area they were forced to give up, quite baffled.

It was around this time that Val, one of the waitresses, happened to be alone in the bar polishing glasses ready for the lunch-time customers.

'Val!' called a male voice.

She looked up, but no one was there. The restaurant and bar were quite empty. Impatiently she put down her cloth and went into the kitchen.

'Yes? What d'you want?'

The chef looked blank. 'Want? I don't want anything.'

'But you just called me, didn't you?'

'No, not me,' said the chef.

Puzzled, Val returned to the bar but there was no one there. She searched the store rooms and cupboard for signs of colleagues playing a joke, but found nothing. It was odd, that's all, and she would probably have forgotten about it had it not happened again, not once but several times.

Soon she was hearing her name called softly whenever she was working alone. It was always the same male voice but since he only said one short word, she couldn't get any clues to his identity. Age and accent were impossible to guess. At first Val found it merely irritating but as the weeks passed she began to get edgy. She wasn't frightened exactly but the place was beginning to give her the creeps.

It was some time before she mentioned it to the Possners. She felt a bit foolish, as if they would think she was going mad. But in the end it was so obvious there was something wrong she had to tell them. And of course they didn't laugh.

By now after six months at the restaurant they were convinced the place was haunted and they were beginning to take the ghost seriously.

They were both young, down-to-earth people, hard-working types who had never given such things a thought before, but this was different. It had reached the stage where the business they'd dreamed of for so long might be at risk.

'Could you come as soon as possible, Doris?' asked Richard. 'This afternoon if you like.'

I laughed. 'Oh dear, I'm afraid I can't come now, I've got somebody coming. What about Monday?'

'Okay. Monday,' said Richard.

And that's how, despite the fact that I was up to my eyes with cases involving children, I came to be sitting drinking tea the following Monday afternoon in a London restaurant.

It was a welcome relief from the pressure of work. These days I get so many thousands of requests for sittings that I have to turn away more than I can accept. For this reason I devote most of my time to bereaved parents because, rightly or wrongly, I believe they are the ones most in need of help.

151

The trouble is, this kind of work is the most emotionally draining of the lot and so, just occasionally, it's nice to get my teeth into a good old impersonal ghost.

Pizza Inc turned out to be a very nice, very unusual restaurant. The minute I walked through the door I could tell that there was nothing evil here. There was a warm, pleasant atmosphere and it felt, and looked, relaxing. The air of tranquillity might have had something to do with the fact that the place appeared to have been furnished with items discarded from churches.

There was stained glass in the windows, pews had been made into bench seats, there were bits of screens and altar rails and even a pulpit.

'Oh, isn't it lovely!' I exclaimed as we walked in.

'Glad you think so,' said Richard, looking pleased. 'We like it anyway.'

'Did all this stuff come from a church?'

He explained that it had been gathered from all over the place but a lot had come from old churches. He went off to get us a pot of tea and I stretched out in my chair.

'Well, this makes a change, doesn't . . .' I stopped and stared in amazement as a monk in a long brown robe walked past.

For a moment I thought they might be extending the ecclesiastical theme to the waiters and waitresses by dressing them as monks and nuns, but then I realized that this was a real monk and he'd passed over long ago.

As I watched he turned, and seemed to glide back past us but, as he drew level, he raised his head and gave us a smile of great serenity. Then he was gone.

Well, I thought to myself, there is a ghost here but he's not doing any harm, he's certainly not fiddling about with switches and making trouble. The monk is responsible for the feeling of peace and tranquillity. He likes to see his old things being put to good use and cared for.

All the same I was very surprised to have seen him. These days I rarely see adult spirits, I only see children. Occasionally an adult will appear, but hardly ever during a sitting. It's usually when I'm not tuned in and when I least expect it.

'Well, there's a monk here, I can tell you that,' I said to Richard as he came back with the tea. 'But it's not him. He's happy to come back now and again to see what you're doing with his stuff. No, there must be something else.'

But I could feel there was something complicated about this case, so I tuned in first to see if Richard's relatives could help. It was Richard's father, I think, who came through. He said how proud he was of Richard and that he had no need to worry because the restaurant was going to be a great success.

'Some of these incidents,' he said, 'are nothing to do with us. They are man-made. There is jealousy at work,' and he went on to name one or two members of staff who had recently left.

'These people had something to do with some of the incidents,' he said.

Richard agreed that he'd always been uneasy about one of the people named and was glad he'd gone.

However, even though some of the mysteries were of earthly origin, it was clear that others weren't. The next step was to find out where the spirit was operating from. Once we'd located him, we could talk to him.

In all these cases, the presence of the spirit is betrayed by a patch of freezing cold air. You have to walk slowly across the floor until you find the cold spot and, no matter how good the central heating, a cold spot will be there if there is a spirit present.

'Now,' I said to Richard and Barbara, 'I'm going to walk round the room and I want you to follow me, putting

153

your feet in exactly the same place that I put my feet. All right?'

They thought it was rather funny but, laughing and chattering, we formed a little procession and wound slowly through the restaurant.

Richard had a feeling the problem might come from the kitchen, so we went there first.

Carefully I padded over every inch of the floor but there was nothing. The temperature was quite even.

'No, it's not here, Richard,' I said. We moved on to the store cupboard. Again, though it was chilly, it was the natural chill of a cool room not the unmistakable sensation of a cold spot in an otherwise normal room.

We backed into the restaurant again and I stepped carefully along the strip of lino behind the bar. Halfway along I stopped.

'I think I've found it.' The room was warm but just here, close to the beer taps, cold waves were rippling over me. Then I realized I was standing next to the ice bucket.

I laughed. 'No. It's probably a false alarm. I'm beside the ice bucket!'

Was it just the ice bucket? I wondered, or was there something else there? I couldn't be sure and unless I was certain I wouldn't say anything.

I returned to the main body of the restaurant. It was fairly large and we patiently pigeon-stepped up and down the aisles. At last, at the far end, I felt another wave of cold air. I stood still. Yes, definitely cold air.

'Barbara,' I said turning round, 'come and stand just here and tell me what you feel.'

I moved aside and Barbara took my place. She paused for a moment, head on one side.

'Yes, it's cold. Just here. It's peculiar.'

Then Richard glanced up.

'Hey, you're standing underneath the fan!'

154

I followed his gaze. There on the ceiling was one of those big old-fashioned blade fans.

'Oh dear, would you turn it off, Richard.'

Richard obligingly went to the switch. The fan stopped and I moved back to my original position. The cold was still welling up like bath water. The fan had made no difference.

'All right, Barbara,' I said, 'come back and we'll try it again.'

Barbara fitted her feet once more into the place I'd indicated.

'Yes, it's still here. It's the strangest thing.' Then she stopped. 'It seems to be going.'

'Going?' I echoed.

'Yes. Now it's gone.'

Quickly we changed places and I realized what she meant. The cold spot had gone and now the area was the same temperature as the rest of the room. This was very odd. Of course spirit entities can move around but since the aim of causing a disturbance is to draw attention to themselves they usually want to be found and they don't whisk about playing hide and seek.

'That is strange,' I said, but time was running out and we couldn't spend hours chasing an invisible ghost. The restaurant would be opening soon for the evening customers and I had to be finished by then.

'Well, never mind, let's see if he'll come and talk to us.'

We returned to our table from which the tea things had been cleared and I tuned in. There was a confusing sort of scuffle as if several people were trying to communicate at once, then a male voice seemed to elbow the others out of the way.

'I was killed,' he said gruffly. 'I was killed here.'

Now we were getting somewhere, I thought with satisfaction.

'Here?' I said. 'What happened?'

Immediately I felt a rushing, falling sensation as if I was falling through the air and my neck and head hurt badly.

'I went right down the stairs,' said the man. 'From top to bottom. That's what did it.'

'Which stairs, dear?' I asked, because we'd just walked round every inch of the restaurant and hadn't come across a flight of stairs.

The man sighed as if I was being unusually dense. 'I'll show you,' he said.

Immediately in my mind I was standing at the top of a flight of steep, narrow stairs with an arch over them. They descended down somewhere gloomy and would need artificial light over them all the time. They were so steep that I could well believe it was dangerous to fall down them.

'I see what you mean,' I told the man. 'But are you sure the stairs are here? I haven't seen any.'

'Of course they're here. Right in this building,' he insisted.

I turned to Richard and Barbara. 'Can you think what he means?'

They exchanged glances. 'Well,' said Richard, 'there's a bar under the restaurant. It's nothing to do with us but it's in the same building and it has its own separate entrance down a flight of stairs just like the ones you described.'

'Do you know if anyone has fallen down them and been killed?' I asked.

He shook his head.

'Well, see if you can find out. I'm sure there has and I'm sure it was a man.'

Having no love link to work from made talking to the man very difficult because he had no special desire to talk

156

to Richard or Barbara and as soon as he grew bored he wandered away. Nevertheless we persevered. He mentioned quite a few names. Some of them meant something to the Possners, most didn't. Then he said Derek, or Eric.

Richard shook his head.

'They don't know him, dear,' I said. But shortly afterwards, as if he felt they really did know, he said, 'In connection with Derek – Bentley.'

Again the Possners couldn't place it. Neither Derek nor Bentley meant a thing to them.

But the vibrations were getting muddled again and I thought I heard another voice come in.

'I was killed, you know,' he said.

'Yes I know, you told me,' I replied, thinking I'd made a mistake and the first man was still talking.

'No, I didn't. This is Billy,' he said loudly. 'I was killed and it wasn't an accident.'

As he spoke I had a brief picture of a young man with flaming ginger hair standing behind Barbara's chair and there was a strong sweaty smell of gymnasiums.

'I was a waiter, you know,' he said, 'and I was killed.'

'This place didn't used to be a gym, did it, or have anything to do with gyms or boxing?' I asked.

'Not as far as we know,' said Richard, 'but we've only been here six months and I don't think the people before us stayed very long. There's no knowing what it was ten or twenty years ago.'

But then the first man was back with more names. They meant nothing to the Possners and I could see Richard looking at his watch. It was time to bring the sitting to a close.

'Now about these things that have been happening,' I said to whoever was listening. 'It's got to stop. You're worrying these young people and it's not fair.'

There was more scuffling then a voice said, 'Didn't mean to do any harm . . . sorry,' and faded away.

'Well, I don't think you'll have any more trouble,' I told Barbara and Richard. 'He says he's sorry.'

They seemed quite happy and we gathered up our things ready to leave as the first customers came through the door.

'Oh, before you go, Doris, would you like to see the staircase you mentioned?' asked Barbara.

I said I would. She led me out into the street and there next to the restaurant was another door. Barbara tried it but it was locked.

'Oh, what a shame,' she said, 'the stairs are behind that door. They're terribly steep.'

I stared at it for a moment or two.

'Would they finish at a point just below your bar?'

'Yes, I suppose they would.'

Immediately I thought of the cold spot I'd felt when I stood behind the bar, the one I'd blamed on the ice bucket. Also the fact that Val had heard her voice when she was probably standing near the same place. I was just about to mention this to Barbara when a band of writing over the top of the door caught my eye. It was the details of the licensee of the bar and his name was written up there, small but clear. Mr Derek Bentley.

'That's the Derek!' I cried in triumph.

Excitedly Barbara came to see and she called Richard. Derek Bentley, as plain as plain, the name that had come through during the sitting.

'I'll be right back,' said Richard. 'There's someone I can ask.' And he darted off up the road.

'Some of the people round here have been in the area several years,' Barbara explained.

Minutes later Richard was back, a big grin all over his face.

'Derek Bentley is dead,' he said. 'He died one night after falling down those stairs.'

Well, that seemed to settle it. John and I headed back to Fulham pleased with the afternoon's work.

But as it turned out, that wasn't the end of the story. Weeks later we heard that though the name calling and trouble with clocks had stopped the mechanical problems were still going on.

Lights kept switching on and off. The stereo kept breaking down, a blade mysteriously flew off a machine landing only inches away from the chef and within an hour of laughing and joking about the ghostly Billy, three of the boys who helped in the restaurant all suffered minor but unpleasant accidents.

This puzzled me until I remembered that if the cold spot behind the bar hadn't been caused by the ice, then there were two cold spots in the restaurant. This would explain why I'd contacted two different men, Derek Bentley and the mysterious Billy. At the end of the sitting when I'd asked them to stop messing about only one voice had agreed and sent its apologies. Looking back I think that voice must have belonged to Derek Bentley. Billy refused to commit himself and it seems Billy is still making his presence felt.

So who is Billy? At the moment we don't know. Richard and Barbara haven't yet found anyone who's lived in the area long enough to give them a clue.

I can see that one of these days I'll have to go along and have another word with Billy.

Around this time I seemed to go into a phase of spontaneously seeing spirit adults. I can't think why this should be unless it's doing so much work with children that's caused it. Maybe because I always see spirit children and I've seen so many of them lately, my psychic eye is getting so highly tuned that it's picking out spirits all over the place.

What with the monk and the flame-haired Billy at the restaurant in Swallow Street I felt sure I'd seen my quota of adults for the year. It's been a long time since my days as a young medium when I was so full of undisciplined psychic energy that I was seeing things all over the place and our homes were full of knocks and bangs and objects flying about. Yet suddenly here it was starting to happen all over again.

I was still rather run down after my operation and was wondering how I was going to get through the string of engagements looming ahead, when Lee Everett offered to give me some healing. Now John is a healer and he was already treating me himself, but I've always believed that every little helps and I accepted gratefully.

As usual Lee arrived with a companion. Not Annie this time but her sister.

'I hope you don't mind,' she said.

'Not a bit.'

I led them into the living-room and Lee's sister and I sat down on the sofa, while Lee sat opposite by the window. We were chatting away and Lee brought me up to date with the latest news, when a sudden movement caught my eye. I glanced up to see a man had appeared in the room.

My sofa is a three-seater. I was sitting at one end and Lee's sister sat at the other. To my amazement the man crossed the room and plonked himself down on the vacant seat between us. My eyes widened . . . I glanced quickly at the other two but they didn't seem to have noticed anything unusual. Lee was in mid-sentence and her sister was listening attentively. So, too, was our unannounced guest.

He wasn't doing any harm so I decided to leave him be.

160

If he wanted to drop in to listen to a bit of conversation I couldn't blame him. He looked so real and solid he had probably not been over long. Perhaps he missed our company.

'Well, I suppose I'd better start the healing, Doris,' said Lee suddenly. 'Change places with me, Bren.'

Obediently Brenda stood up but as she did so the man laid his hand on her knee.

'Don't go, Bren,' he said sadly.

But of course Brenda couldn't hear him or see him. He failed to stop her and, as she stood, his hand went right through her knee. The man disappeared.

Yet the sadness in his voice touched me. The man hadn't dropped in for a chat. He belonged to Brenda and he wanted to see her. Therefore I felt I must say something.

'Look, Brenda, I don't know what to do about this,' I said slowly, 'but it's so definite I must tell you. There's a man been sitting between us and as you got up to go he said, "Don't go, Bren." '

One look at her face told me I was right to mention it.

'Oh dear, it's your husband, isn't it?' I added.

She nodded, her eyes full of tears. 'He only passed last Friday,' she whispered.

Well, what could I do? After the healing session Brenda and I had a sitting and her husband was able to return with messages of love and reassurance.

Shortly after this there was a small gap in my diary and since the weather was fine, John suggested it would be a good idea if we went down to our caravan for a few days.

For a long time we've been dreaming about moving out of London. John would like to have a garden to potter in and I must admit it would be nice to live somewhere where you could hear the birds singing and when you walked out of your front door you breathed lungfuls of fresh air instead of traffic fumes.

We've finally had to face the fact that it would never happen. I need to be in a central position for my work, or people wouldn't be able to find me, and we can't afford anything else in such an area. It looked as if we would have to give up our dreams for ever. Then someone told us about caravans. Apparently you could buy them on country sites complete with furniture and some of them even had little garden plots attached. It sounded ideal for us.

'We could do with a bolt hole,' said John. 'This place drives you mad at times with the phone going non-stop.'

He was right. Often the phone rang all day and although we don't give out our full address people find us and come to the door on spec. It would be marvellous to have somewhere quiet to escape to now and again, where we could rest well away from the pleading eyes which were so difficult to refuse.

Terry was just as enthusiastic about the idea, and he kept bringing us advertisements of suitable places. Eventually we picked out a place in the middle of nowhere about an hour's drive from the flat.

Terry took us down to see it one weekend and we were all thrilled with it. It was in a small, green park surrounded by fields and it had two bedrooms, a bathroom, kitchen, living-room and a little garden. When you stood still and listened you could hear nothing, nothing but silence and birdsong.

'Oh, John,' I sighed, 'I don't care if we go bankrupt. Let's have it.'

So we did.

Soon John was pottering happily in the garden, I could sit out in a deckchair and watch him when the weather was fine and Terry was making lots of new friends. We all enjoyed it for different reasons.

Down in the country I tried not to think about my work at all so I was very surprised when I walked into our sitting-room one morning to find a strange lady sitting in the chair by the window, waving through the glass at the passers-by.

For a moment I wondered if I could have wandered into the wrong caravan by mistake, it was still so new to us. Then I realized that it was our chair she was sitting in and those were our flowers in the vase on the table.

Maybe she was one of our new neighbours. I took a step closer and she heard me. She turned and gave me a lovely smile.

'Hello, dear,' she said as if she'd known me all her life.

'Hello, dear,' I replied and then I blinked. She disappeared like a puff of smoke.

Even though I'm used to such things it's always a surprise when it happens because spirit people look so real. Often they look no different, no less solid than the people you pass in the street. I don't know where this idea of ghostly beings drifting about in long white sheets comes from but it's certainly not inspired by real contact with the spirit people.

'D'you think she could have had the van before us?' I asked John later when I'd explained what happened.

'Probably,' he said, 'but the neighbours are bound to know. We can ask them.'

'We'll be careful how we put it though, John. They don't know us from Adam and if we start saying there's a ghost in our caravan they'll think we're crackers!'

John laughed but he took the point. We made our enquiries as discreetly as we could, but even so it was rather difficult to get the phrasing right.

'You wouldn't know if a lady ever passed over in this van?' I asked our neighbour soon afterwards.

He nearly choked on his tea.

'What makes you say that? I've been here two years and I've not heard of anyone dying.'

I'd obviously not handled the subject very well.

'Oh I just wondered that's all – about who had the van before us, I mean.'

'Oh, I can tell you that,' he said and launched in to a description of the previous owners who were very much alive and kicking.

Nothing more was said and it seemed as if the identity of our elderly visitor would remain a mystery.

Then on another visit a few weeks later we met the people whose garden backed on to ours. They had been away on holiday when we were last down so we'd not had a chance to talk to them. We soon put that to right. Not long after we arrived we were chatting over the fence like old friends.

'Of course, old Mrs So and So died in the bedroom there,' said the woman suddenly.

I was instantly alert. 'You mean in our van?'

'Oh yes,' she said.

'Tell me, did she used to sit by the lounge window waving to people?'

The woman stared at me in amazement. 'Why, how did you know? She was in a wheelchair and she used to wave to me when I took the dog for a walk.'

So that was it. The van used to belong to her and she'd come back to have a look at us and see that we were taking care of it.

Incidentally, if anyone who has read my last two books wonders what we did with our cat, Matey, while we made our jaunts down to the van, I have to explain that we didn't leave him behind and we wouldn't have dreamed

164

of leaving him behind. Sadly, he passed over before we got our country retreat, which is a shame because he would have loved the garden.

One day he simply disappeared. He didn't come in for his meal as he normally did and when he hadn't turned up by nightfall I was fearing the worst.

'He's probably got shut in somewhere,' people suggested to cheer me up. Or, 'It's spring. He's probably having a last fling on the tiles.'

But the next day there was still no sign of him. John and I searched the walkways and the courtyard around the flats and found nothing. Matey seemed to have vanished into thin air.

That afternoon I felt terribly tired.

'I think I'll have a lay down, John,' I said yawning and, unusually for me, I was asleep in minutes. But it wasn't a restful sleep. Dreams came almost at once and in my dreams I saw a very tall man holding the body of a ginger cat in his arms. I couldn't see the man's face but the cat was Matey and I'm pretty sure the man was my father.

When I woke up I knew I'd seen the truth.

'We can put away Matey's bowls,' I told John. 'He won't be coming back. My father's taken him. He's on the other side now.'

We never saw him again.

It's sad because Matey missed his garden when we moved to London and he would have enjoyed stalking about in our little plot at the van. On the other hand I know he's got all the space he wants on the other side, because animals live on just as humans do and we shall see our pets again one day.

It wasn't many weeks before we discovered that even deep in the country we couldn't escape entirely. Word

165

got round in that mysterious way it has and some people were arriving unannounced. I discovered too that, even in the country, I wasn't to escape the lessons Ramanov wanted to teach me.

One evening I was watching television and John had gone round to our neighbour to take back a clothesline we'd borrowed, when I heard a commotion outside. I lifted up the corner of the curtains and saw a lady, a man and two youngsters all coming down the lawn.

'Perhaps they think the place is still for sale,' I thought. Oh well, they'd soon realize their mistake. I went back to my programme.

A few minutes later John came back.

'Hey, love!' he said putting his head round the door. 'There's a lady outside and she doesn't want to bother you but she wondered if she could have a look at you just to make sure it was you.'

'What d'you mean, make sure it's me?' I asked.

'Well somebody told her you were staying down here and she said she wouldn't believe it unless she saw it for herself. She says she doesn't want to be a nuisance, but could she just look at you for a moment.'

Well, what could I do? It was vain but I couldn't resist it. Up I got and out I went onto the verandah and, despite the fact that I was wearing an old sun dress, slippers and no stockings, I stood there feeling like the Queen. My admirers gathered round to gaze at me in awe and I have to admit it was very flattering.

I enjoyed myself thoroughly and granted them much longer than a minute or two. And what was the result of my vanity?

As I stood there on the verandah holding court like the Queen, a mosquito bit me three times.

The next day the bites swelled into hot red lumps that

kept me itching and scratching for days. And as I rubbed away at the blazing skin I couldn't help smiling.

Well, that'll teach you, Doris, I said to myself. What does Ramanov say? 'Your gift is for helping others not for your own self-aggrandisement.'

That's what comes of being vain!

CHAPTER 10

'Rawlinson,' said a voice.

Startled, I looked up to see who had spoken but even as I did so I realized my mistake. Despite the fact that I wasn't tuned in, it was a spirit voice I was hearing.

'Rawlinson,' it said again. 'Rawlinson.'

The car was speeding along the motorway, engine roaring, tyres loud on the tarmac, yet above the noise I could hear the quiet voice quite distinctly.

I was on my way to a public demonstration in Maidenhead and, as the Berkshire countryside flashed past the window, the name was repeated again and again. It was quite obvious to me that Rawlinson, whoever he or she may be, was going to be important at the coming meeting.

All right, I told the voice in the end, I understand. I'll see what I can do when I get there. I've sometimes wondered in the past how much comfort people can get from mass meetings. I know they are very useful in awakening interest and getting people to ask themselves questions that might never have occurred to them before but can you give much help to individuals? Is it better to give a lot of people a little or a few people a lot? In Maidenhead I got my answer, with the Rawlinson case.

As with all the answers I get in one form or another from Ramanov it was vaguely disconcerting. I was to stop bothering about things I didn't understand, do my job and leave the rest to the spirit world. How much or how little help I thought I was able to give was irrelevant because my messages weren't an end in themselves, but just another link in the chain the spirit world was building.

As far as I was concerned, I wasn't able to give the

168

Rawlinsons much time, but the spirit world was already at work with them and the information they got from me, on top of the things that had already happened, was all part of a process that was to change their lives.

When I went on stage at Maidenhead I chatted to the audience for a few minutes and told one or two jokes to help them relax. Then as the laughter died away and I could feel a general loosening up all round, I reckoned it was time to start work.

'Now, before I begin,' I said, 'is there anyone here by the name of Rawlinson or who knows anyone called Rawlinson? I've been hearing the name all the way down here so I know it's important.'

There was a stunned silence for a moment, then a man raised his hand.

'I'm Rawlinson.'

Immediately the voice came back, a young man's voice eager to communicate and clearly delighted to have got through first. The names tumbled from him so fast it was difficult to keep up.

'He's talking about someone called Margaret.'

'That's my wife,' said Mr Rawlinson.

'And Joe, or is it John?'

'My daughter's called Joanne.'

'Then there's Paul,' I continued. Then I stopped. The man nodded, yes he knew Paul, but he was clearly very upset. The young man came close in and I realized there was a great tragedy here. He was only nineteen, he said, and there'd been a car crash. In the background other voices were clamouring to be heard. I didn't want to start the evening on too sad a note and I didn't want to embarrass Mr Rawlinson.

'I'll have to move on, I'm afraid,' I told him. 'They're all trying to get through, but don't worry. I'll come back to you.'

As it turned out though, I didn't. There were so many spirit people determined to talk to their friends and relatives in the audience that our time ran out before I was able to return to Mr Rawlinson.

Wearily I left the stage and headed for the kitchen where my customary cup of tea was waiting. I felt rather bad about Mr Rawlinson but I have to go where the spirit voices lead me and that night his son, for I was sure it was his son, had not led me back to his father.

What I hadn't realized, of course, was that Glen, as I later discovered his name to be, was doing it the other way round. He was leading his father back to me.

I was deep into my second cup when suddenly the kitchen door opened and there stood Mr Rawlinson. He hesitated in the doorway obviously unwilling to disturb me.

'It's Mr Rawlinson, isn't it?' I said, motioning him to come in. 'I'm sorry I didn't come back to you but it was too sad. Your son tells me he was only nineteen and he was in an accident. He was coming round a bend, he says, and there was a head-on collision. Two people went over and three ended up in hospital.'

Mr Rawlinson look dumbfounded. 'Yes, that's right. My son and the other driver were killed and three passengers were taken to hospital.'

Glen was back now, loud and clear. 'I was killed instantly,' he said. 'I didn't suffer but I'm so sorry it happened. I shouldn't even have been there. I wouldn't have been there if it hadn't been for Kevin.'

Mr Rawlinson nodded. 'Yes, he was giving Kevin a lift home to Cookham.'

'I'm so sorry for the upset I caused just when I was doing what Dad wanted me to do,' Glen went on. 'Now they're shattered, especially Mum, because I didn't say goodbye.'

170

'Yes, that's what upset her the most,' said Mr Rawlinson. 'He always said goodbye when he went out but that night she was upstairs and for some reason he didn't call out to her.'

Glen was worried about his mum. 'She's falling apart and she's got to stop because I'm all right. I'm alive and I'm happy. Oh, and tell her Margaret, called Maggie, is looking after me.'

This was gratifying because apparently one of the things that most worried Mrs Rawlinson was that if there was an after life, Glen would be alone because very few of his relatives had gone over. The only one was his grandmother, Margaret, nicknamed Maggie.

On a lighter note Glen added, 'Tell Mum there's lots of sunshine here because she is a great sun fanatic, and tell her that I spend a lot of time in the halls of music. Not just with pop music, good music too.'

Mr Rawlinson drew in his breath. He recognized the phrase. 'In his spare time Glen was a DJ,' he said, 'and he always said, "I don't just play pop music, you know. I play good music." '

Glen went on to give more family names, then he returned to the accident. 'I wouldn't have minded,' he said, 'but I'd only sold a house that morning.'

Apparently Glen was an estate agent and the day of the accident he was particularly happy and excited because he'd just sold his boss's house and he was going on holiday to the South of France the following weekend.

That was about all I was able to do that night and it seemed little enough to me. I was particularly sorry that Eric Rawlinson's wife Margaret wasn't there. Apparently, Glen had only passed a month before and the grief was so strong she felt she couldn't face a public meeting.

What I didn't realize was that the whole family was to

experience a real change and a new world was opening up to them quite literally.

My communication, while not much in itself, fitted neatly into what they were finding out, and was further confirmation of the truth.

Several months later Eric and Margaret explained what happened.

'Glen was something special,' said Eric, a property developer and insurance broker. 'He was a positive, lively young man who was great with people. So many people loved him. In fact afterwards, when we were looking through the old photographs, it was difficult to find a picture where Glen didn't have his arm round someone.

'It was impossible to have an argument with him because he always apologized and put his arm round you. He gave out so much love. We're still finding out about the things he did for people and at the hospital where he was a DJ in his spare time, they are putting up a plaque in his memory because they were so fond of him.

'After his death the family were devastated. He was such an extrovert that there was a great void in our lives. Even today nothing can fill it.

'Yet some incredible things have happened. Four days after his death I had the most incredible spiritual experience. I've never known anything like it in my life. It is very difficult to put into words. All I can say is that on Thursday afternoon after the accident I was sitting in the kitchen in a terrible state. I was so distraught, so unhappy.

'Then suddenly the kitchen started to fill with light, a tremendous light like coming out of the fog into bright sunshine and I heard Glen's voice say, "You have to die to be born."

'All at once everything fell into place. Life, death, everything. I knew. I understood. Yet if you ask me what I knew, I couldn't tell you. At the time I felt uplifted, tremendously elated. I've never been so happy in my life. I wanted to rush out and open bottles of champagne.

'I turned to Margaret and she said, "Yes, I know. It happened to me last night." But when I mentioned it to a friend later, thinking he'd understand, he thought I was going out of my mind.

'I wasn't. I've never been saner. I'd seen the truth. Suddenly I understood what all those old clichés like "seen the light" really meant. The elation didn't last. The next day I was depressed again, but the truth remained.

'I don't believe any more. I know.'

The experience caused Eric to read as much as he could on spiritualism and philosophy and everything he read seemed to confirm his feelings. Although he'd never read these subjects before, he instantly recognized what they said. Even the philosophy was familiar.

In the past he'd been a forceful, down-to-earth businessman with little time for such matters. He didn't even know that the spiritualist church existed. Yet when the family came back from a holiday Eric had taken them on to get over the shock of the accident, he found two tickets for the meeting at Maidenhead waiting for him.

'A neighbour got them for me,' he said. 'She had read *Voices in My Ear* and *More Voices* and she thought that seeing Doris might help. There was never any question in my mind that I shouldn't go. I knew I had to go and I knew Glen would contact me. When Doris called out my name I was shocked but somehow not surprised, if you see what I mean.'

Of course, as I found, and as every parent I've ever spoken to has found, Eric discovered that you never get over the loss of a child, but you do learn to live with it. He also realized that it helped to talk about it, and the more he talked the more he became aware of a dimension he'd never noticed before when he was deep in his money-making schemes.

'People are embarrassed to talk about their beliefs,' he said, 'but once you make it clear that you understand, they come out with the most amazing stories. I've discovered that about sixty or seventy per cent of the people I've spoken to are spiritually motivated.

'One man I've known for years wasn't at all surprised by my experiences. "I know you're right," he said, "because of what happened to my brother."

'Apparently his brother had been extremely fond of their grandfather, but while he was away in the Navy, the grandfather died. When the brother's ship docked, the whole family went to meet him and once the greetings were over their mother said, "I'm afraid there's some sad news as well."

' "If it's about Grandad, I know," said the brother. "I know he's gone. He came to me on board and told me."

'The family were astonished but the brother stuck to his story. "He appeared to me on the ship and said goodbye," he said.

'The strange thing is,' Eric added, 'I've heard dozens of stories like that ever since.'

Margaret Rawlinson knows exactly what he means. Although she didn't feel able to attend the Maidenhead meeting, she, too, was learning and discovering.

'That meeting was too soon for me,' she said. 'I was still in the depths of grief. Yet I'm glad Eric went because the things he was able to tell us afterwards helped the whole family so much. We knew nothing about the subject at all. We were feeling terrible, then suddenly there was this joyous news. It brought us such comfort to know that the person we loved was still there and that we'd meet again one day.

'We've been reading books ever since and talking to

people and we have been told the most amazing things. One woman from the village told me that she knew there was life after death because she'd been to the other side. She had been involved in a terrible accident and she had "died" for several minutes. She says she can remember what happened in great detail. She said she was in a tunnel and there was a bright light at the end and she could see all these loving people waiting for her. She was moving along the tunnel towards them and she knew that once she reached the light she would be "over". Then suddenly she was pulled back again and the doctors revived her.

'She also believes she has visited her grandmother – in a dream that she is convinced wasn't a dream. She was very sad because her grandmother died and she hadn't said goodbye. One night she "dreamed" she met her grandmother in a beautiful place. Her grandmother was looking much younger than she remembered her and they hugged and kissed and said goodbye. Most people would say it was a dream, but this woman is quite convinced it actually happened.'

For Eric Rawlinson the tragedy has had far-reaching effects.

'The most important thing that has happened to me since the accident is that I'm no longer afraid of dying. I used to be terribly afraid. I used to wake up in the night in a cold sweat imagining black eternity and vast, endless space. For years I'd been living in terror of death. Now I don't fear it at all. Quite the opposite. I know that death is simply rebirth on a higher level, to a world of beauty and love.

'But it isn't something you can get over to other people. Before all this happened, if you had told me this I wouldn't have believed it. I wouldn't have listened. You can't tell people. It's something they have to experience for themselves. Because of what's happened to me, I know.'

What's more, the experience has made Eric question his values and way of life. He is a successful businessman with a talent for raising money and now he would like to use his talent to help other people.

'I suddenly realized that in his short life, my son had achieved more than I have done in the whole of mine,' he said. 'Now I would like to do something worthwhile for others. In fact, I know I will. When the time is right it will all fall into place and I will see what I have to do.'

After talking to the Rawlinsons I will never again doubt the place that my little snippets of information have in the overall scheme of things and I have been going to public demonstrations with new enthusiasm ever since.

I'm often invited to speak at the Spiritualist Association of Great Britain's headquarters in Belgrave Square, and the last time I was there I had some very vivid communications. At one point I glanced up and saw a little girl dancing round the feet of a woman in the audience. It was quite clear from the way she moved and the way no one took any notice of her that she was a spirit child.

'My name's Helen,' she told me, giggling. 'And this is my mummy.'

Then she skipped up to the platform and got hold of the necklace I was wearing.

'Look round Mummy's neck. Look round Mummy's neck,' she instructed excitedly.

But I was too far away to see her mother's neck or what she was wearing. Helen wasn't going to give up though. After the meeting she accompanied her mother to the front to see me and round her mother's neck I noticed a chain from which hung a tiny picture of Helen.

During the same meeting two young people, a boy and

a girl, came to say hello. They were called John and Lorraine, and John's mother was in the audience.

'What happened, love?' I asked John and in reply he gave me what I took to be two contradictory sensations. I could smell gas very strongly but I was also surrounded by water, lots of water. That confused me. Were they gassed or drowned, or was one gassed and the other drowned?

John's mother explained. 'They were on a boat, Doris, and one of the gas bottles was leaking.'

'I tried to get help,' said John, 'but I couldn't make it. I collapsed. It's a good thing Mum didn't look at me afterwards. We were strawberry coloured.'

It was horrifying, of course, yet these two lovely young people were still together and happy.

You hear so many tragic stories on these occasions yet, strangely enough, there is usually a lot of laughter as well. I remember when I gave a similar demonstration shortly afterwards in Hitchin, Hertfordshire, one lady was astonished when I was able to tell her she'd got £42·50 tucked away in a tea caddy. The audience rocked and her face was a picture.

'Yes, I have,' she gasped. '£42·50 exactly!' And she stared at me with great suspicion as if she thought I'd been peeping through the window.

When I was working with a live audience on the Granada television show, *An Evening With Doris Stokes*, we hardly stopped laughing all night. An elderly man with a walking-stick came along to talk to one lady and I could hear his stick tap-tap-tapping in the background.

'He used to use a stick, didn't he?' I said. 'For walking and getting in and out of chairs.'

'Not just for that, either,' she replied tartly. 'He used to whack things with it as well.'

177

Everyone laughed but the man who had a strong York-shire accent wasn't put off.

'When's she going to get rid of that blue hat that's been standing on the wardrobe all these years?' he said. 'She gets it out and puts it back. Why doesn't she throw it away?'

'He's right,' the woman chuckled. 'It's still in its C&A hat bag.'

Then there was the dear old lady who had relatives halfway across the world.

'You've got relatives in Australia, in Melbourne, and relatives in Christchurch, New Zealand,' I told her.

'Yes I have,' she agreed happily.

'And next year they're all coming over to see you for a special celebration.'

'Are they?'

At this there was an irritated hissing in my ear.

'It's a surprise. A surprise,' said a voice. 'You weren't supposed to tell her.'

'Oh dear, I wasn't supposed to say that,' I apologized. 'It's a surprise.'

'It's all right,' the old lady beamed. 'I didn't hear a word.'

The animals got a look-in as well. A little later in the middle of something serious I had to break off and turn to someone else.

'There's a dog called Barney just turned up,' I said to a lady with tight dark curls. 'Do you know Barney?'

'Barney? Why, yes, I do,' she said in surprise. The last contact she'd expected was from her dog.

That was all for the time being, but a few minutes later I was dragged back to her. Oh no, I thought, when I heard what the voice wanted me to tell her. That sounds ridiculous. But the voice insisted.

'All right,' I said in defeat. 'Well, you know Barney,

well, with Barney was there a parrot? They're saying something about a parrot and Barney.'

A great hoot of laughter filled the studio and even the woman giggled.

'A stuffed parrot, yes,' she said. 'Over Barney's basket.'

There were sad cases as well, of course. There was a little boy no more than four or five running up and down the aisle. His name was Anthony he said and he had leukaemia. His parents weren't in the audience but a friend of theirs was. Anthony wanted his parents to know that he was all right now and his hair had grown back.

Then there was the baby girl who was a cot death victim. She'd gone over leaving behind her identical twin, Collette, and the seven-year-old girl whose mother had put a rose and a teddy bear into the coffin with her. Even Barney's owner was there for a more pressing reason than contact with Barney. She had been waiting for twenty-one years for news of her daughter who had never recovered from an operation to repair a hole in her heart.

There were warnings too. One woman was told of her relative's great concern over the cellar steps.

'He's very worried about these steps,' I said. 'Something about a door at the top and a child falling down. He wants you to put a bolt on the door as soon as possible.'

Another woman, there with her young daughter, was warned of a motor-bike.

'There's something about a motor-bike,' I said. 'There's a boy here who was killed on a motor-bike.'

The woman shook her head. 'No, I don't know anyone.'

'No, it's something to do with your daughter. Do you know anyone who was killed on a bike?'

She said she didn't.

If I hadn't been so certain this message was meant for them I would have thought I'd got the wrong contacts. As it was I knew it fitted in somehow.

179

'Who wants a motor-bike?' I asked.

'I do,' said the daughter.

'She's always on about it,' said her mother.

That was it. No, they were saying emphatically on the other side. No, and they pointed to the boy who had been killed.

'No way,' I said. 'She mustn't get a bike. They've brought this boy back as a warning of what could happen. She mustn't have a bike.'

The girl looked distinctly fed up as if she wished she had stayed at home.

'I shan't be allowed to have one now,' she muttered gloomily.

I felt a bit sorry for her but I wouldn't take back what I'd said. I've seen the parents of so many children who've lost their lives on motor-cycles.

Last year I was also invited to appear on the *Russell Harty Show*. Russell was a lovely boy but he seemed a bit nervous at first and he tried to rush me round to too many people in the audience.

That's the trouble with television. Producers don't like it if you stay too long with one person or if the messages are not evenly distributed round the audience. I can see their point but unfortunately I have to go where the voices take me and I can't force or hurry them.

I was a bit disappointed with my work that night for this reason. I didn't feel I had time to establish a rapport with the audience before Russell was rushing me again.

'Now,' he said, 'we have a surprise mystery guest here tonight. We thought it would be a bit of fun if Doris could discover her identity.'

Well, I was certainly surprised. I'm a medium not a mind reader, after all, but I hate to refuse a challenge.

'I can't promise anything,' I said slowly, 'but I'll have a go.'

The mystery woman was sitting in another room speaking to the studio by telephone. We only had a couple of minutes but soon I was listening to a warm Irish voice.

I've been to Ireland a couple of times and the accent sounded identical to me to the accents I'd heard on my travels, yet something made me wary.

'It's not genuine,' Ramanov whispered. 'Be careful.'

'I don't think this lady usually speaks with an Irish accent,' I said slowly. But, even as I was talking, spirit voices were drawing close, hoping for contact with her. One of them muttered something about the stage.

'I think this lady is something to do with the stage,' I said.

Then I heard the name Minnie.

The mystery woman said she knew someone of this name.

Next came the name Pat.

'And I'm getting the name Pat. Do you know anyone called Pat?'

There was a tiny pause as if she had taken a deep breath before answering.

'Yes, I know a Pat,' she admitted.

I began to relax. The contact was there. It would be all right.

'Well, I'm sorry, Doris,' said Russell Harty, so suddenly I jumped, 'but that's all we've got time for. And now here is our mystery guest.'

I was brought so swiftly back down to earth my mind was spinning and before I fully realized what was happening, the actress, Pat Phoenix, was walking towards me. I was thrilled. Pat was one of my favourite characters from *Coronation Street* and I never missed an episode if I could help it.

'Hello, Doris,' she said, smiling in such a friendly way

I felt as if I'd known her for years. But then I suppose in a way I had. She'd been coming into my living room twice a week for as long as I could remember.

'You know, if you'd have had more time you would have got me,' she said. 'You were getting so close.'

She was just as nice and natural as I'd always imagined and we became friends. To this day Pat regularly phones to see how I am and she gave me an autographed copy of her book which has pride of place in my bookcase.

Yes, my work does take me all over the place and into some very unlikely situations, from large halls to television studios and radio phone-ins, as well, of course, as my own living-room which has to double as a 'sitting' room, since it's our only reception room. When I'm working, poor John and Terry are banished to the kitchen!

Perhaps one of the loveliest aspects of my work is when I'm asked to be the medium at a naming service. This is the spiritualist version of a baptism, I suppose, but we don't baptize our children with water, because water is supposed to wash away sin. We believe that every newborn child is pure. They come straight from God or the spirit world and therefore they know no sin.

We name them with white flowers as a symbol of their purity. The other unusual feature of this service is that the child receives two names. The name his parents have chosen for him and his spirit name. This is the name he was last known by in the spirit world before he was born. To find out this name, a medium has to be present to tune in and ask.

This service isn't only for children, adults can take part too and I was 'named' myself in a lovely ceremony on the Isle of Man. It is not essential but I thought it would be a nice thing to do, a sort of public affirmation of my faith. The medium told me my spirit name was Lena, and John was given the name Samuel. Quite a coincidence that,

182

since my father, who still helps me, was called Sam.

I took part in a very moving but informal naming just a few weeks ago, but it came about most unexpectedly. We have known Del Robinson, president of the Wimbledon Church, for years. When we came back from Australia last time it was Del who arranged a wonderful welcome home party for us. So naturally we were very excited for him when he told us he was about to become a grandfather for the first time.

The event was very close when Del's partner, Reg, happened to be visiting us. We were changing our car and he had brought the new one down to us. Anyway we were standing in the kitchen having a cup of tea when he asked if he could make a phone call.

'Jackie's been taken into hospital today, you see,' he said, 'and I wondered if there was any news.'

'Help yourself, love,' I said. 'You know where the phone is.'

He turned and went out into the hall but before he reached the phone, Rose, Del's mother, came bustling through.

'He needn't bother,' she said proudly. 'I can tell you. It's a fine big boy. A *big* boy. It's here. He's been born,' and I thought she said they were going to call him Alec.

'Reg,' I called, 'phone by all means, but Rose has just told me the baby's here and it's a fine big boy.'

A startled look crossed Reg's face as if he didn't know whether to believe me or not.

'Well, I'll just check, if it's all the same to you,' he said with a sheepish grin.

I laughed and went back into the kitchen as he began to dial. It was 1.40 by our kitchen clock.

Reg was connected immediately and his voice floated in from the small hall. We could hear him getting more and more incredulous with every word until John and I had to put our hands over our mouths to stop ourselves from laughing out loud.

'Already . . .' said Reg. 'What? A boy . . . Really? That's a big one . . . and when . . . half past one? You mean ten minutes ago? Well, I'm blowed.'

This went on for some time. Then there was a click and a bemused Reg came back to the kitchen.

'You were right,' he said reaching for his tea. 'It's a boy. Born ten minutes ago and he is a fine big lad too, nine pounds, seven ounces.'

There was just one thing wrong. I thought Rose had said he was going to be called Alec. But he wasn't. It was Ashley.

The story didn't end there. Del Robinson was so delighted he asked us to go to see the baby.

We had a marvellous time. The little flat was full of white flowers and Ashley was the sweetest little fellow you ever saw, with smooth creamy skin, a tiny button nose and a few thistledown tufts of fair hair. I took him in my arms and tuned in.

Rose came over immediately for another look. 'Isn't he lovely? My great grandson,' she sighed.

Then another, firmer, voice took over and I realized I was dealing with someone on a much higher plane. He spoke with kindness and yet there was authority in his voice, too. It was the sort of voice you obeyed instinctively.

'I am the baby's guide. My name is Clear Water,' he said. 'His spirit name is John.' Then he was gone.

I passed this on to the parents and as I spoke I could hear cameras clicking away. The proud grandparents wanted to make sure that every event in Ashley's life was well documented.

We moved on to the tea and sandwiches and I kept Ashley on my knee for as long as Jackie would allow.

'Isn't it strange?' I said to Del. 'Ashley's spirit name is the same as my baby's earth name.' And because of this I felt a strong bond with him.

There was another surprise in store. A couple of weeks later the photographs were developed and Del noticed something strange about the picture that was taken as I named Ashley. There was me, quite clearly in the foreground with Ashley in my arms, but up near the ceiling to my left was a large ball of white light and if you looked closely you could make out the face of a baby in it. The light was hovering in front of the dark brown curtains and Del couldn't understand it at all. There was no glass or mirror anywhere near that could have caused a reflection.

He asked the photographer for an explanation but the photographer was equally baffled.

Since then we've shown the picture to many people and without telling them why we ask them what they can see, if anything, in the light. Most of them say without hesitation 'A baby' although some look at it for a long time twisting it this way and that before at last it falls into place.

'Oh yes, I can see it now,' they say. 'It's funny once you've seen it, it jumps out at you and you can't understand why you couldn't see it before.'

What's the explanation? I don't really know. My own guess is that John Michael was present and showed himself in the form that I would best remember him – as a baby, not much bigger than the one I was holding in my arms.

The spirit world loves babies and I often get news of them before the parents know themselves.

When I was working on the Granada programme, I

185

was talking to one of the men connected with the show and I said, 'You've got two children, haven't you?'

He laughed. 'No, only one, Doris,' he said.

'Well, they're telling me two,' I said. 'If you've only got one at the moment, you're going to have two soon.'

He shrugged it off. Anyone can say that. But a week later his wife told him she was pregnant.

In Australia they were tickled pink because I was able to tell them that the Princess of Wales was pregnant before the official news came out.

It was on 6 October 1981 and some Australian reporters had come to interview me. The royal wedding was still in everyone's minds and they were talking about the young couple.

'When d'you think they'll start a family?' asked the reporters.

'Well,' I started to say, 'I think they'll wait until . . .' but then I stopped. That was just Doris Stokes guessing, but over the top of my opinion came something more substantial from the spirit world.

'No, I don't think,' I corrected myself, 'I know. She's pregnant now.'

As I said it I nearly had kittens, because I don't go round predicting things and I don't profess to be a fortune teller. But this came through so spontaneously I had to say it.

Well, of course, it caused a great stir. The Australian papers splashed the headline all over the place. 'Doris Stokes says Princess Di is Pregnant!' and the Sydney *Sunday Telegraph* reported, 'Mrs Stokes, who predicted the marriage of Prince Charles and Lady Diana Spencer . . . predicts the birth of a Royal babe about July next year.'

It frightened the life out of me. Supposing I was wrong?

186

Boy, was I relieved when a few weeks later Buckingham Palace released the official news.

And what did the Australian papers do? Across the front pages: 'How Doris Stokes Knew Before the Queen!'

CHAPTER 11

In the distance I could hear a train coming.

It was dark and cold and the noise was getting louder and louder. Beneath my feet the rails were vibrating, the whole line singing with the approaching train. Suddenly lights filled the night, a blast of air shook my body and my senses were drowned in a terrible roar.

I had a brief glimpse of a motor-bike with a crash helmet placed neatly on the saddle. Then the picture went out as if a bulb had blown.

It is always a tragedy to lose a child but the worst tragedy of all is to lose that child through suicide.

All parents suffer guilt, but the parents of children who have chosen to die face unimaginable torment. For the rest of their lives they will be tortured by endless questions. 'Why?', 'Why did he do it?', 'Why didn't I realize?', 'How could he have been so unhappy without me knowing?', 'Where did I go wrong?', 'Was there something else I could have done?'

The questions never stop because there is no answer.

Other parents can find comfort in the thought that accidents will happen, illness strikes anywhere. But the parents whose children commit suicide have only the knowledge that the life they gave was deliberately thrown away because it became intolerable. Their love just wasn't enough . . .

Or at least that's how it seems to them. If only they could understand that they are not to blame. Neither are the children. The children who do these terrible things are as sick as they would be if they had leukaemia. This is understood on the other side where they are not punished but nursed back to health. And when they are well again these children are horrified at the suffering they have caused.

Nigel Cox was a loving, apparently happy boy who one night stepped in front of a train. When he realized what he'd done he was so distraught he couldn't rest until he received his mother's forgiveness.

In addition to her grief Betty Cox was haunted by an impression of Nigel standing behind her, sobbing. She thought she was going out of her mind. In fact the bond between mother and son was so strong she was simply sharing his anguish.

It was Betty's friend, Lois, who first contacted me. She was afraid for Betty, she explained. Since the tragedy she'd been unable to get over her grief and they were afraid of what she might do. She so loved Nigel that she felt her life was not worth living without him.

It was obvious that Nigel was a special child – well, listen to Betty's description:

'He was a wonderful baby, Doris. He was so contented. He never cried. He grew up to be a happy lad with a great sense of humour. We had a lot of fun together. I miss the laughs. He was very generous even to the point of being taken for granted, but he enjoyed helping others. The last two years he loved to help his friends with their bikes and they loved him so much that over a hundred of them came to his funeral.'

Nigel was there as soon as I tuned in and it was clear his grief was as strong as his mother's. He was sobbing and all I could hear was, 'Forgive me, forgive me.'

Until he heard his mother say the words I couldn't get anything else out of him.

'Of course I forgive you, Nigel,' Betty said at last when she realized the problem. Immediately the atmosphere changed. A weight had been lifted from Nigel's shoulders.

'I'm so sorry for what I did,' he told me. 'I must have had a brain storm.'

As we talked, he explained that he had everything to live for. A loving family, lots of friends and the prospect of a good job when he finished college. Then things started to go wrong. One evening he went out on a recently acquired motor-bike and he was stopped by the police. He didn't have an MOT certificate for it and he was very worried that they would take him to court over this.

Had he been his normal self this wouldn't have been an insurmountable problem but he wasn't his normal self. A few weeks before he had been attacked in a disco and he had suffered a broken nose and concussion.

'Everyone thought I had recovered from the attack but I hadn't really,' Nigel told me. 'I changed after that. My personality changed.'

'Yes, he's right,' said Betty, 'he did change. He used to shout a lot over little things which wasn't like him.'

'But Nigel, why did you do it, love?' I asked. 'What happened that night?'

He sighed. 'I don't know why. It was like a brain storm.' Suddenly everything seemed too much for him. That terrible scene at the railway track flashed into my mind. Nigel rode to the railway line. Stood his beloved bike beside the track, placed his crash helmet on the saddle and walked in front of a train.

'Why didn't they do a post mortem on my head?' he cried. 'They would have found a blood clot in my brain. That's what did it.'

But he was all right now, he wanted to assure his mother. The only thing that made him unhappy was her unhappiness. He was being looked after by his grandmother and he often visited his family at their cottage in

190

Leicestershire. He knew about his sister's wedding and he wanted her to know that he would be there.

By the end of the sitting both Betty and Nigel seemed calmer and afterwards Betty wrote to me:

'Lois and I were on cloud nine coming back from London, so excited by the marvellous contact. Lois said I was looking different, the strain of sadness gone from my eyes. Funny that, for my friends at work today said I looked happier . . .

'Now I feel at peace that Nigel is safe with my mother and all the family. I am content to wait to join him when only a few weeks ago I felt I could not live without him . . .'

Margery Foden-Clarke was in a similar state to Betty when she came to see me. Her son, David, went out to the kitchen one Sunday afternoon to make a cup of tea, or at least that's what he said he was going to do. Instead, he hanged himself.

It seemed so senseless. He was surrounded by loving people, his mother, his sister, his wife and his two beautiful daughters. He had a nice home and a good job. What's more, he was a considerate man. What on earth could have made him bring such distress to his family and horror to his wife who found the body?

It was a question that whirled round Margery's head endlessly. She sat in my living-room fiddling with her tea-cup explaining the things that most bothered her about the tragedy.

'Well, let's see what David has to say,' I said and tuned in.

At once I heard a man's voice, very warm and loving yet there was tension underneath.

'I tried very hard, you know,' he said. 'I tried so hard with my life . . . but there was something at the back of my mind. I thought I had a brain tumour.

191

'I was ill. I wasn't kidding. Sometimes I felt as if my head would burst. I used to hold my head in my hands, but I couldn't make them understand . . .'

Margery agreed that David had been worried about his health but the doctor could find nothing wrong with him.

David went on to give more family names, then he returned to the day of the tragedy.

'I was going out to make some tea and then suddenly it was all too much for me. I said I feel like ending it all, and I thought someone said, "Why don't you?" The pain came back so I took some tablets and I don't remember much more.' That's when he hanged himself.

'I just wanted peace and quiet,' he said, 'and I wanted the pain to stop but it didn't work out like I thought. I was still alive. I went to hospital over here and I slept.'

When he woke again on the other side the pain had gone and he had time to realize what he had done to his family. He seemed happy in the spirit world but he wanted his family to be happy too.

'I wish my wife well,' he said. 'I hope she meets some nice man who will look after my children. Could you ask my mother to go out and do some voluntary work or something? She gets very lonely. She lives alone with just her little dog.'

Like Nigel he was sorry for what he had done.

'Can you forgive me?' he asked his mother. 'I'm afraid I left a lot of chaos behind . . .'

I still see Margery from time to time. She has her bad days, of course, we all do. But she feels close to David. He often makes his presence felt in the house and she knows that whenever she needs him, he's not very far away.

CHAPTER 12

Edinburgh
1 September 1982

Dear Doris Stokes,

Last night my daughter and I went to the Assembly Rooms to see you.

Whilst we were waiting in the queue to get in I said to my daughter, 'If all these spirits are lining up to give messages your father will be saying, After you, After you. He's so bloody polite he'll either be last or miss it altogether.'

Well, I was the last person you spoke to. The one who lost a wallet with £25·00 in it and who has an anniversay coming up this month. And then you said I must finish now. Oh, the frustration of not being able to hear more!

Anyway, my daughter and I were both so thrilled at the little you told us we came away from the town hall feeling so happy.

Is there any chance of a private sitting? I'm keeping my fingers crossed.

Yours very hopefully
Mrs Miller

Edinburgh
6 September 1982

Dear Mrs Stokes,

Because of the way you coped last night in what must have been very difficult conditions I must thank you and Ramanov.

You got through to me (I was in a blue dress seated on your 'actor's' right) through 'someone in a brewery'. This was my father who died in the 1914 war along with three of my mother's brothers. A whole family of young men slaughtered.

The other name, Duncan, amazed me so I thought immediately of Frank Duncan (you gave me Frank later) but I remembered after I left the hall how when I was very young, Isadora Duncan, the great dancer, was brought through as a guide. You also gave me Louise and as we have French ancestry this is likely.

The two wedding rings was right and the necklace.

I intend returning tonight. I have never had my Dad come through before.

Much love to you
Jean Bruce

Edinburgh
9 September 1982

Dear Doris,

I attended two of your meetings in the Assembly Rooms this month. I have read both your books and look forward to the one you are writing at the moment.

I listened to you speaking to the young woman whose mother had passed on with leukaemia. It was a privileged experience. Then just after that you had us laughing heartily about the couple who had been left to look after a very spoiled pussy cat!

Thank you for coming to Edinburgh.

Yours
Mary Sleight

Strathclyde

10 September 1982

Dear Doris,

I had to write to you. I was the lady whose little girl was there Monday and Tuesday night. Thanks a million, Doris. I was too full to speak much. I would love you to have a photo but I cannot part with the one I have.

I see my little one often. I am one of the fortunate ones who have seen spirit in body.

Oh, Doris, thanks a million. I tried for a reading but I know the ones who were lucky are the people most needing comfort. Please remember my wee one at your Christmas party.

God bless you
Rose Keenan

Dumfries

11 September 1982

Dear Doris,

It was so nice to meet you and you looked much younger than the picture on the books.

I will never meet anyone who could reassure me more that I will meet my darling Morag again. I'm sorry I was so dull and upset. I need the drugs to help me through my days and work.

A lot of the names you gave me meant nothing at the time but afterwards I remembered a lot of them. Derek is Fiona's boyfriend. I wondered what Morag would have said about that.

You will see from Morag's photo that she is just as you described. How I wish the accident never happened and we could all be struggling on together, but at least I know that one day I can put my arms round her again.

195

I am so grateful that someone like you, Doris, has been given this gift.

God bless you,
Moira

One of the most exciting things I did last year was to take part in the Edinburgh Festival and these letters are just a handful, chosen at random from the hundreds I received after my visit.

Now what, you're probably wondering, was I doing at the Edinburgh Festival amongst all that ultra-modern culture and talent? I can only say I often wondered the same thing myself.

The place was full of weird people. Very nice people, as it happened, but definitely weird to a lady of sixty-three like me.

I couldn't understand it at all. Take the frog, for instance. What would you say to a frog who approached you in the restaurant as you were quietly sipping your morning coffee? There I was, just back from the hairdressers, all nice and relaxed after a soothing spell under the drier and I looked up from my coffee to find a frog standing there. Well, it wasn't a real frog. Underneath, I think there was a young girl but her feet were painted green, her hands were painted green, she was dressed in a brown baggy suit and she was wearing a great papier mâché frog's head over her own.

I think I put my cup down with rather a clank at this extraordinary sight, but the girl didn't seem to notice anything unusual. Making no reference at all to her appearance, she said:

'I just wanted to tell you that I saw your show the other night. I thought it was marvellous. When I saw

196

you sitting here I just had to come over and speak to you.'

'Oh,' I said. 'Well, thank you very much.'

Somehow my eyes remained fixed on this great papier mâché head and I couldn't think of anything else to say.

She smiled, at least I think she did under that mask; if she didn't, her voice certainly smiled, and wished me luck. Then she was off to wherever she'd come from. I looked across at John but for once I was lost for words.

There were many other strange sights that fortnight but gradually we got accustomed to them. When I walked into the foyer and saw two girls dressed from head to foot in black, patiently painting each other's faces with multi-coloured squares, triangles and circles, it hardly even struck me as unusual.

Edinburgh was a beautiful place. The wind was freezing and there were steep, cobbled streets that were a bit difficult at times but one look at that great rugged castle all floodlit on its rock and you forgot the cold. And I must say the bracing air certainly did me good. Despite the fact that I was working hard, I went home without the dark circles under my eyes that had been there for so long I thought they were a permanent feature of my face.

It would be much nicer this time if we stayed in a self-contained flat rather than a hotel, John and I thought. That way we needn't worry about bothering people for meals at odd hours and we could come and go as we pleased. So we asked some friends to find us a flat for the fortnight.

I must say they did us proud. The place they found belonged to a Mr Wong and you could have put our flat in London into the sitting-room and still have had space to spare.

When we walked in for the first time we just dropped

197

our suitcases and gaped. One wall was covered entirely with mirror tiles. Another was orange with curtains to match and on another wall was a full-length picture of Gordon Jackson dressed as the butler from *Upstairs Downstairs*. As for the kitchen, it was so smart and modern I reckoned you'd need a pilot's licence to operate the gadgets. Wouldn't it be lovely if I could take it home with me, I thought.

We were certainly comfortable, the city was beautiful and the atmosphere in the streets was friendly and exciting. Nevertheless, I was apprehensive.

I couldn't see how I fitted into this modern young festival. Surely the sort of people who came to see all this experimental theatre and dance wouldn't be the sort of people who would be interested in a granny like me. Supposing nobody came to the demonstrations? I'd look a proper Charlie then.

Ramanov must have been grinding his teeth in frustration to hear me doubting again. He had always told me to trust. If I would only trust I would have no worries. And, of course, I should have known it would be all right. The spirit world would not have sent me to the festival if they didn't think it was important.

That first night I had to work hard to get a rapport with the audience and then when I did, I seemed to be getting the wrong messages.

A young girl came through. She said her name was Morag and she gave me a Scottish surname as well, but I've been asked not to mention it. She said she was looking for Moira and that she had Robert with her. This information caused a great silence to fall over the audience. Nobody could place a Morag.

'Sorry, love,' I said. 'There's no one here who knows you.'

Reluctantly Morag went away and after that the other messages flowed.

The next night, however, Morag was back. She was a persistent girl. She seemed to think Moira ought to be present, but still no one claimed her and I had to send her away without making a contact. Again the sitting went well after she'd gone.

Soon afterwards, however, a lady who said her name was Moira telephoned me. Someone had told her about the unclaimed message and she thought it might be for her. Her daughter's name was Morag and Morag's father, Robert, was also on the other side. It sounded pretty conclusive to me and she asked if she could have a private sitting.

'All right, love,' I said, flicking through the crammed appointments in my diary. 'Could you manage next Friday at twelve?'

She said she could.

In the meantime the public demonstrations were attracting quite a following. I remember one at 5.00 in the afternoon when the rapport was so good I couldn't seem to stop and the mood changed from happiness to sadness and back again with every message that came through.

A young mother who had gone over at an early age with leukaemia came back to talk to her daughter. She gave several family names and then she said that one of the girl's sisters, Donna I believe it was, was getting married.

'Would you ask her to put one small rosebud in her bouquet for me?' she asked. 'And say "That's mum. Mum'll be there." '

At this the girl suddenly broke down in tears and as I glanced up, pausing to give her a moment to compose herself, I saw that the audience was a forest of handkerchiefs. Even the men were crying.

Five minutes later there was a complete contrast. The spirit light bounced over to two old ladies sitting side by side. They were sisters, alike as two peas, and a voice told me their names and various personal details.

Every time I said something that was right, they dug each other in the ribs, almost knocking each other off their chairs, and they were laughing so much they could hardly speak.

Suddenly whoever was talking from the other side said, 'And tell them we know they've got the big ginger cat and they're having to look after it.'

There was a gasp at this and more tremendous digs. Then they went off into hysterics.

'Is that right?' I asked. 'The cat belongs to your sister and she's gone off to Australia?'

'Yes,' spluttered one of them. 'She has and she's left me the cat to look after and blooming expensive it is, too. She didn't tell me it was on a special diet!'

Well, the place was rocking so much heads kept appearing round the door to see what on earth we were doing.

During a later meeting I kept hearing something about a sum of money. £50 it was.

'You've paid it out for something,' I said to the woman I'd been talking to, but no, she couldn't understand what I meant.

I moved on, but halfway through a message for someone else I had to stop and go back. The £50 wouldn't stop coming until we'd pinned it down.

'I'm sorry,' I said, 'but this £50 is for you and it's something to do with a gas cooker.'

The woman gasped and clapped her hands to her mouth.

'Oh, my God. She's only been over two weeks and I bought her gas cooker. I did pay fifty pounds for it.'

We'd got there. A feeling of satisfaction flooded out from my houseproud contact on the other side.

'She's got a bargain there, too,' said the voice. 'It was nearly brand new.'

'Yes, it was,' agreed the woman. 'Thank her very much.'

Word spread about what was going on and soon other performers would slip into the hall after their own shows and sit quietly on the steps or stand at the back. Little presents started arriving at the theatre for me just as they used to when I was in Australia. One lady gave me a crystal vase just big enough to hold flowers for my spirit children. Someone else brought me a brooch with feathers in it and one old lady gave me some lovely mother-of-pearl shells, all cleaned up and polished. I've put them in my cabinet.

Some people clearly had mixed feelings to start with. I came out of my dressing-room one evening and almost bumped into a woman who was standing determinedly outside the door. She had had no intention of coming she told me. She'd read about my work and thought that if God was going to give anybody a gift like mine he would have given it to priests and nuns not to ordinary housewives.

Yet at the last minute she changed her mind. Something had made her come along to the theatre to see for herself and after the show she was so impressed she felt compelled to come and talk to me. As we chatted I heard a young man's voice in the background. It turned out to be her son who had been killed.

Well, what could I do? I could hardly turn her away so I gave her a quick private sitting. As soon as I tuned in I got a falling feeling as if I'd been thrown and then

I landed on the floor with my fingers across my neck. Apparently it was a car accident and the boy's brother had been driving. Someone called Donald had gone over at the same time.

I wasn't to leave Scotland, however, without stirring up a bit of controversy. It seems to be getting a habit these days, although I don't do it on purpose.

Quite a few reporters came to interview me for the Scottish papers while I was there and during one of these interviews I was asked how I felt about God.

'I mean I don't believe in God,' said the girl turning to a fresh page in her notebook. 'Do you?'

'Oh yes,' I said. 'Without God I couldn't exist and I certainly couldn't do my work.'

The girl frowned. This was obviously not what she wanted to hear.

'Well, how do you stand on the question of Jesus?'

And I told her what I believe. I don't ask anyone else to believe it. I'm not saying it's a hundred per cent right. It just happens to be my view, that's all.

'Well, I think Jesus Christ was the greatest medium and healer who ever lived and that he was put to death for political reasons by the people in the church,' I said. 'They were afraid of him because they realized he had something that the church couldn't offer.'

The girl was scribbling furiously. 'So what about the crucifixion?'

'Well, it happened,' I said, 'but I don't believe that because Jesus was crucified he can wash me free of sin. He can't take responsibility for what I do. Only I can do that. If I do something wrong I can't just walk into church and have the slate wiped clean and go out and do it again. I am responsible for my actions and if I do something wrong I have to pay for it.'

The reporter seemed quite satisfied with this and after

202

a few more questions she packed up her things and left. But when the paper came out, blazed across the column were the words: 'Doris Stokes Doesn't Believe That Jesus Was the Son of God.'

This upset a lot of people and in particular it upset one of my sitters. For three months before the Festival a certain gentleman had been writing to the promoter's office regularly to arrange a private sitting. Then as the Festival drew near he began ringing every few days to check that the booking was still all right. He was assured it was. His appointment was for 12.00, Thursday.

The day of the sitting happened to be the day this newspaper story came out. I was feeling irritable because I'd been misunderstood, but when the doorbell rang at 12.00 I made myself calm down. It wouldn't be fair to take it out on this poor man who had been waiting so long for a sitting.

John went to the door but was surprised to find a young girl standing there.

'I've come to see Doris Stokes,' she said.

'No, I'm sorry there must be some mistake, dear,' he said. 'She's expecting a gentleman any minute now.'

'Oh he's not coming,' said the girl. 'He's given his booking to me.'

Apparently this man had been so angry at what I was supposed to have said in the paper that he refused to come, but since this girl was curious about what I did he said she could go in his place.

John doubtfully let the girl into the hallway and came to talk to me. Rightly or wrongly I was furious when I heard. I thought of all the desperate people in Edinburgh whom we'd had to turn away because all the bookings were taken. All those people who had lost children, or husbands, or wives, and were craving for reassurance. People who would jump at the chance of a cancelled booking, and he thought it would be all right to send someone who was merely curious.

'No,' I said to John, 'I won't do it. I'll save my energy for someone who actually needs help.'

Unhappily John went to relay this message to the girl in the hall. By the time the front door had slammed behind her I was already regretting my harsh words. Maybe I was being unfair. After all, it wasn't the girl's fault. Perhaps I had been too hasty.

Miserably I began leafing through the paper with that unpleasant sensation in my stomach that's caused by a bad conscience. The doorbell rang again. If it's that girl back maybe I should see her I was thinking, when John put his head round the door.

'It's Moira,' he said, 'she's got the date mixed up. You said Friday at 12.00 but she wrote down Thursday at 12.00.'

I sighed with relief. I had done the right thing after all.

I got up and went to the door.

'Never mind, love,' I said. 'You come in.'

I was very glad I was free to see Moira that day. She had travelled a long way to meet me in Edinburgh and she was so heartbroken at the loss of her daughter that she had thought about taking an overdose.

When Morag came to talk to me I felt myself flung violently into the air then there was a pain across my throat. Apparently Morag had been travelling in a car when the door came open and she was thrown out. She hit the pole of a bus stop and was killed instantly. During the sitting she gave the names of her brother and sister and her sister's boyfriend. She also mentioned a photograph that her mother had.

'The jumper I'm wearing in the photo is the one Mum took out of the drawer and held to her face,' she said.

She was very concerned about her mother because of the pills she needed to keep her going in her grief. 'Please don't, Mum,' she kept saying. 'Please don't.'

She was so distressed her mother promised to try to cut down although she didn't feel she could do without them entirely.

Strangely enough while I was in Edinburgh I got the chance to help someone who was normally to be found working only ten minutes away from my home in London.

The producer of the *Jimmy Young Show* had been ringing all round Edinburgh in a desperate attempt to find me. Apparently Jimmy was supposed to be leaving for a publicity tour to publicize his new book but at the last minute he refused to go.

Two incidents had convinced him that he would be in danger. A medium had rung the BBC to say that she had seen a black cloud hovering over Jimmy Young and she thought it was a warning. Then a friend of Jimmy's had gone to a healer and the healer had told him he could see a man connected with him in a plane crash. He saw a small plane and a man slumped inside with a gash on his head.

Jimmy put these two messages together and came to the conclusion that his small plane was going to crash as he travelled the country on the tour. The publishers were desperate. Would I be able to help put his mind at rest?

'Well, I'll talk to him,' I said, 'but if I feel he's in danger I'll have to say so.'

'Well, yes, of course,' they said, 'we don't want anything to happen to him after all. We just wondered if he might be over-reacting.'

I was quite excited as I waited for Jimmy Young to come on the phone. I've always liked his prog, as he calls it, and he has some interesting people appearing.

I was sitting there with the receiver in my hand daydreaming about whether I should ask him to play a Jim Reeves record for me, when a bright breezy voice suddenly crackled in my ear.

'Hello, Doris? How are you?'

It was Jimmy and sounding exactly like he does on the radio. He explained in more detail about the warnings and how he felt about them.

'Some people might think I'm crazy, Doris,' he said, 'but I don't want to take the risk.'

'Well, just a minute. Let's see if we can find any of your relatives on the other side and ask them,' I said.

I tuned in and after a moment or two I contacted Jimmy's father.

'Tell him not to take any notice,' said the father. 'He'll be all right. I'll be with him and he won't come to any harm.'

I passed on the message along with several other bits and pieces and the result was that Jimmy went on his book tour and afterwards flew on to Australia as well. He sent me an autographed copy of his book as a souvenir.

People still have some strange ideas about our work. When I returned to London I got a letter from a woman who said her vicar had told her she was wicked to read such evil books as mine. I have had quite a few letters like this over the years. The writers are usually upset about the unsympathetic attitude of the clergyman but determined to carry on reading nevertheless.

'I don't care what he says,' they often write, 'nobody else has been able to give me the comfort I've found in your books.'

It's a pity but at the moment the orthodox church can't make up its mind about mediums. Some clergymen regard us as servants of the devil, while others think we're wonderful. On many occasions I've shared the platform with vicars and I even gave the Bishop of Southwark a sitting in Southwark Palace.

Yet funnily enough that incident illustrates the confused attitude of the church to spiritualism. A friend of mine, the Rev Terry Carter, had taken me to meet Mervyn Stockwood who was Bishop at the time. Terry was due to appear on stage with me at our Easter service.

We drove through the enormous gates of Southwark Palace and we were led through beautiful rooms to see the Bishop. I don't know what I expected, but Mervyn Stockwood was certainly no disappointment.

He was sitting on his ornate Bishop's throne in a splendid purple robe and I felt as if I was meeting the King. I was rather nervous to start with but nevertheless we had an interesting sitting and afterwards we fell into general conversation.

Terry Carter had told the Bishop about his plans to conduct the Easter service for us but there was one point on which he needed advice.

'Do you think it would be all right if I wore my collar, Bishop?'

The Bishop thought for a moment or two. 'Oh, I don't think so,' he said doubtfully. 'No, I don't think it would do.'

He wasn't actually forbidding it but his reaction made me cross.

'Well, I think you're a hypocrite,' I burst out before I could stop myself.

The Bishop raised his eyebrows. 'Why do you say that, Doris?' he asked politely.

I'd done it now, I thought, so I might as well have my say. 'Well, look at you,' I said. 'There you sit in all your purple with your Bishop's ring on while I give you a sitting and yet you say Terry shouldn't wear his collar to conduct a religious service. I think that's hypocritical. It ought to be left up to Terry to decide for himself.'

I think he was rather surprised at this outburst but the Bishop was very good about it. He agreed that I had a point and that Terry should let his own conscience guide him on the matter.

And on Good Friday as we prepared ourselves for the meeting at Brixton, the Rev Terry Carter climbed bravely on to the platform wearing his dog collar for all to see.

CHAPTER 13

The last time I was in hospital an Irish friend came to see me.

'You always seem to be in hospital, Doris,' he said. 'How many operations have you had now?'

Briskly I totted it up on my fingers.

'It must be twelve now,' I said. 'I've had my boob off, my thyroid out, my gall bladder out, my ovaries removed, a hysterectomy and seven other minor operations.'

My friend listened to this impressive list with awe.

'Well, you know what it is, don't you?' he said at last.

'No. What is it?'

'They want you over on the spirit side but they can't have you because you're too busy so they're taking you over piece by piece!'

Well, I just roared with laughter. It was the funniest thing I'd heard in ages. I laughed so much I had to make my friend promise not to crack any more jokes – it was too much for my stitches.

Yet afterwards it set me thinking. At my age and with all the operations I've had I couldn't help wondering how much time I'd got left. Was this operation going to be my last? I asked Ramanov.

'Ramanov, can you tell me how much time I've got left?'

There was a long silence. Then came one of his typically enigmatic answers.

'You will have enough time to do the work God wants you to do.'

So I wasn't to know. Well, it didn't really matter. I'm not afraid to die. I know it's a great adventure I've got to look forward to and though I'm not in a hurry to leave John and Terry and all the people I love on earth, I'm happy to think that one day I will see my John Michael again. I will be able to take him in my arms and we will never be parted again.

So to all those parents like me who have lost children, I would just like to say, please don't leave your child's room as a shrine. Please don't turn away from those who are left.

Put his toys and clothes to good use. Hug the children who remain, and thank God for the joy of that special child lent to you for a little while, in the sure and certain knowledge that one day when your work is done you will see him again.

Do not stand at my grave and weep . . .
  I am not there – I do not sleep,

I am a thousand winds that blow,
I am the softly falling snow,
I am the gentle rains that fall,
I am the fields of ripening grain.

I am in the morning hush,
I am in the graceful rush
Of beautiful birds in circling flight,
I am the starshine of the night.

I am in the flowers that bloom
I am in a quiet room.
I am in the birds that sing,
I am in each lovely thing.

Do not stand at my grave and cry –
  I did not die . . .

Mary E. Frye
1932

WHISPERING VOICES

Chapter One

It was a hot summer day the first time I saw the house.

'Come and look at this Doris,' said Laurie and I walked up the road, puffing a bit because the heat was bouncing off the paving stones and making the air go swimmy and what I really longed for was a shady chair to rest my back and a long cool drink.

But then I saw it and for a moment the heat melted away.

Set back from the road and on a slope so you looked down at it, the house was blue and white with tiny lattice windows that glinted in the sun and a strip of garden ablaze with roses. There were matching blue gates folded neatly across the sloping drive and a pretty cottage-style front door.

'Oh it's gorgeous!' I cried in delight, and then with a pang I realized that a house as lovely as this would be far too expensive for me. 'Oh Laurie,' I said, suddenly disappointed, 'I wish I hadn't seen it. I could never afford that.'

But Laurie's not one to give up easily. He just shrugged and grinned his unstoppable grin. 'Well let's go and see shall we . . .'

It was a strange feeling, this house hunting for the first time at my age. In the past John and I had always been very grateful for whatever rented accommodation was offered to us. It might not look like something out of a glossy magazine but we filled it with our bits and pieces, put our pictures on the walls and made it home. Now, suddenly to be given a choice was a bit bewildering. And this business of walking into someone's home and wandering about inspecting the decoration – well I just couldn't get used to it. It always seemed so rude somehow to say no.

Yet it had to be done. It was the answer to a problem that had been worrying me for months. When John and I came to London we'd managed to get a flat in a block for disabled ex-servicemen because John is a disabled veteran of Arnhem. It wasn't a palace – in fact some people said the blocks were ugly – but it was comfortable and convenient and we soon had it looking cosy. We even made a miniature garden outside the front door with rows of plants in pots along the balcony and on summer evenings John and I could sit there in deck-chairs amongst our geraniums and busy-lizzies and pretend we were in the country.

In 1982 things got even better. As flats fell empty, the management began putting bathrooms into them. Until then we'd used a tin bath in the kitchen, but after a long wait, John, Terry and I were moved up the corridor to one of the converted flats. We paid a bit extra and had a shower installed as well and after a couple of weeks we couldn't imagine how we'd managed without it.

The improvement was so great that the blow that fell soon afterwards was doubly unexpected. The whole site was going to be completely redeveloped, the tenants were told. Our block was to be demolished to make room for a garden. The other blocks were to be modernized and in many cases two flats were going to be made into three.

We had a choice. We could live on a building site for the next five years while we waited for a flat in one of the other blocks to become available – though they couldn't guarantee we'd get another two bedroomed place – or we could find another home.

Now the spirit world has always told me not to worry – just to trust and we shall be provided for. But I couldn't help worrying. How could I do my sittings with the noise of building work going on all day? And how could we turn Terry out if at the end of five years we were only offered a one bedroom flat? The mobile home we'd bought as a country retreat might be a solution, but it was tucked away in a quiet little backwater near Ashford in Kent. Lovely for holidays but it would be very awkward to carry on my work from there.

I lay awake at night wondering what on earth we were going to do, and all Ramanov my spirit guide would say was 'Trust, child.' Which was all very well for him but for me it was easier said than done.

John, who's not a worrier like me seemed to be just as unconcerned. 'Don't worry yourself love,' he used to say soothingly. 'It'll work out. You'll see.'

But I didn't see. The months went by and nothing seemed to happen except that I developed a very bad back. London became very hot and dusty the way it always does in summer and John and I were very glad when our holiday came round and we were able to go down to the van for some fresh air.

And then when I least expected it, the spirit world stepped in. It was an overcast day and my back was playing me up badly so when John said he thought he might go out for a bike ride I told him to go because all I felt like doing was sitting about with a hot water bottle. Yet no sooner had John pedalled away than I was bored. I'd finished my book the day before and I'd got nothing else to read. There was no one around to talk to and nothing on TV.

Dejectedly, I fiddled around with the remote control buttons. Terry had got us linked up to the Oracle and he was always looking at it, but I'd never used it. I wonder if I can get Russell Grant's stars? I thought. I always enjoy horoscopes. I pressed a few buttons and sheets of information began flashing across the screen but half of it was double dutch to me and there was nothing that resembled a horoscope.

Impatiently I pressed more buttons and then suddenly one of the bright pages caught my eye. It was nothing to do with Capricorn. It was a list of properties for sale at a London estate agents, and one of the houses in South London had three bedrooms and was surprisingly cheap.

I did a quick bit of mental arithmetic. If we sold the van and added our life savings I reckoned we could afford that house. It would be the answer to all our problems.

Excitedly I dialled Laurie's number. I don't think I've introduced you to Laurie. He's the latest addition to our team. To say he's my manager sounds rather grand and it's not really like that. In the last couple of years my work has snowballed so much that what with personal appearances, radio and TV, as well as my normal sittings, I couldn't cope with all the organizing. People kept saying you need a manager Doris but it sounded so official I dithered. Then one day I was introduced to Laurie O'Leary, and we hit it off straight away. Laurie had actually given up a management career for a more peaceful life but when he saw what a mess I was in he decided to go back to management to help me. So now Laurie looks after the bookings, sees to the travel arrangements and all the other bits and pieces that take up so much time. He's much more than a manager. He's like one of the family.

Anyway, on the phone that morning I told him I'd read about this house I thought I could afford.

'Okay, Doris,' he said, 'I'll come and fetch you tomorrow and take you to see it.'

Well John wasn't bothered. 'If it suits you, girl, it'll suit me,' he said. But he didn't want to interrupt his holiday to go trailing through a house. He'd much rather potter about with his roses in the garden at the van. And in truth I knew he'd feel like a spare part – after all women are much more interested in that sort of thing than men.

Instead, Nancy our good friend and neighbour from the flats, said she'd come with me. As it turned out that first house wasn't right. A young couple lived there and they'd worked very hard on it but it was too arty for me. There was a bare white room with one sofa

8

in it and flash shelves. They'd stripped down the doors to bare wood and built a big stone fireplace. It was beautifully done and would have been perfect for a young couple but not an old fashioned sort like me.

I wandered about making polite noises but Nancy, bless her heart, is a bit forthright.

'Well that'll have to come out for a start,' she said shaking her head at the fireplace. And, 'Oh no you don't like those doors do you, Doris? They'll have to be painted.'

It was obvious we'd have to spend a fortune on decorating to get it to our taste and I don't suppose the young couple were too pleased at the thought of us tearing out all their improvements. I think it was a relief all round when I explained it wasn't quite us.

The area was very nice however: convenient for the shops and central London but green and open with trees and flowers in every garden and the countryside an easy drive away. Laurie checked with another estate agent and this time we were in luck. The first house we were sent to was very nice but somehow it didn't feel right.

'We'll think about it,' I promised. My back was killing me by this time and I was quite prepared to go home again but that was when Laurie called me to look at the blue and white house he'd found.

I fell in love with it on the spot.

'Come on then, let's have a look inside,' he said ignoring my protests about the expense and the fact that we didn't have an appointment.

A tiny little lady opened the door and when she saw me her eyes flew wide in astonishment.

'Oh Doris Stokes!' she gasped. 'I never ever thought I'd meet you.'

Her name was Hilda and she led us round chattering brightly. The house was as lovely inside as out. There was a beautiful kitchen with work tops all round – no more trying to balance half-a-dozen plates on the kitchen table – there were patio doors looking out onto

9

the garden and a spacious bathroom. The bathroom was a bit of a problem though because it was downstairs.

'There's no way I'll get down stairs with my legs crossed first thing in the morning!' I said doubtfully.

'Don't worry about that, Doris, you could have a loo put in the bedroom,' said Laurie.

The other problem was that with my bad back I could hardly lift one foot from the ground let alone tackle those stairs. Never mind, said the others, they'd look at the bedrooms for me.

They clattered away and Hilda and I stood chatting in the hall. It was a particularly nice hall. Square and airy with a rich blue carpet and sunshine streaming in through the windows on either side of the front door.

'I do like this hall, and such a beautiful carpet.' I was saying, when out of the corner of my eye I saw a blur of movement. Someone else was heading up the stairs to the bedroom. It was a frail old man, taller than Hilda and rather stooped and by the way he hauled himself from step to step, pulling heavily on the handrail, I guessed he had difficulty walking. A flash of intuition told me that this was Hilda's husband and substantial as he looked – he was a spirit person.

'Excuse me, love,' I said suddenly to Hilda, 'but was your husband an invalid?'

'Well, yes he was,' she said in surprise.

'I thought so,' and I glanced back at the stairs. They were quite empty. The man had vanished. So I was right. He'd passed over but came back from time to time to visit his wife and his old home. Well that was alright by me. I've never minded sharing a place with spirit people as long as they don't make a nuisance of themselves.

There was a lot of clumping overhead and then the others, unmistakably of this world, came thudding down again.

'The bedrooms are lovely, Doris,' said Nancy, 'and

the one at the front looks right over that little green outside.'

But still I hesitated. I'd love the house. I didn't need to go upstairs to know I'd be happy here but I wasn't at all sure we could afford it.

Hilda must have read my mind. 'Look, Doris,' she said, 'I'd like to think you lived here. As it's you I'll bring the price down.'

'She'll take it!' said Laurie instantly.

On the way home of course the doubts set in. Oh dear what have I done? I kept thinking. Our life savings and I haven't even been up the stairs. I hope I'm doing the right thing. Our friends in the mobile home park thought we were mad. There they were selling their houses to move into mobile homes and here we were selling our mobile home to move into a house. At our age! But then John and I have always been impulsive. We married a week after we met and they all thought we were mad then. In fact I couldn't convince my family it wasn't a joke. When they discovered after the wedding that we were only too serious they shook their heads disapprovingly and said it wouldn't last. Yet here we are 40 years on, still going strong.

You know you're doing the right thing when everything goes smoothly, however, and soon it was obvious that the spirit world wanted us to have this house. The legal side went through without any bother and just when we were trying to decided on a moving date, another piece of good luck came along. I was talking to *Woman's Own* magazine on the phone one day and I told them I'd let them have my new address as soon as possible.

'I've got my house at last!' I said happily.

'Oh wonderful,' they said, 'you will let us design it for you, won't you?'

Design it for me? The idea of having a house designed had never crossed my mind, but the more I thought about it the more exciting it seemed. It was true that Hilda's colour schemes wouldn't go very well with our furniture, but I haven't a clue about decorating. As long as a place is clean and comfortable I'm happy. But if someone else would sort out the paint charts and wallpaper . . . well, yes, it *would* be very nice to have everything matching and colour co-ordinated, as they say these days.

Well the house became legally ours by the end of the summer but we put off the moving date until December to allow time for the decorating to be done. In between we went down again with Deborah, nicknamed Dobs, from *Woman's Own*, to discuss the colours. Dobs had great plans. I couldn't quite picture what she meant half the time but she seemed to know what she was talking about so I thought it best to let her get on with it. At this point, though, I still hadn't been up the stairs and Dobs was very insistent that I should.

'Come on, Doris, you'll have to come upstairs,' she said. 'I must show you what I have in mind.'

My back was still twinging and I hadn't had any stairs for twelve years but it did seem ridiculous, so I held my breath and took a run at it. I flew up those stairs as if I was on a wire and when I got to the top I turned round and saw everyone was killing themselves laughing.

'You went up those stairs like a two-year-old!' giggled Dobs.

I couldn't help smiling. 'Yes well I didn't dare stop,' I confessed. 'If I'd run out of steam half way up I'd have been stuck.'

The planning stage didn't take very long because John and I were about to leave on the publicity tour for my book *A Host Of Voices*. We were going to be away three weeks and when we came back we were going straight into our new home. Terry was going to organize everything he said. He'd pack up all our things and arrange the whole move. I must admit I was a bit apprehensive. I was afraid I'd never be able to find anything again, but Terry told me not to fuss. He was quite capable of managing.

Well John and I set off on the tour, but back at the house things were far from tranquil. The first we knew about it was when Steve, the electrician, refused to work in the place on his own. He wouldn't say much about it but we gathered he heard strange noises when no-one was there and his tools were always being moved about. He could never find them where he left them.

Laurie was the next one to realize something odd was happening. He and Steve left the house together one evening and before leaving they turned the lights off at the mains, as an additional safety measure. They banged the front door shut, went out to the car and as they glanced back they noticed that the light was on in the loft.

Bewildered, they went back and checked. But the electricity was still off at the mains. Puzzled, Laurie went up to the loft and switched off the light. Then they locked up again and went outside. By the time they reached the car, the loft light was twinkling brightly. Back they went, rather nervously by now and switched the light off once more, and this time they headed for the car at a near run.

'Come on, Steve, let's go for goodness sake,' said Laurie, 'or we'll be here all night.' And they sped away without looking back.

About an hour or so later Terry called at the house on his way home from work. Afterwards he phoned Laurie.

'Did you know you left the loft light on?' he asked.

Finally Terry discovered for himself what they meant. Arriving first at the house one morning, he went in, locked the door behind him and wandered into the living-room to see what the decorators had done. But as he stood there admiring the paint work, he heard the front door open again. Thinking it was Laurie he stuck his head into the hall to say hello but

13

to his surprise the hall was empty. The front door was wide open and no one was in sight.

Crossly Terry closed the door and was just walking into the kitchen when there came a great crash from upstairs. A portable light on a long cable had disengaged itself for no apparent reason and come smashing down onto the floorboards.

On later visits to the house with Laurie and Steve, the three of them were startled by further unexplained crashes and even the sound of footsteps crossing the boards above when everybody was downstairs.

In the end it became a joke. They christened their unseen visitor George and when he became particularly troublesome Terry would say, 'Oh pack it in George, or I'll turn the old woman on you!'

Funnily enough, since John and I moved in George has been quite peaceful. Occasionally a door will open silently and close again when there's no-one visible and we say, 'Hello, how are you.'

Recently I decided it was time we had a chat to get things straight, so I waited until the sitting room door opened all by itself and then I tackled George.

'Your missis doesn't live here any more,' I told him because I was certain it was Hilda's husband, and in case he was confused I explained where she'd gone. 'It's our house now,' I added gently.

He said his name wasn't George but Edward, nicknamed Ted, and the house used to belong to him. He couldn't understand why we were here stripping off his wallpaper and knocking things about. Once I'd explained he seemed quite happy.

'We don't mind you popping in whenever you like, Ted,' I said, 'but don't move things about. It makes life so difficult.'

And there have been no problems since. Ted wanders in from time to time but he doesn't bother us at all.

Not long ago we had another spirit visitor as well. I don't think we are particularly unusual in this. I think

14

that probably most houses are visited by previous occupants and people who were closely linked to the building, it's just that most people aren't aware of it, or dismiss strange noises and unexplained draughts as the wind, or the people next door.

Anyway on this particular occasion we'd had some bricklayers in building a garden wall and I put a strip of plastic down in the sitting-room to protect the carpet from their muddy boots. I was sitting there by the fire winding down before going to bed when I heard footsteps quite distinctly walking across the plastic. Everyone else was in bed and the sound definitely came from just a few inches away. What's more one foot came down much more heavily than the other so I knew this person walked with a stick or a pronounced limp.

'Who's that?' I asked.

'Reggie,' said a man's voice and then the steps faded away and he was gone.

Reggie? I thought. How odd. I was sure the man who used to live here said his name was Ted. So the following day when our next-door-neighbour Margaret came in, I asked her about it.

'Did the man who used to live here walk heavily on one side?'

'Oh no,' said Margaret, 'he was an invalid. You never saw him walk. He was either in a chair or in bed.'

'That's strange,' I said, 'I heard this man walk across my sitting-room and he came down very heavily on one foot so he must have had a limp or walked with a stick. He said his name was Reggie.'

To my amazement Margaret burst into tears. 'That's my husband,' she whispered dabbing at her eyes. 'You've just described my Reggie.'

So now we know that Margaret's husband has been in to have a look at us to check that we're the sort of people who'll be nice to his wife.

It certainly was marvellous to come back from our tour to a lovely new house. Terry had done very well

15

with the move and, though there are still one or two things I haven't found yet, practically everything was safely in one piece. Dobs had worked wonders and for weeks I kept wandering around reminding myself that this magnificent place really belonged to us and we wouldn't have to leave it soon and go home. It still seems a bit unreal.

Dobs' *'pièce de résistance'* was my bedroom which was done up like a beautiful birthday cake in pink and white with mirror doors on the wardrobes all along one wall to make it look twice as big. When she'd suggested the mirrors and all the other bits and pieces I hadn't the faintest idea what it would look like and I must say when I saw the end result I was staggered – in the nicest possible way!

I sat there in my pink chair with the frill round the bottom and looked at myself in the mirrors, all thirteen-and-a-half stone of me and I said, 'Sixty-five! You could have done with this girl when you were twenty-five! All these frilly pillows and scatter cushions and pink satin bows on the pictures, and all they've got to look at is Doris in bed with no teeth in and her indigestion pills!'

I was appearing on TV AM with Derek Jameson not long after this and I couldn't help telling Derek about my beautiful bedroom and the mirrors. Derek's an earthy straightforward man with a great sense of humour and I knew he'd enjoy the joke.

'Well you know, Doris, twenty-five years ago those mirrors would have done your sex life a bit of good,' he chuckled, and of course I was in fits again.

A few weeks later on our wedding anniversary the delivery man came to the door with two packages. One was a single red rose in a long flat box with a card saying: Happy Anniversary, John and Doris, from Derek Jameson. The other was a square box which said: Happy Anniversary, John and Doris and the wardrobes. Also from Derek Jameson.

And the wardrobes? I said to myself. What did that

mean? Intrigued I tore off the wrapping paper. Inside was a crimson box with two black tassels on the top. What on earth could it be?

'D'you think it's an orchid?' I wondered aloud.

Laurie who'd just popped in suggested it might be stationery. John hadn't got a clue.

So I opened the box and inside was a black lace suspender belt, a pair of black silk stockings and a tiny wispy object that Laurie explained was a G string. The black tassels I'd thought were for opening the box were in fact to go on your boobs!

What a sight for the wardrobes that would have been, if only I'd been able to get them on!

Chapter Two

It was a very eventful summer that summer of '84 before we moved into our new house, and quite by chance we found ourselves caught up in a tragedy that moved the whole country.

The weather was very warm that year and so John and I, who're not well suited to the heat, tried to escape to our mobile home whenever we could. I was always glad when I could work from the van instead of our stuffy flat in London, and one particular week the van proved specially convenient because I was doing a demonstration at Tunbridge Wells – just up the road.

The show went well and afterwards I felt very drained, the way I always do, and I sat in my dressing-room drinking tea while the clamour of spirit voices faded away and the ordinary day to day world re-established itself in the the forefront of my mind. There were a lot of people milling about nibbling sandwiches but I didn't notice anyone in particular until Laurie came up.

'Doris, I'd like to introduce you to an old friend of mine, Ted Roffey.'

Ted was a slim, dapper man, he lived in the area and Laurie had sent him tickets for the show. He seemed to have enjoyed himself and he was very kind. He'd never seen anything like it, he said, fascinating. Certainly made you think. Then he steered a young a couple in my direction.

'They're dying to meet you, Doris,' he said. 'This is my nephew Tony and his wife Janet.'

They were a lovely couple. Very young, dark and a little shy and Janet of course was heavily pregnant. A pregnant woman is a wonderful sight I always think,

18

so full of hope for the future, and yet when I looked at Janet it was as if a cloud passed quickly over the sun. There was a sudden coldness and I felt afraid for her for no reason I could put a name to. I looked at her carefully trying to work out what was wrong and noticed that she was wearing high heeled shoes.

'You want to get those shoes off, love, and put flatties on,' I said. 'You've only got to go over . . .'

Tony who was standing slightly behind, put his arms round her. 'I'll buy her some flatties tomorrow, Doris,' he promised and as he said it he leant forward and kissed the top of her head and there it was again. That quick pang of fear. There and gone again, before I could identify it.

'That's right. Give her all the love you can,' I said without realizing what I was saying. 'She's going to need all the love you can give her in the next few months.'

They just smiled at each other, so young and so very much in love, and Tony brushed her hair with his lips again. They didn't realize how seriously I meant it. But how could they? I didn't really know what I meant myself. All I knew was that every time I looked at Janet I wanted to go and put my arms round her and support her in some way. I was sure there was something wrong somewhere. Yet she looked the very picture of health and Ted said the doctors were very pleased with her.

Oh stop being fanciful, Stokes, I told myself sternly. You're imagining things. What you need is another cup of tea. And I went to fill the kettle, pushing that shadow firmly to the back of my mind.

Half an hour later as she left the theatre, Janet stumbled on an uneven paving stone and went straight over. Fortunately there was no harm done, but Ted and Tony, remembering my warning, made her take off her shoes then and there and walk the rest of the way to the car in her stockinged-feet. In a way I was relieved. Perhaps it was just the potential danger of her high heels that I'd picked up.

Weeks passed and at last came the news that the baby had been born. Janet had had a little girl and they were going to call her Hollie. Mother and baby were doing well we were told. It was good news, of course, but it didn't banish the feeling that there was something wrong somewhere. Every day, when I thought of the Roffeys and little Hollie that shadow seemed to grow stronger.

Well I'm not going to ring up and worry them, I told myself, you're just being over-imaginative because of John Michael. And it's true that after losing my own baby at 5 months, I've always mentally held my breath over other people's babies until they're a year old. It might seem illogical but I tend to feel that anything can happen in the first 12 months of life. Once a baby has reached a year I let out a sigh of relief and feel that he's safely on his way.

Then one day I opened the paper and there was a story about the baby who was to become the world's youngest heart transplant patient. It was a baby girl and her name was Hollie Roffey. The paper slipped from my fingers and with a cold sinking feeling, I realized that this was what I'd sensed from the start. Apparently at birth, Hollie had appeared quite normal and healthy but as the days went by her colour didn't look quite right and she was taken off for tests. The day Tony and Janet hoped to bring her home the results came through. They were told that the left side of Hollie's heart was missing. The defect was too drastic to attempt a repair. Hollie's only chance of survival was a heart transplant – if a suitable donor could be found.

Everybody worked very hard to save little Hollie. By the time I phoned Ted, a donor had been found and the family were at the hospital pacing the corridors and drinking strong coffee while the operation took place. Ted's son, Simon, answered the phone.

20

'Simon, I don't want to intrude,' I said, 'could you just tell your dad that I rang and that we're praying for Hollie.'

I don't know how the Roffeys got through the next few days. It was such a tense time. Little Hollie's plight touched the whole country. The newspapers, radio and television carried regular stories about her and her brave struggle for life melted the coldest hearts. Amazingly for such a fragile little thing she hung on for 17 days after the operation. She was a born fighter.

At one point she seemed to rally, she started to suck and all the signs were hopeful. The whole nation held its breath. The length and breadth of the country people were rooting for Hollie.

Tony and Janet had spent every day at the hospital but at last Hollie's condition was so encouraging they were persuaded to go home for a rest. Tragically, while they were away their baby took a turn for the worse and before they could get back to the hospital she was gone.

John and I were at the van when we heard the news. I wasn't surprised, yet at the same time it was a shock and I felt desperately sorry for poor Tony and Janet. I knew exactly how they must be feeling. It was the story of John Michael all over again.

I know some people back away from tragedy. They don't know what to say so they don't say anything at all and you even hear of people who will cross the road rather than face someone who's suffered a bereavement. Yet the strange thing is, if you do face it, the words come and it means so much to the bereaved to know that people care.

It didn't even occur to me not to get in touch. Sadly, I dialled Ted's number.

'Ted, I'm so very sorry,' I said when he answered.

At the sound of my voice he seemed relieved.

'Oh Doris. Tony and Janet are here with us now. Can we come? Can I fetch you?'

21

How could I refuse? Scarcely half an hour later Ted arrived and whisked us back to his home. I think he was very glad that John and I happened to be in Kent that day because he was finding it difficult to comfort Janet and Tony.

They were in a dreadful state as anyone would have been. I put my arms round them both, then I sat them down and tried to talk to them. I don't know how much of what I said actually got through but we talked for about 3 hours.

'Listen, darling, Hollie's not dead,' I said. 'And she's done more in her short life than all of us put together could do in ninety years. She's paved the way to show that these operations can be done on tiny babies. Thanks to her, who knows how many lives will be saved. Just be proud you were chosen to be her parents.'

It's odd how in times of tragedy people often focus on one tiny detail which seems to take on an importance out of all proportion to the greater horror of what has happened. With Tony it was his baby's hair. Distraught as he was he was particularly upset because they'd shaved Hollie's head.

'She was so beautiful, Doris,' he sobbed, 'but they shaved her head. Why did they have to cut off her hair?'

He didn't really want a medical answer, of course, though doubtless there was one.

'Look Tony it doesn't matter,' I said, 'she's beautiful again now. She's got all her hair again on the other side. That wasn't Hollie you saw when you went back to the hospital, just her old overcoat.'

I didn't even attempt to do a sitting for them. It was too soon. Grief is natural, it's part of the healing process and I think it's better to let it out and adjust a little to the loss before contacting a medium. In the Roffeys' case though the spirit world wanted to clear up that one small point.

Suddenly as I was speaking I felt a small jolt as

22

something was put on my lap. I looked down and there was Hollie. Now I love babies and they all look beautiful to me, but Hollie was one of the most beautiful children I've ever seen. She was gurgling happily to herself and her head was a mass of tiny red gold ringlets, glossy as a new conker.

'There, isn't she lovely?' said a woman's voice. 'Tell Tony he can take it from me that she's got all her hair back now and I'm looking after her.'

It was Tony's grandmother and I gladly passed the message on. Only one thing puzzled me. The red gold hair. Both Tony and Janet were dark and I'd have expected Hollie to be dark like them or else baby fair with the kind of hair that darkens as the child grows. Yet Hollie's hair was bold and distinctive and quite unlike her parents.

It was only a few days later when I met Tony's brother that I discovered the answer. As soon as I saw his deep copper head coming towards me I realized that the colour ran in the family, and for some reason had bypassed Tony.

But the Roffeys' ordeal was far from over. The baby's body was taken to the undertakers and Tony and Janet had arranged to see her there. They told me about this and they kept hovering round until at last I realized what they'd left unsaid.

'D'you want to ask me to go with you?'

They exchanged relieved glances. 'Would it be imposing too much to ask you?' said Tony.

'Not a bit, love. Come and pick us up when you're ready.'

Well, it was an experience I'll never forget. I couldn't believe it. We drew up outside a bike shop, and at the side was a window, bare but for a vase with a few dusty artificial flowers in it. In we went and a man emerged from the shadows at the back.

'We've come to look at our baby,' said Tony painfully while Janet clung to my hand.

'Oh yes,' said the man. 'Follow me.' And he led us

out through the back of the shop, across a yard filled with old bikes, to a desolate little room at the end.

'In there,' said the man standing back.

Tony and Janet, quite numb, didn't move. 'Would you go in first, Doris?' Janet whispered.

'Yes, all right love,' I said and I'm very glad I did. The first thing I saw as my eyes adjusted to the light was a tiny white box no bigger than a shoe box, and a dead carnation lying on the top. Fortunately before we left the van that morning I'd cut a white rosebud, just starting to open and, quick as a flash, I whipped off the carnation and laid the rosebud in its place. And then there were those two poor kids standing beside me, Tony repeating, 'It's not fair. It's just not fair,' over and over again while Janet sobbed her heart out.

There was nothing to be done, of course, there never is, and at last I kissed the poor cold, uncomprehending little face and touched Janet's arm.

'Come on, love,' I said gently. 'It's only her old overcoat. She's not there you know. She's safe and happy.'

And, finally, we persuaded them away from that dismal place and took them home.

There was still the funeral to be got through and I was dreading it. Tony and Janet wanted us to be there and we wouldn't let them down for the world, but the whole sad episode was bringing back such vivid memories of the loss of John Michael that I found it very painful. After all, one heartbreakingly small white box looks very like another and day and night I found myself reliving the worst moments of my life.

'Now look,' I told Tony and Janet just before the funeral. 'The worst part is when you see that little box disappear into the earth. Just keep telling yourselves that's not Hollie. Hollie's safe.'

But it was a heart-rending affair nevertheless. There was a terrible moment when two hefty men came into the chapel with this pathetic little white box carried

24

on a canvas sling between them. There was something ludicrous about two such burly figures sharing such a tiny burden. Why couldn't one of them have simply carried the coffin in his arms I wondered? At John Michael's funeral we had a little fair, curly-haired boy carrying my baby's box in his arms. It was simple, touching and appropriate. You don't need pomp and ceremony for an innocent little baby.

Yet although it was sad, that funeral underlined what a special child Hollie was and how in just a few short days she'd won the affection of so many people. The church was packed and magnificent floral tributes poured in from all over the country. Hollie's grave looked as if it was set in a carpet of flowers and to that blazing sea of colour John and I added our own little contribution. We'd cut every bud from every white rose bush in our garden, wrapped them in a white doily and added a little card. 'To Hollie. You didn't know the world but the whole world knew you.'

Afterwards, back at Ted's home, Janet and I strolled in the garden as she tried to calm herself. It was a warm day and crowds of mourners drifted outside for some air. We walked slowly back and forth and suddenly through the chatter I distinctly heard:

'I don't care what you say. Hollie's not there. Read Doris Stokes' books. I'm telling you . . .'

I couldn't help smiling. How nice to know that my words hadn't fallen on deaf ears. I moved towards the speaker, a pleasant-faced, middle-aged man to thank him for his recommendation but just as I reached him he noticed me. His words died away, his jaw dropped and his skin went a little pale under his tan.

'B-b-b-but it's her. It's Doris Stokes. Where did you come from?' he stammered for all the world as if he thought I'd just materialized out of thin air.

'I came to the funeral,' I said, 'I'm a friend of the family.'

He looked relieved and his healthy colour returned.

'Well, Doris! how lovely to meet you. Come and talk to us.'

Janet and I joined the group and although I hadn't intended to work, the day had been too emotional already, I found that the man's wife had arrived unseen from the spirit world and wanted to send him her love.

'And give my love to our Mary,' she said, 'and as for him, tell him to talk to Mary. They haven't spoken for years.'

Apparently there had been some sort of family disagreement and the man had fallen out with his sister-in-law. As the years passed it became harder for either of them to break the ice and although they sometimes went to the same functions, they behaved as if they'd never met. It turned out that Mary was at the funeral too and the prompting from the other side was all they needed. Before the afternoon was over that man was crouched beside Mary's chair, sheepishly making up for years of silence.

Once people find out that I'm a medium they're usually full of questions and after a while one of the other men in the group, Micky Dallon who'd been listening quietly, finally plucked up the courage to raise a subject that must have been bothering him for some time.

'When my mother was dying I sat with her holding her hand,' he said, 'and at one point I wanted to jump up and shout for the doctor, but at the same time I didn't want to leave her. In the end I stayed with mum and she died. Ever since I've been wondering if I did the right thing. If I'd got the doctor then, perhaps we could have saved her.'

I shook my head vigorously.

'No, love. You were right to stay and comfort her. It wouldn't have made any difference who you called. If it was your mother's time to go over she had to go and no one could have prevented it.'

Micky seemed satisfied and the conversation moved

on but I couldn't concentrate on what they were saying. A woman had joined us and she was bending forward to whisper to me.

'Give my love to Micky,' she murmured.

'Who are you?' I asked.

'It's Lilian,' she said and she was gone.

'Sorry to interrupt,' I said quietly out loud, 'but I just got something for Micky. It's not much. Lilian sends her love, that's all.'

It was the tiniest of messages but the effect was amazing. The colour just drained from Micky Dallon's face and he went so white I thought he might faint.

'It's such an unusual name . . .' he blurted through pale lips, 'you could never have guessed my mother's name was Lilian . . .' and he blundered away to get a drink to steady his nerves.

There are two sequels to the story of Tony and Janet, one rather strange and inexplicable, the other perfectly explicable and down to earth but just as wonderful.

The first occurred during that same long hot summer. The Roffeys spent quite a lot of time with us in our mobile home and naturally the subject of Hollie came up frequently. Tony seemed to be particularly anguished. He couldn't come to terms with the tragedy at all.

'I believe you, Doris,' he said time and time again. 'I believe everything you say but if only they could give me a sign that my baby's all right, then I could rest.'

His words used to tear at me because I wanted to help but there was nothing I could do. I'm only human after all. I could pass on messages I heard, and tell him what I knew about life on the other side but as to signs that he could see for himself, well that was out of my hands entirely.

'Well, Tony, be patient,' was all I could advise. 'If they think you need a sign, perhaps they'll send you one. Who knows?'

27

A week or two later when my back was less painful I decided to get on with some housework around the van. I pulled out our nest of tables and was giving them a good polish when suddenly I dropped the duster in surprise. There on the table we used most, the pattern of the wood had re-arranged itself, that's the only way I can describe it – into the face of Jesus complete with beard and crown of thorns. The little picture was about four inches long and in the opposite direction to the grain and what's more it had certainly not been there before. I blinked, looked away, and looked back again but it was still there.

Quickly I went into the bedroom where John was hoovering and touched his arm. 'John switch it off and come and look at this and tell me what you see.'

Puzzled he followed me into the living-room. Without saying a word I pointed at the table. John looked, then frowned, looked away and looked back, just as I had done.

'It's the face of Jesus,' he said. 'That's what it looks like to me. But I've never noticed it before.'

It's very easy to let your imagination run away with you in cases like this and John and I are so closely attuned I couldn't be sure I wasn't influencing him, so we decided to call in other opinions.

'If anyone'll know what that table used to be like it's Phyllis and Doreen,' I said.

Phyllis and Doreen were two of our friends on the site who used to air the van and give it a quick going over before we arrived if we'd been away for some time. We invited them in and without mentioning what was going on we asked them to look at the table. Both spontaneously saw the picture of Jesus.

'Well I've polished these tables I don't know how many times,' said Phyllis, 'and I've never seen that before.'

Finally, when we'd heard enough exclamations of astonishment to know we weren't seeing things, we told the Roffeys. They came, looked, and Ted was so impressed he took the table away to be photographed.

'Well, Tony,' I said, 'I'm not saying it is – but you did ask for a sign . . .'

Several months passed before the second sequel. I was very busy with the arrangements for moving and with the tour and so quite a few weeks went by before I saw the Roffeys again. Then, just before Christmas I did a very exciting demonstration at the London Palladium (more of that later) and afterwards, to my delight, Tony and Janet walked into the dressing-room. They both looked well and much happier than the last time I'd seen them and I was instantly reminded of my parting words in the summer.

'Well this time next year I hope I'll be able to come and have a drink with you at your christening.'

Janet was still as slim and agile as ever and yet there was something about her . . .

'Yes the baby's on its way,' whispered a voice in my ear and I beamed at the kids.

'I'm still keeping the summer free for the christening,' I joked.

Tony laughed ruefully. 'No, Doris. I'm afraid you'll have to wait a bit longer. We've had no luck yet.'

I stared at him in surprise. 'But I'm sure they . . .' then I saw Janet frantically signalling behind his back and I stopped. 'Oh well never mind, love,' I finished lamely, 'it'll happen in good time.' And I left it at that. I didn't want to spoil Janet's surprise.

Sure enough, a few days later on Christmas morning, Tony came downstairs to find a plain white card amongst his brightly wrapped parcels.

'Dear Tony,' it said. 'Sorry you'll have to wait another 33 weeks for your present. Love Janet.'

Tony, who must have been celebrating rather freely the night before, didn't get it. 'Thirty-three weeks?' he said puzzled, 'why will I have to wait thirty-three weeks?'

'Because I'm pregnant you idiot!' cried Janet and the next second he was swinging her round, very gently, in delight. It was the best Christmas present they could have had.

Win Webb and Flo Hodson with my mum (far right)

Meeting Stoksie with Freddie

The wonderful poster for my tour

The first Christmas in our lovely new home

Happiness and tears after contact

A proud moment. Princess Anne opens the Westminster Children's Hospital Bone Marrow Transplant Unit. Here with the Princess are Pauline and Brendan McAleese who lost their son, David, to bone marrow disease

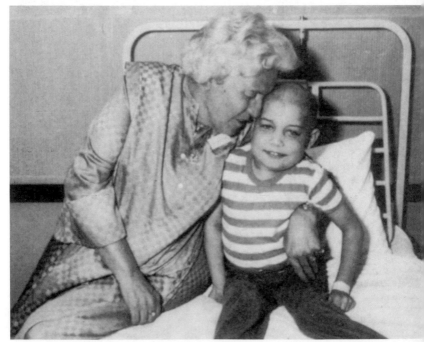

Cuddling lovely little transplant patient Matthew Hardy

SHE'S MAGIC!

Doris Stokes at Lewisham Theatre. (Picture Jim Selby)

"I THINK your name should live for ever," Freddie Starr told her. "Let me give you something."

"That's not necessary, Freddie love," Doris Stokes replied. "I'm just happy I was able to help."

"No," he insisted. "I must let you have a gift. I know — I'll give you a racehorse."

And so he did. It's a yearling named, after some discussion, Stokey and currently housed at Freddie Starr's stables.

Freddie, distressed by the suicide of his close friend Alan Lake after the death of Alan's wife Diana Dors, was inconsolable until a journalist acquaintance advised him to seek a sitting with Doris Stokes. What she told him after conversing in his presence with long-dead Diana and Alan gave Freddie comfort, peace of mind and the abiding conviction that she was the most wonderful person in the world.

Doris Stokes is a permanently cheery 65-year-old spiritualist. She's grey-haired, grey-eyed, a 13½ stone dumpling. Her weight, she says, goes up and down like a yo-yo because of thyroid trouble – not to mention a train of other medical problems that beset her, including cancer. Yet despite her chronic ailments and not all that glamorous appearance, Doris is the world's most reclaimed medium. She isn't clairvoyant, that's to say she doesn't – except very rarely – see any of the dear departed, she's clairaudient. Like Joan of Arc she hears voices. The dead speak to her and she talks back in the matey-est

of terms with occasional prompting from her spirit guide, a Tibetan named – as near as she can spell it – Ramanee.

This sweet, elderly lady, who only needs a floral pinny round her tummy to look like the archetypal sensible suburban grandma, could earn as much per annum as Freddie Starr himself, probably the highest paid artist in Britain. She doesn't rake in that much because, unlike the hyper-energetic eight or nine shows a week Freddie, her health allows Doris to appear twice, or at most only three times a week, but the sure posting of Doris's name over a marquee can fill a theatre faster than most pop stars.

Last year, she packed London's huge Dominion Theatre solid for three successive nights. This summer she is taking over the Palladium for a series of Sunday evenings. The first three dates to be announced were July 14, August 4 and September 1 – but don't apply for tickets, they went ages ago. Her first London Palladium appearance last year likewise sold out in less than two hours.

There can't be a more modest theatrical presentation than hers. After a brief introduction Doris sits in an easy chair with the stage to herself and her voices. She simply pours affection as the desperates love and solace to everyone in the worlds – this one and the next, for she recognises no line of demarcation. To Doris there is no death. As a survival medium she is convinced that the world of the spirits, is merely a continuation of ours. When she speaks of her many

friends in show business who have passed over like Dick Emery, Alan Lake or Diana Dors, it's always Dick-"is", Diana "is". Never "was". The past tense doesn't exist for her in this connection.

Doris doesn't pretend to be anything other than an old lady, maybe specially gifted as well, who plucks voices out of the air talking to them as friends about neighbours who identify themselves by disclosing how much one woman paid over the odds for a new gas stove, or why another hid her blue hat on top of the wardrobe. Hardly world-shattering revelations, but to a crowded standing-room-only house itching for the slightest sign of contact with departed loved ones, they become riveting dramas in which they are themselves intimately involved. No fancy talk. No tricks, no illusions, no ectoplasm, no make-up or costumes. No telling fortunes. The dialogues with unseen dead proponents might appear to sceptics to be largely imaginary, but unquestionably even for them Doris Stokes, alive on stage is real magic.

She can't understand why everyone makes so much fuss over her. Why she was flown recently on a special plane to Australia for a jam-packed appearance at Sydney's prestigious Opera House.

"The dressing room there was bigger than my whole flat in South London," she confided to me. Dismissing this unwarranted luxury she continued: "Though my books sell very well, and my appearances make money, much of it goes in taxes and donations to charities. What do I want lots of money for, anyway? I've got my husband, John, my son Terry and my spirit family over there waiting for me – with probably not so long to wait either," she added with a genuine chuckle. "After all, I'm only a simple old country woman."

She's about as simple and uncomplicated as that other country woman, Margaret Thatcher whose parents ran a grocers shop across the way from the Stokes in Grantham.

"We didn't have much to do with them," Doris recalled, "or rather they with us. We Stokes were very poor and they were the 'quality Roberts'. Her father was a lay preacher, Methodist, I think. Very strict. My father was a Romany, the first of his tribe to quit wandering and settle down in a permanent home. My mother and the rest of us were Church of England. I used to get a ha'penny from the Methodist elders to attend Sunday Services in their Chapel. I would clutch the coin in my hot little hand and listen to sermons about hell fire and damnation wishing all the time I could rush into the street and spend it on gob-stoppers.

"As for Margaret, quite a few years younger than me, she was a proper little madam. Never went out scrumping in the orchards with the other kids her age. Always immaculately dressed. Never a stain on her pressed school uniform. Not a hair out of place. Come to think of it" – with another guffaw – "she hasn't changed much!"

The robust speech and good humour of ordinary working folk has never deserted Doris. She is not above telling

some obstreperous other-world sprite in public not to be a silly sod and stop shoving. She may even start off sessions with jokes like the two mediums who meet by chance at Tesco's where one tells the other: "You're all right. How am I doing?" Or the story about the fitness fanatic who asks if they have any sports up there and is told to come back a week later when he is greeted with good news and bad news. The good is that they play cricket and football. The bad is that he will be captain on Sunday.

Danny La Rue is another great friend of the Stokes family. When both Doris and Danny were in Birmingham appearing at different theatres, they regularly visited each other's dressing rooms between shows. On one such occasion an enterprising photographer asked to take a picture of the famous pair together. Doris at first, refused. Although without a trace of vanity, she didn't want to be photographed in day clothes since a recent mastectomy had removed one of her breasts and she felt she looked a little lop-sided without its temporary replacement.

"I told Danny about my missing boob", she recounted without affectation. "I thought for a moment he'd say – I'll lend you one of mine. But he posed me carefully behind a large vase of flowers, called in the photographer and all was well."

On another mutual date in Birmingham Doris was in the audience with some friends when she noticed Danny's long-time manager Jack Hanson waiting in the wings. He wasn't backstage however and when she mentioned it to Danny, he told her Jack had just died in hospital. This was one of those rare moments when Doris was truly clairvoyant. Usually it's only voices, with the single visual indication of something or someone from another world present in the audience in the form of a light burning, strongly for a person who has passed over a long time ago, and faint and flickering for a recent bereavement.

Doris's voices never let her down. Before an evening session she spends the whole afternoon tuning into the spirit world, praying desperately that her voices will come through. They always do. Sometimes the voices she conjures up on stage will describe ordinary events that can build up into high drama. At the Dominion she asked a woman: "Have you still got that blue hat and matching gloves?" The answer "Yes?" "I see the bag is still behind the wardrobe". . . "Yes! Yes!" "She's met Ted after all." – "Yes!" "In Australia" – "Yes! Yes!" "They've been together all the time. Didn't you think a penny" – "Yes! Yes!–Yes!" The tension rose like Molly Bloom's randy Ulysses monologue to culminate in a great orgasmic affirmation.

Doris receives more than 1,000 letters every week, each of her four book have been best sellers and she is constantly in demand for TV and radio shows. She has recently recorded an album on the LIPP label which has introductory music by the famous guitarist Bert Weedon, and contains a poem recited by Doris and dedicated to her dead son, John Michael.

The Palladium!

Chapter Three

The garden of the mobile home was looking lovely as I showed Lady Michaela Denis Lyndsay round and all about us was the scent of roses. Roses are my favourite flower. We'd planted dozens of bushes when we bought the van and now they were all out and blooming like mad.

It was so beautiful that Michaela and I quite forgot the cameras whirring away in the background recording every move and we drifted towards the seat beside a glorious 'Blue Moon', chatting as if we were alone.

'Oh look!' I cried as we sat down. 'There's Minnie the mongoose!'

The late Minnie had been a very special pet of Michaela's and now I saw her as plain as I saw my roses, snuggled on the bench against Michaela's leg, a little ball of fur with a pointed face and bright eyes.

'Oh yes,' said Michaela in delight, 'I see her. She's often with me you know.' And she stroked Minnie's head fondly. I reached out to pat Minnie myself and as I did so I smiled up at the cameramen. This must make a lovely scene for them, I thought, what a bit of luck, and then I noticed that far from smiling back, they had turned distinctly white and nervous and were staring at the seat uneasily.

That was when it clicked. Of course, Minnie was invisible to them. They must have thought we'd gone stark raving mad, patting and talking to a patch of thin air!

I bet they won't forget that particular edition of *Forty Minutes* in a hurry! I was tremendously flattered when BBC2 rang to ask if they could make me the subject of the programme. As most people probably know the programme takes its name from the length of screen

31

time allotted to it but it takes a great deal longer than forty minutes to make.

The documentary team seemed to follow me round for weeks filming everything, until in the end they became like members of the family and I hardly noticed the cameras at all. They filmed in our flat, in our mobile home, at public demonstrations and church services and even in Bert Weedon's garden. Bert Weedon of course is the guitarist who wrote and played the background music on my LP. They couldn't use half of what they'd filmed, of course, because they must have recorded hours and hours of material, but I was very impressed with the finished programme. They'd made an interesting, intelligible documentary out of a great hotch-potch of different topics.

They said they wanted to cover just about every aspect of my work and beliefs and they certainly did. To explain my spirit guide, Ramanov, they decided to focus on the name plate of the mobile home which we'd named in his honour and then show me explaining the origin of the name to Michaela.

I've known Michaela for years and since she happened to be in England at the time they thought it might be nice if she appeared. A lot of people remember the wonderful wild life programmes she used to make with her first husband Armand. When he passed over she married Sir William Lyndsay which is why she is now a titled lady. Sir William too is now on the other side and these days Michaela lives alone in Kenya surrounded by her beloved wild animals. What few people realize though, is that Michaela is also a medium and every year she comes to London to attend the SAGB dinner dance and visit her spiritualist friends.

Michaela and Minnie did eventually reach the screen but many other scenes did not. At one point the producer got quite excited about the news that I could do sittings over the telephone.

'D'you think you could do one for us this afternoon?'

he asked. 'If we pick a letter from your post bag could you phone them and do it straight away?'

'I can try,' I said.

So one of the team delved down my huge pile of letters and came up with a note which included a phone number. To make doubly sure that I knew nothing of the contents she even dialled the number herself and then passed me the receiver as the phone was answered.

'Hello,' I said to the woman at the other end. 'This is Doris Stokes. I believe you wrote to me asking for a sitting.'

'Oh yes,' she said.

'Well,' I explained, 'I can do one on the phone for you if you don't mind the BBC recording it. They're here now making a documentary.'

'Oh,' she said, 'what time?'

The producer signalled impressively.

'It's got to be half-past-one.'

'Oh dear,' said the woman, 'couldn't you make it four-thirty. I go to bingo at half-past-one.'

But the producer was adamant and the woman seemed reluctant to miss her bingo so another letter was drawn from the bag. This time I tuned in as they were dialling the number and instantly I heard the name Doug.

'Look I don't want to know what's in the letter,' I whispered, 'but just tell me, is the name Doug mentioned?'

They skimmed through it. 'Yes.'

Thank goodness for that. I'd contacted the right person and not someone connected with the TV crew. It's so easy to get crossed wires when there are a lot of people about, because their friends and relatives in spirit are often so close to them.

This time we were in luck. The woman on the line was only too delighted to help and 1.30 suited her perfectly. It turned out that Doug was her husband. He was only fifty-four and he'd died suddenly of a heart attack.

'Who's Jenny?' I asked.

'My daughter-in-law,' said the woman.

'Doug tells me that you were with Jenny when it happened.'

'Yes I was,' she agreed.

'They were out Christmas shopping,' said Doug. 'They were in Marks and Spencers' buying me a sweater when I passed. I tried to tell them not to bother because I wouldn't be needing it but I couldn't make them hear.'

The woman was dumbfounded when I told her what her husband had said.

'That's exactly what we were doing,' she gasped when she got over her astonishment. 'We were in Marks buying him a sweater! Oh I'm so glad he knew.'

Unfortunately Doug and his sweater never did reach the final programme, there simply wasn't time, but I'd like to let him know that he's not forgotten!

The demonstration I gave at Poplar fared better on the screen. I can't say that every message I gave was shown on the programme but a good proportion did make it. There was a lot of laughter that night and one message in particular tickled the audience. A pair of women were standing together at the microphone and one of their relatives – I think it was their father – was chatting away in my ear.

'And when they knocked the wall down it all went wrong,' he tutted.

'Are you doing some building work at home?' I asked them. 'He's saying something about a wall knocked down and everything went wrong.'

The women looked at each other and giggled.

'Yes!'

'What a mess,' the man went on. 'And when they got the tiles for the floor, there weren't enough!'

I passed this on and by now the women were practically in tears of laughter.

'Yes, but it wasn't the tiles, it was the glue we ran out of!' they corrected.

'Oh well, tiles, glue whatever, they ran out and had to rush off to the shop to get some more,' said the man. 'And at home they daren't move till the glue arrived. What a mess! I cleared off till it was all finished.'

There were the usual moments of confusion too, which I've learned I just have to put up with when I'm working with a big audience. I can normally tell who a message is intended for by the light I see shining close to them, but often there are so many spirit people eager to talk to their loved ones that the place is packed with lights. What's more the theatres are usually so crowded, with the seats packed so close, it's impossible to say exactly which person I'm looking for.

That night in Poplar, a woman called May told me she was looking for a young lady in a red dress. There was a light hovering near a woman in the front who seemed to fit the description.

'Yes that must be me!' she shouted eagerly hurrying forward.

But I wasn't certain. Something didn't seem quite right. In the background someone gave me the name Fred.

'D'you know someone called Fred, spirit side?' I asked.

She shook her head. She was the wrong contact. As soon as I mentioned the name Fred, Fred himself came in drowning May altogether.

'It's my daughter I want,' he said, 'and she's wearing red.'

Suddenly I was aware of a hand waving frantically near the back of the hall.

'I know a Fred,' she called.

'Are you wearing red, love?' I asked because, dazzled by the lights, I couldn't see the back.

'Yes I am,' she called and came running down to the microphone.

I wanted to make absolutely certain however that I'd

35

found the right person so I asked for further identification. 'Mention working for the Co-op,' he said.

'Who worked for the Co-op?' I asked.

'My father,' said the girl in wonder, 'he was a milk lorry driver.'

I breathed a sigh of relief. We'd found Fred's daughter.

'Tell her that Eva's here with me,' he said.

The girl gasped. 'That's my mother! They're together? Oh I'm so glad.'

'She's our baby,' said Fred and you could hear all the love and affection in his voice. They must have been very close. 'And she's wearing her mother's ring. She's got it on tonight.'

His daughter's smile was dazzling. 'Yes I have.'

All at once the crowded hall faded and before my eyes I saw a glorious lilac bush. Not the spindly, insignificant little tree that you see in so many gardens, but a really lush, magnificent shrub. Then the picture was gone. Now why had Fred shown me a lilac bush I wondered.

'You haven't got a lilac bush in your garden have you?' I asked the girl.

'Why yes. A really beautiful one.'

'That's it,' I said. 'They've just just shown me a beautiful lilac bush and they're saying when the lilacs are out in the spring cut a spray and say Mum and Dad's here.'

'Oh, thank you, I will,' she assured me her face lit with joy.

All evening the spirit people came flooding through. Some were marvellous communicators, others quite overcome by the excitement. One grandmother was so thrilled to be able to tell her daughter that she had seen the grandchildren she'd never lived to meet on earth that all she could do was babble their names over and over again. 'Rachel and Rebecca! Rachel and Rebecca!' she kept telling me in delight.

Another young lad who was killed in an accident

seemed to think that the name of his favourite pub was all the information necessary to convince his sister that he was really there.

'Just mention the Green Man,' he said confidently.

And some messages seemed puzzling to me but made perfect sense to the recipients. At one point I got the name Proctor and not one, but two ladies claimed it. It turned out they were the Proctor sisters, a bubbly duo full of fun.

'Well, this is very odd,' I told them, 'I've got a lady here, I'm sure it's a lady, but they're calling her Henry.'

The sisters collapsed into each other's arms all laughter and dimples. 'Yes that's right. It's Henrietta but Father always called her Henry.'

'And now I've got another lady but they're calling her George.'

The sisters could hardly speak for mirth. 'That's right,' they spluttered, 'Georgina!' and the whole theatre laughed with them.

The Proctor sisters were obviously enjoying themselves immensely. So much so that the next day when they were on a day trip to Clacton they decided to buy me a present. They'd read in my books that I'm specially fond of gold roses and passing a florist's they saw the very thing they were after. A pretty arrangement of roses in the very shade I'd described. The only snag was that the shop was shut but the Proctor sisters weren't going to be defeated by a tiny detail like that. They went all the way back to Clacton the next day and bought it.

Soon after the Poplar demonstration the Forty Minutes' team followed me to Deal where I was doing a church service. I try to attend a church as often as possible because I think it does me good. It reminds me what my work is all about. The big theatres and the assorted messages are only a small part of it. The rest is as much about living your life now, as life after death.

I must say our services are usually quite lively. We

have hymns and prayers, of course, like other churches but it's all very informal, not a bit holier than thou. Then when the religious part is over there's a short demonstration.

It was lovely to visit Deal. A pretty little town on the South coast with the salt tang in the air you always get by the sea and a fresh breeze blowing. The church was bright and welcoming and full of flowers and the congregation was squeezed in so tightly it's a wonder they had enough breath to sing!

After a relaxed service I did a demonstration. This was the time when I was suffering with my back and the actual details of the demonstration have faded, all I can recall is the dull ache that I hoped didn't show on my face. One thing does stand out though. A boy came through saying that he was connected with the navy and that he'd taken himself over. He was claimed immediately by a woman in the congregation but once again it seemed slightly off key. Many of the details didn't mean a thing to her and thought she was eager for the message to be hers I had an uneasy feeling I was talking to the wrong contact. But my back was aching, the heat was increasing and other spirit voices were jostling to be heard. So instead of working at it and trying to sort out the confusion as I normally do, I passed on to the next message. I might have known, however, that Ramanov wouldn't let me get away with such sloppiness.

After the service I noticed out of the corner of my eye a woman and young man approach the producer. They stood talking to him for some minutes and then he brought them over to me.

'They were so disappointed, Doris, not to get a message,' he said and the woman pressed a photograph into my hand.

'That's him, Doris,' she told me pleadingly.

She was a handsome blonde with clear, creamy skin but the expression in her blue eyes told me she'd lost a child. I looked at the picture. A smiling, suntanned young man looked back at me and as I stared I realized that he was with us.

'I'm here,' he said, 'I've been trying to get through.'

'What do I call you, son?' I asked silently.

'Stephen,' he said.

'I hear the name Stephen,' I told the couple and the other boy clutched the woman's arm.

'That's him. That's my brother!' he said.

'He's wearing all my jewellery and stuff,' said Stephen, 'but I don't mind. It's no good to me now is it?'

'That's right I am,' cried the brother.

The woman's face lit up. 'He's been waiting for that for a year,' she said. 'He used to be frightened of spirits and things but he's read your books and he felt sure you could help.'

The case was not a clear cut one though. Around Stephen's passing I could sense a great deal of mystery and confusion. It wasn't the sort of thing to be tackled in five minutes before lunch I felt.

'Look,' I said impulsively. 'I think there's a lot to be gone into here. I've got a day off tomorrow. Why don't you come and see me at the van and we'll see what we can do.'

They agreed eagerly and when we got started on the sitting I was very glad I'd asked them to come back.

As soon as I tuned in, the feeling of confusion swept over me more strongly than ever. This was no ordinary accident victim or sufferer from an illness. This poor mixed up boy had taken his own life.

I chose my words carefully in an attempt to spare the mother's feelings.

'There's a great deal of mystery and confusion here,' I said, 'Stephen wasn't killed, he was found.'

His mother bit her lip. 'Yes, I found him.'

I caught a fleeting glimpse of a teenage bedroom.

'You found him on his bed?'

She shook her head. 'No, on the floor in his bedroom.'

So that was why he'd shown me the room, but

39

Stephen wasn't quite ready yet to discuss the details. He was still ashamed to have caused his family so much pain and he kept shying away from the subject whenever I brought it up.

'Don't forget to remember me to Gary,' he said ignoring my question.

'Who's Gary?' I asked out loud.

'One of his best friends.'

I tackled Stephen again. 'Now look I know it's difficult love,' I told him silently, 'but I do need to know your last impressions. Can you just give me some idea what happened?'

All at once the confusion swamped me and there was an uncomfortable feeling in my head. My head hurt and my chest felt constricted.

'I feel as if I've got something over my head,' I said thinking aloud, 'and I can't breathe. Did he take an overdose or something?'

His mother shook her head. 'No he shot himself.'

I was surprised. The strange feeling in my head was a very strong impression. I don't deny that I sometimes make mistakes but when spirit people give me a clear impression it's never wrong. My interpretation of it may be way out but the impression itself is always correct.

'Well this feeling in my head seems very definite,' I insisted.

'It's funny you should say that Doris,' said Stephen's mother, 'because for a couple of weeks before he died he'd been complaining about his head.'

'I'd got it into my head there was something wrong,' said Stephen, 'I must have been mad. What a stupid thing to do. But it felt as if the top of my head was coming off. I thought I was ill.'

Then he gave me the name Joan.

'Who's Joan?' I asked.

'I am,' said his mother beaming.

Stephen went on to tell them that he played the

40

guitar on the other side, which pleased them very much.

'He always wanted to play the guitar,' said his brother, 'he used to stand in front of the mirror and pretend.'

Stephen also started talking about a dinner service which puzzled me rather because young men aren't usually bothered about things like that. It wasn't at all clear though and I wasn't sure what he meant.

'Why's he talking about a dinner service?' I asked. 'He's saying it's connected with work. You know plates and things, he's saying.'

His brother was thrilled. 'I think he means me. I've just started work as a steward. I work with plates and things.'

Finally, right at the end of the sitting I realized it had been Stephen trying to get through during the service in Deal with the message about the navy. He was talking about his funeral and he wanted to thank his family for the anchor of flowers they'd given him. It turned out that his father was in the navy. I'd found the right contact at last!

Not long after the *Forty Minutes* documentary, I had another phone call from the BBC, but this time it was from BBC Radio 2. Would I like to do *Desert Island Discs*? they asked.

For a minute I thought there must be some mistake, because surely they only have highbrow people on *Desert Island Discs*? But no, they said, they were quite certain they wanted Doris Stokes the medium. All I had to do, they explained, was pick out eight of my favourite records, records which meant something special to me, and talk about them.

Well it seemed easy enough and I love music. But when it actually came to narrowing down my favourites to just eight tunes it turned out to be more difficult than I'd imagined. Just when I thought I'd been really ruthless and pruned down my list as far as I could go,

I'd suddenly think of a really lovely piece I'd forgotten that I couldn't manage without.

It took me days. I got through pages of my writing pad with lists, revised lists and endless crossings out. But at last I settled on eight lovely tracks.

Presenter Roy Plomley, and producer, Derek Drescher, were lovely men. They invited John and I out to lunch to plan the programme but I explained that we don't really feel comfortable in posh restaurants.

'We just can't manage a big meal in the middle of the day,' I told Roy. 'We'd really much prefer tea and sandwiches in the office if it's all the same to you.'

So tea and sandwiches it was and we spent a lovely hour listening to all my discs and picking out the bits they were going to play because, of course, they can't play the records right the way through. Then it was time to record the programme with me talking to Roy between the music.

'I warn you I can woffle,' I told them but they thought I was joking.

'I'd sooner have a woffler than someone who doesn't say a word,' said Roy and away we went.

We started on a light note. Roy asked if I played a musical instrument and I explained that I didn't, though I'd always wanted to and I was hoping to learn in the spirit world.

'What will you play?' asked Roy. 'A harp?'

My first record was *One Day At A Time Sweet Jesus*. I go for the words every time and this song sums up how I've learned to live my life since I had cancer. Next was *I Love You Just Because* for John, because he's always there and when I'm tired or ill I don't always remember to let him know how much I appreciate it. *Morning Has Broken*, because it's such a beautiful song and it captures the pleasure I feel to see each new morning. Then there was *Mother Kelly's Doorstep* which always makes me smile because whenever I hear it, it reminds me of the time Danny La Rue came on stage at Birmingham Odeon to help me hand out flowers and got me singing a duet with him of *Mother Kelly's Doorstep*. Now I can't sing a note, there's no two ways about it but the audience loved it. I think they treated it as a comedy routine!

After that there was Freddie Starr singing *Have I Told You Lately That I Love You* because whenever he phones, he serenades me with this song. Then I changed the mood completely and played *May The Good Lord Bless and Keep You*. Some people might think my reasons for choosing this rather sad but I don't. When I pass over I'm going to be cremated and I'd like this song played for my family because I'll be all right. I'll be away and happy with my loved ones on the other side. It's the ones who're left behind who will need help and comfort.

Finally I ended with *My Way* followed by my own reading of the poem that was given to me when I was mourning the death of my baby John Michael: *In a Baby Castle*. The words brought me such comfort at the time that I like to pass them on to every mother grieving for a lost child, in the hope they'll do the same for her as they did for me.

And then suddenly it was all over. The programme was recorded and I realized I'd been enjoying myself immensely.

Derek Drescher's head appeared round the door. 'That went on a bit too long, Roy,' he said.

I laughed. 'Well I did warn you I can waffle.'

And Roy, bless him, just grinned and leaned across the desk. 'Ah, but such magical waffle,' he said.

I seem to have been involved in a lot of programmes lately but with one of the most recent, *Glass Box*, which is only shown in the Granada TV area, I wasn't sure if I'd make it on to the screen at all.

Glass Box is recorded at the TV studios in Liverpool and it's a sort of visual *Desert Island Discs*. The idea is that you select a number of film clips that you particularly enjoy or that remind you of some special moment in your life and instead of taking them to an imaginary

43

desert island, you seal them into a glass box to preserve them for ever.

I'd met the presenter, Shelley Rohde, before and we got on well and after enjoying *Desert Island Discs* so much I knew I'd enjoy *Glass Box*. I was looking forward to it. The choosing of the film clips had not been so difficult for me because films somehow don't seem to have such sentimental associations. There were some clips from the *Dambusters* to remind me of my airforce days, a piece from *Yield to the Night* with Diana Dors to remind me of our friendship and everyone else what a wonderful actress she was, some beautiful ballet because I've only recently learned to appreciate it and finally a scene from a horror movie because horror movies make me laugh so much. The whole thing would be great fun, I was sure.

Unfortunately, though, Liverpool went wrong from the evening we arrived. Some time before, a little girl of ten had written me a touching letter. She'd lost her Daddy she told me and she knew I could speak to him because she'd read my books. Could her Mummy bring her to see me because she wanted to tell her Daddy she loved him? I saw from the address that she didn't live too far from Liverpool and I realized that we might be able to combine a meeting with the *Glass Box* trip, so I asked Laurie to see if he could arrange for her to come and see me at the hotel.

This he did. 'But do remember to be there by six o'clock,' he said, 'because Doris has to go out at half-past-seven.'

We were meeting the producer of *Glass Box* to plan the next day's show and it was something that couldn't be put off.

Well we waited and waited. Six o'clock came and went and there was no sign of the little girl and her mother. At six-thirty I was convinced.

'They're not coming, Laurie, I'm certain of it,' I said.

'But they must be, they were so keen,' he insisted. 'Perhaps they're stuck in traffic somewhere.'

We waited until seven o'clock and then I had to get changed.

'Give me a shout if they arrive and I'll see if I can do something quick,' I said, 'but I've got a feeling Laurie. They're not coming.'

By half-past-seven even Laurie was forced to admit I was right. And it wasn't until the next night that we discovered what went wrong. They'd got the dates mixed up and come a day late. By the time they arrived in Liverpool I was almost home. I felt so sorry for that poor little girl. She'd been looking forward to talking to her Daddy and it had ended in disappointment. I'm still hoping we can meet one day.

The mishaps continued. That evening, no sooner had the meeting ended than Laurie hurried away to bed. It's most unusual for Laurie because normally he's a night owl, but his face was pale and drawn, despite the fact that he was complaining of the heat.

'Aren't you feeling too good, Laurie?' I asked, 'you don't look well.'

'Oh I'm fine, fine,' he insisted because he hates to admit to being ill. 'I only need a good night's sleep.'

'Looks like the 'flu to me,' said John when he'd gone.

'But it came on so suddenly,' I pointed out. 'He was all right at the meeting.'

We fully expected to find no sign of Laurie at breakfast the next morning but there he was, as bright and cheerful as if nothing had happened.

'Yes I'm fine now,' he said. 'But oh did I feel rough last night. At one point my legs just went to jelly. I could hardly stand up.'

Well, apart from shaking our heads over the peculiar bugs that go around these days we thought no more about it. Liverpool was like the North Pole that day with a wind that must surely have been blowing from a glacier and the weather was the main topic of conversation.

Earlier Laurie had taken a short stroll to the studio to check one or two points. It was only up the road from our hotel but the cold was so intense he couldn't face the walk back and had to take a taxi instead!

'Well if it's as bad as that I'm certainly not walking.' I said, 'I'll be blue by the time I get there!'

So at mid-day we climbed into our immaculate limousine for the two minute journey. They were very kind at the studio and had laid on a beautiful lunch in the directors' dining-room. Everyone tucked in hungrily except Shelley Rohde and I. Neither of us could eat a thing before working so we just pushed our food around on our plates and watched the others.

Then at last the meal was over and I was taken away to be made up. But half way down the stairs I went all dizzy and I swayed towards the make-up girl who was leading the way.

'I'll have to hold on to your shoulder, love,' I explained. 'I've come over a bit dizzy. I expect it's the heat.'

For it was very warm in the studio after the icy weather outside.

And settled in the comfortable chair in front of the big make-up mirror I felt fine. The girl soothingly combed my hair and put in heated rollers and then she put my face on. I did look a bit pale I thought but the foundation cream soon cured that.

At last, five minutes before I was due on the studio floor, I popped into the ladies. I was all ready. I've only got to slip into my dress and I can go on I was thinking, when suddenly without warning my legs went to jelly and my head spun. Anxiously I grabbed at the wall to steady myself. I was so dizzy I didn't think I could stand upright let alone walk coolly into a TV studio and talk intelligibly for half an hour.

Panic rising I waited for the attack to pass, but it didn't. My God, I thought, here I am with my make-up on and everything and I'm not going to be able to do it. They'll be calling me any minute and I don't think I can even get out of the loo.

In desperation I sent out a prayer to the spirit world.

46

'Please spirit friends just see me through this bit. Just see me through this hour. I don't mind what happens afterwards if I can just get this show done.'

And as always they turned up trumps. Even before I'd finished the prayer my head started to clear and my legs felt a little stronger.

By the time they called me to the studio I was wobbly and going hot and cold, but I was upright and walking and I got through that show as if there was nothing wrong with me.

The only one who had any idea was Shelley Rohde.

'You're not feeling very good are you, Doris?' she said afterwards.

'Oh dear, was I dreadful?' I asked.

'Not at all, it went marvellously,' she said. 'No one else noticed a thing. It's just that we're old friends and I could tell.'

And in fact when I saw a tape of the show afterwards I was relieved to see she was right. I don't look my best I'll admit. I look rather tired and drawn about the eyes and despite the make-up my colour's not good. But I don't think anyone would know that only five minutes before the cameras started rolling I could hardly stand up, let alone make light-hearted conversation.

The mystery bug hadn't finished with me of course and the journey back to London was pretty miserable but I couldn't complain. I'd asked the spirit world for the strength to see me through the show and they'd given me exactly what I'd asked.

People often comment about how frequently I seem to fall ill. Well all I can say is I'm as fed up about it as anyone I can tell you! I can't understand why I seem to be so unlucky in that respect. I can only think it's the spirit world's way of forcing me to slow down when I'm doing too much.

Yet ironically when I appeared on the Wogan show it wasn't me who was ill – it was Terry Wogan!

I was filled with trepidation when I first received the invitation to appear on the show. After all Terry can be a bit, well not sarcastic exactly, but cheeky with his guests and I thought I might be an ideal target. Nevertheless I've always had a soft spot for Terry Wogan. I think he's a gorgeous man and so I couldn't help but agree to go on his show just to get the chance to meet him!

I'd been keeping my fingers and toes crossed that I wouldn't get a cold or anything before the show and I was in luck. But when I arrived at the studio poor old Terry was all flushed and snuffling and struggling to get through the show despite a nasty bout of 'flu.

He gave me a terrific build up – psychic superstar and goodness knows what else – and then when I walked on he took both my hands in his and kissed my cheek. Well, even at my age it sent shivers up my spine!

'Terry,' I said when we sat down, 'before you start I must say that I think you're gorgeous – and I'm old enough to be able to say it!'

He looked at me with that wicked twinkle in his eye but he was very good. He asked me sensible questions and let me answer them. He was tickled to death when I told him about the Sod It Club – the club I'd formed with fellow cancer sufferers with one aim in mind – to say sod it, I'm not going to have it, to the dreaded 'C'.

Terry rocked back in his chair when I explained that Sod It didn't stand for anything, it simply meant sod it.

'I thought it was to do with psychic things!' laughed Terry.

Our interview lasted fourteen minutes I'm told and I enjoyed every second of it. Afterwards we met Terry again in the hospitality suite and I realized that he wasn't at all well.

'Why don't you spend the weekend in bed love?' I asked.

'I wish I could, Doris,' said Terry, 'but I've got to work.'

It was a very happy evening. What I particularly

liked about the programme was that every guest had a person to look after them throughout. They met you at the door, took you to your dressing-room, then on to make-up. They took you to the set, waited for you to come off and then took you back to the hospitality suite. It really made you feel they were pleased to have you on the programme.

All that and Terry Wogan too!

Chapter Four

The demonstration was going well. I was standing on the stage at Birmingham Odeon, the audience seemed to be enjoying themselves and the voices were coming through thick and fast. Once again, though I'd been tired earlier in the evening, energy seemed to flow from nowhere and I was skimming along on a wave of psychic power getting through more work than I'd have thought possible a few years ago.

'I'd like to ask a question,' said a neat little lady at the microphone on the floor below me.

'Go ahead, love,' I told her.

'I'm a widow and I'd like to know if my husband knows I go to the graveyard every week and that every time I go there's this little robin. If he's not there when I arrive, he comes soon afterwards and I take him something to eat.'

I was just about to tell her that I was sure her husband knew, because our loved ones stay close to us and continue to take an interest in all our activities, when a scornful Brummie voice interrupted my thoughts:

'Does she think I've come back as a bloody *bird*?' he asked.

Well I burst out laughing and when I explained why, the audience roared. The woman giggled too.

'Yes but I'll tell you something strange,' she said as the laughter subsided. 'Before he went over we used to discuss things and I used to say when I go over I'm going to come back as a bird so I can poop on all the people who pooped on me in my life!' (Sorry about that but that's exactly what she said.)

Anyway the audience fell about and the atmosphere which was already happy became almost euphoric.

Well I like to share everything that happens with the audience and I thought this story was fun, so the following night when I was appearing at the Odeon again, I told them about the robin, only I thought I'd better clean up the punch line a bit.

'. . . and she said, "I'd like to come back as a bird so that I can **** on all the people who **** on me in my life," ' I quoted.

As I expected, the audience roared, but as the commotion died away I saw a neat figure waving wildly from the front row. It was the little widow.

'I'm here, Doris! I've come again!' she shouted. Then she turned round to the rest of the audience: 'It's quite true. Every word – only I didn't say ****. I said "so that I can poop on all the people who *pooped* on me!" '

And of course the theatre practically exploded.

Yes we have a lot of fun one way and another. I think people who come along to demonstrations for the first time are quite surprised. They expect gloom and doom and instead they get jokes and laughter. There are tears as well, of course, but they are tears of joy and emotional release, not sorrow.

Sometimes it's the spirit people who say funny things. During one demonstration I'd been talking to a man on the other side for some time when suddenly he said rather mischievously, 'Mention the mountain goat.'

I thought my powers were going peculiar.

'Mountain goat?' I queried silently. 'Did you say mountain goat?'

The man assured me that he did.

It was one of the unlikeliest messages I've ever been asked to pass on but he was insistent, so feeling a bit of a fool I took a deep breath.

'Well I don't know if this means anything to you, dear,' I said, 'because it sounds strange to me, but he's saying something about a mountain goat.'

To my surprise the girl just fell apart. 'You couldn't

have given me better proof,' she said. 'That's what we used to call my father-in-law – the mountain goat!'

Sometimes the messages leave me tongue-tied because they're so forthright. I stand there dithering and stalling while I try to translate them into a tactful phrase. After all I don't want to embarrass anybody.

'Will you tell my daughter to make up her mind,' said one irate mother. 'She's living with two men. One's on nights and one's on days.'

Well how could I say that out loud in front of hundreds of people?

Just as often though, it's the people who're still with us on this side who provide the fun. Not long ago we did a book signing session in a big Midlands store. Afterwards we ran through the rain to the car and as I got in I noticed a very pretty blonde lady beckoning to John.

He went over to see what she wanted and she took his arm and walked him up the car park. The next thing we saw, she had her raincoat open and John had his head inside.

Laurie and I exchanged glances. 'What on *earth* is my husband doing!' I exclaimed.

A few minutes later John came trotting innocently back. 'She's got a cut-out under there!' he said climbing into the car and grinning from ear to ear.

'You dirty old man!' said Laurie.

John looked puzzled. 'Why? What have I done now?'

'We saw you with your head in her coat,' teased Laurie, 'and now you tell us she had a cut out dress.'

'Cut out dress?' said John in surprise. 'She didn't have a cut out dress. She had a cut-out of Doris.'

And he looked so wounded we couldn't help laughing. Back at the bookstall we'd noticed a few large cardboard cut out photographs of me on a stand and this lady had obviously whipped one and smuggled it out of the shop under her coat.

We were still laughing as we swung out of the car

park. We rounded a bend and there on a traffic island in the middle of the road was the blonde and a few of her friends, waving this cut-out over their heads and chanting, 'Doris Stokes! Doris Stokes!' just like a football crowd. They waved merrily as we went by and we all waved back.

What they made of our car I don't know. Since Laurie has been looking after us we've taken to travelling long distances in grand style. We often have to travel hundreds of miles to an appointment and in the past when we had to go by train and taxi I've arrived so exhausted by the journey I've not been sure whether I'd have enough energy left to work. Laurie changed all that.

'You can't do your job if you're worn out by travelling,' he said, 'you need to travel in as much comfort as you can.'

And he promptly hired us a grand midnight blue Daimler, complete with TV, telephone and cocktail cabinet for our next long journey. We've used it on our tours ever since. It's the most beautiful car you've ever seen and I feel like the Queen rolling up at theatres in it. I suppose we must look very impressive as we bowl along the motorways, but what other motorists don't see is that we're sitting there with our shoes off and our feet up, eating tuna fish sandwiches, drinking tea out of paper cups and singing our heads off. It's the only way to cover the miles. If we didn't have a laugh and a sing-song we'd go mad.

'You don't drink *tea* out of paper *cups*!' said one horrified friend. 'You should have champagne in a car like that.'

But we'd sooner have tea than champagne any day and we're not interested in the car as a status symbol. It's simply the next most comfortable thing to my armchair at home. Mind you, although I'm not out to impress anyone, I had to laugh at the reaction of an old cousin of mine recently.

We happened to be in my home town of Grantham,

and this cousin I hadn't seen for years, came up. We chatted for a while catching up on old times and when it was time to go he walked out to the car with us.

The sight of the limousine nearly took his breath away.

'Ee, is this what you came in, Dol?' he asked.

I assured him it was.

He walked round it a couple of times, ran a reverent hand over the gleaming bodywork and peered through the window for a look at the palatial interior.

'I say, Dol, is that a TV you've got in there?'

I nodded.

'And is that a telephone?'

I had to agree that it was.

The information took a second or two to sink in and even then he clearly found it difficult to believe.

'Ee,' he said at last, shaking his head, 'bloody 'ell you could live in there!'

Yes the last few years have brought a great deal of fun but it wouldn't be true to say the growing fuss hasn't brought problems as well. I find the letters very worrying. Every week I get literally hundreds of letters. Soon after we moved to our new house I breathed a sigh of relief because there had been no mail that morning. But I spoke too soon. Minutes later there was a knock at the door. It was the post girl.

'Could I possibly have a drink of water,' she said, 'I've almost finished then I'm going home for the pram.'

The pram? I thought. Surely she wasn't going to bring a baby out in this weather. It was bitterly cold and there was a freezing wind.

'Oh no,' she said, 'it's for your post. There's so much I can't carry it all so I'm going to put it in the pram and wheel it round.'

You can see the problem. I get pram loads of mail every day. If I spent each day doing nothing but answering letters I still wouldn't finish them and the next morning there would be another batch. It's impossible to deal with. What's more, the letters themselves are heartrending. Each has a tragic story. Every correspondent starts by saying they know I'm very busy and that I can't see everyone and then goes on to explain why they should be a special case. The trouble is, I know everyone's a special case but I can't see everyone.

Sometimes it makes me despair. There's so much sadness out there and I want to help but I feel as if I'm trying to empty the ocean with a tea cup.

Even more of a worry are the people who get fed up with waiting for a reply and come calling instead. A couple of weeks ago I had my first day off in two months. It was a wonderful luxury. Our glamorous hire car might seem like the height of good living to some people, but for me there is no greater luxury than sitting at home with absolutely nothing to do.

Right, I thought, that morning. I'm not going to do a thing. I'm not going to talk to anyone, tune in to anyone, I'm not even going to open a letter. I'll just sit in my chair and watch a bit of television. But I must have been more exhausted than I knew, because no sooner had the programme started than I fell asleep. John woke me up with a sandwich at lunch time but afterwards I drifted off again.

All around me I was vaguely aware of the sounds of the house, but they could have been a thousand miles away. Then at some point in the afternoon I heard a bell ringing.

'Oh it's the phone,' I thought sleepily. 'John'll get it.'

But it wasn't the phone, it was the front door and I was abruptly woken by John leading a complete stranger into the room.

'I thought you'd better see her, love,' he said. 'She's come a long way.'

Apparently this lady had set out from Hertford early

55

that morning determined to find me despite the fact she didn't have my address. She'd read in the books that I lived in some disabled ex-servicemen's flats and she was under the impression they were in the Kensington area, so she went to Kensington and walked the streets looking for the flats and asking if anyone knew of them.

At last a newsagent told her he thought the place she was looking for might be in Fulham and he told her which bus to get because Fulham is quite a distance from Kensington. But the lady was too impatient to wait for a bus. She ended up walking all the way to Fulham and after more tramping about she found the flats. Now there are a great many flats in the complex where we used to live. There are several long blocks, each block four storeys high, but undaunted, she started knocking on doors until she stumbled across one of the three people who knew my new address and persuaded them to give it to her. Then she caught two trains and walked another fair step, until she reached my door.

What could I do? I was not at all pleased, but after such a long journey I felt I had to give the poor woman a cup of tea. The one thing I wouldn't do though was give her a sitting. There was a time when under similar circumstances I'd have relented but not any more. Now I realize that it wouldn't be fair to all those people patiently and politely waiting, some of them for two years, on the waiting list. So I chatted to this lady, gave her tea and let her phone her family because they'd had no idea what she was up to and she'd be very late home and then I gently explained that we were about to start our supper and she would have to go.

I felt a bit guilty about it afterwards but also annoyed. Why should someone make me feel guilty about having a day off? It wasn't fair. Even vicars are allowed time off. I'm sixty-five years old now and surely I'm entitled to a rest now and then.

The great ocean of grief all around is just too much for me to handle so I've had to be sensible. Now I concentrate on mass demonstrations because I can give a lot of people a little comfort in the time it used to take me to comfort one. As for private sittings, I still do a few, but I let the spirit world guide me. They let me know which people are most in need of help which people I must see. Sometimes I'm going through a sack of mail and one letter will literally leap into my hand. Occasionally the feeling of urgency is so strong that I immediately drop what I'm doing and phone the sender right away, although it's not always clear to me why speed is so important. Sometimes the sender will be a distraught mother almost out of her mind with grief over a lost child, but other cases are less straightforward.

One morning I was sifting through the mail as usual when a small envelope addressed in a round childish hand almost flew into my lap. It was from a sixteen-year-old girl in Scotland who'd recently lost her much loved Nanna. A sad but not unusual story you might think but there was more to it than that. From the other side there was a great rush of urgency and I got the impression of a woman trying to push me to the phone.

I looked at the signature on the letter. The girl's name was Cheryl and she obviously needed help. I put down the rest of my postbag and dialled the number she'd printed beneath her address.

Cheryl herself answered the phone and once she'd got over the surprise, the sad story came pouring out. Brought up chiefly by her grandmother she'd been devastated when the old lady died. Now she was unhappy at home. She didn't get on with her stepfather and to comfort herself she'd started eating vast amounts of food.

'She always was a big girl,' said a strong Scots voice in my other ear, 'but now she's gone up to nineteen

57

stone and she won't go to school. She won't leave the house. It's such a waste.'

Cheryl admitted it was true. 'I can't go to school. The other kids laugh at me because I'm so fat,' and she started to cry.

I realized that if something wasn't done quickly there could be another tragedy.

'Now, Cheryl, listen to me,' I said, 'you're making your Nan very unhappy. She's here now and she's telling me you're such a beautiful child she can't bear to see you letting yourself go. If only you'd lose some weight and make yourself smart, everyone would want to know you and you wouldn't want to hide away at home.'

'If you'd just stop buying sweets and biscuits and nibbled at an apple or a carrot when you were hungry you'd soon lose weight. If you do that, I promise you that before the year's over you'll be having a wonderful time. You're only sixteen for goodness sake. Your Nanna wants to be a great-grandmother and she's not going to do that if you're shut up in the house . . .'

Cheryl sniffed and sobbed but eventually she agreed to try a diet.

'It's not easy, Cheryl,' I said, 'I've got thyroid trouble and I'm sixty-five and I have to be really strong with myself or I'd be twenty-one stone. But your Nanna says there's nothing physically wrong with you – it's just insecurity. So if you could just stick to a diet for a few months you'd see the weight roll off.'

Cheryl promised to do her best and I gave her my phone number so that she could ring me with progress reports or just for a chat if she felt desperate.

'And remember, Cheryl,' I added at the end of the conversation, 'when things get difficult just put out your hand and your Nanna will be there to help you. She's not far away and she's watching over you.'

Afterwards I could only pray that I'd got through to that poor child and helped her back on the path to a normal life. The spirit world had done their bit, I'd done mine, and now it was up to Cheryl to find the strength to pick up the pieces.

Occasionally, however, my post bag brings me news of even more disturbing matters. Another of the letters that forced itself to my attention contained a very alarming story. It was from a woman whose hotel business was almost ruined despite the 'advice' I'd been giving her for so long through a 'mutual friend'. She wanted to thank me for the work I'd done on her behalf, but she'd now sadly come to the conclusion that the business was beyond redemption.

Horrified, I skimmed through the letter again. I had never heard of this lady or her hotel and the name of our 'mutual friend' meant absolutely nothing to me. What on earth was going on? This time I didn't need the spirit world to prompt me. I was instantly on the phone.

'Oh thank goodness you phoned,' said this poor woman when I explained who I was and that I was quite mystified by the whole thing. 'It was my daughter who suspected there was something wrong. She read your books and then she read your predictions and she said you know Mum these sound as if they were written by two different people. There's just no comparison.'

'Predictions?' I asked more alarmed than ever. 'What predictions? I don't make predictions I'm not a fortune teller.'

'Oh yes this friend says she knows you and that she regularly visits you to discuss people's problems and that you make predictions about what they have to do. Just a minute, I'll read you some.'

She went away and came back with a piece of paper.

'It says here, "I, Doris Stokes, do hereby declare . . ." ' and she went on to read out the worst load of rubbish I've ever heard. It included instructions to sweep up the leaves from the hotel yard, put them in a jar and keep them in the bathroom. This utter nonsense was apparently signed with my name and these so called messages from me had been arriving almost every month for some time.

'I feel such a fool now,' said the poor woman, 'but she was so plausible. She described you and your home. She even said things like, "d'you like my dress? Doris Stokes gave me this." We followed all her instructions thinking they came from you and now we're just about ruined.'

I was appalled. 'But I've never met this woman in my life,' I said. 'She's probably seen me and my flat on television or in pictures.'

There was little I could do to help save their business. I could only sympathize and suggest they throw away the dead leaves in the bathroom and anything else I was supposed to have instructed them to collect. Finally I asked for the address and telephone number of our 'mutual friend'. She must be stopped. How could people be so wicked? And how many other people was she ruining in my name?

Furiously I dialled the number and got through right away. My 'old friend' sounded quite taken aback to hear from me.

'Now look,' I said, 'I've never met you, I've never spoken to you and you've never been to my home.'

'Eh. Well. No. But we have met,' said the woman faintly.

'Where?' I demanded, 'I don't recall ever meeting you.'

'We met in a previous life,' she insisted, but I think it sounded ridiculous even to her.

Well I'm afraid I told her what I thought of her. I told her that her friend would probably lose the hotel and that what she'd done was quite wicked.

'And how many other people have you been sending predictions to?'

She hesitated. 'Eh well, not many. I only do it to comfort them you know. I didn't mean any harm.'

I was too angry to think straight at that, so I brought

60

the conversation to an end intending to ring back when I'd cooled down. From then on, however, the phone was permanently engaged. In the end I had to be content with sending a strongly worded solicitor's letter forbidding her to pass on any more messages in my name.

The lengths people will go to and the nonsense they are prepared to come out with constantly amazes me. Why they do it I can't imagine. Perhaps they're trying to get attention, perhaps they've got problems, but whatever the reason they've got no right to take advantage of gullible people looking for help.

A newspaper rang me recently to ask if I could help with a reader's query. This woman had written in to say that her husband had gone missing and she'd consulted a medium to find out if he was dead or alive. The medium had taken her money and told her that the husband was definitely on the other side but that he couldn't talk to her because he'd been killed by a blow to the head and he was delirious. The newspaper wanted to know if this was possible! Now I ask you? It would be funny if it wasn't so serious.

Another woman sent me a tape recording of a sitting she'd had with a so called medium who had spent most of the time singing hymns.

'I was so upset and felt so dreadful after that sitting,' she wrote, 'that I felt like coming out and throwing myself under a bus.'

As I read the letter I heard the name Mark, very clearly, so I phoned her straight away.

'I'm so sorry you had such a bad experience,' I said, 'but as I was reading your letter I heard the name Mark and I knew it was important.'

'Yes that's right. That's what I was waiting for. Mark's my son.'

'Well, love, he took himself over didn't he,' I said because Mark had just told me he was very ashamed of what he'd done.

'Yes he did,' she admitted in astonishment.

'And he tells me he did it away from this country.'

'Yes.'

'Tell them I'm sorry,' Mark begged me, 'I hadn't been married very long.'

'Only four months,' sobbed his mother, but despite the overwhelming emotion she was pleased. 'That's all I wanted,' she said. 'That's why I went to a medium in the first place. I didn't want to bother you because I know you're busy, but I felt so dreadful after this other sitting. It was awful. All I wanted to do was get out. I felt sick.'

She was quite content with the few scraps I was able to give her but I felt very sad that she'd been treated so badly, especially by a person who called herself a medium.

Sometimes I just don't understand people at all.

I suppose the most depressing reading of all though, comes through the letter box every morning in the shape of the newspaper. Is it just my imagination or is the news getting worse? Every day people seem to think of new and more horrible ways of being nasty to each other. But at least now I have a little money behind me I sometimes get the chance to put right, in a very small way, a few wrongs.

Some months ago I was upset to read about a poor little boy who was set upon by louts who smashed his expensive hearing aid. How they could be so cruel to a child who has enough problems to contend with anyway, I don't know, and my heart went out to the little boy. He must be so confused and disillusioned with life.

Impulsively I sat down and wrote him a note. I promised to buy him a new hearing aid and added; 'Just to tell you there aren't all nasty people in the world – there are some nice people too, people who love you and want you to be happy.'

I couldn't undo the pain and misery he'd gone through but perhaps I could cheer him up a little, and help restore his faith in human nature.

It's worth all the hard work and tiring journeys to be able to make little gestures like these and I know my dad would be pleased. As he used to say to me when I was a girl: 'If you want to keep love, Dol, you have to give it away.'

Chapter Five

Diana Dors was unmissable. There she was, large but glamorous in a sleeveless black dress, her blonde hair falling round her shoulders, her long, long, eyelashes almost brushing the glass in her hand and her infectious laugh brightening everybody in the room. The place was packed and all the guests had dressed up, yet it was Diana you noticed. The slender figure of the fifties sex symbol might have disappeared for ever but Diana was still every inch a star.

John and I were a bit over-awed to tell the truth, so we just said a polite hello as we passed and moved on to mingle with the other guests. It was certainly a splendid do. Robert Maxwell who owns the company which publishes my books had invited all his authors to a reception at his beautiful old home, Headington Hill Hall near Oxford. It was a magnificent house, built like a castle with a massive staircase and a minstrel gallery, and the Maxwells had gone to endless trouble over the arrangements. A toastmaster announced the guests as they entered the solid oak door; there were waiters circulating with trays of champagne and wine and there was a bar for those who wanted something different. Outside there were two bands playing, one by the swimming pool and one by the marquee and the buffet lunch, spread out on huge tables, was quite dazzling.

Feeling slightly overwhelmed by it all, John and I decided that the first thing we'd better do was cool down with a drink and since neither of us touches alcohol we had to make our excuses to the waiters and I went up to the bar for fruit juice.

'Two orange juices, please,' I said and as two glasses

tinkling with ice appeared on the bar a deep voice at my shoulder said, 'Are you on the wagon too?'

I looked round. It was Diana's husband, Alan Lake. 'No, it's just that we can't drink,' I explained. 'It doesn't agree with us.'

But Alan wasn't listening. He was staring at me as if he couldn't quite place the face. Then his frown disappeared.

'You're Doris Stokes, aren't you! I did enjoy your book. Do come and meet Diana.'

And that was how John and I became friends with Alan and Diana. We never did get around to visiting each other's homes, but we bumped into each other at functions and TV stations and when we heard that Di had cancer, the dreaded C as we called it, I rang her regularly.

Diana was a great fighter and at first it looked as if she'd won. As anyone who's had cancer knows, you have to keep going back for check-ups and no matter how healthy you feel, it's a worrying business. It can easily play on your mind and so to boost our morale at these difficult times, Diana and a couple of other friends and fellow sufferers, Julie Goodyear, the actress from Coronation Street, Pat Seed, who wrote the lovely book *One Day At A Time*, and I formed the Sod It Club. We used to get on the phone, have a good laugh and advise each other to say: 'Sod It! I'm not going to have it!' I don't know whether, medically speaking, laughter and defiance is the best way to react to the dreaded C, but it certainly made the four of us feel a lot better. In the nerve-racking days that surrounded the regular check-ups and tests those phone calls were like a tonic.

Diana seemed to blossom again. She went on a diet, exercised every day and swam in her pool and the pounds fell off. I bumped into her at TV AM one morning towards the end of her diet and I could hardly believe my eyes. Glamorous as ever, she was half her former size and she looked sensational.

'You make me want to spit!' I joked when I saw her

because we'd both been fighting a losing battle with our weight for months and now she put me to shame.

Diana laughed, delighted. 'You're never too old, Doris! You're always telling me that! You could do it too if you tried.'

'I never stop trying!' I wailed. 'And look where it gets me!'

They were a devoted couple, Alan and Di. They were always together. At parties and receptions they didn't split up and talk to people separately the way some couples do. They preferred to move round as a pair, Alan very dark and handsome with the cravat he always wore, and Di bubbly and full of fun, the silvery blonde hair bouncing when she laughed.

They'd had their problems, of course. Alan was an alcoholic and at the height of his illness he became very violent but Di stood by him.

'They always turn on the one they love,' she said and knowing that she stayed and helped him to beat his addiction. She was a very wise lady. Diana was the strong one in that partnership and, as the old saying goes, she really was his mother, lover, friend and wife. For his part, Alan worshipped her.

The last time I saw Di was at Robert Maxwell's. The annual reception had come round again and it was beginning to be a regular date in our diaries. There was no sign of the Lakes when we walked in this time, but as we loaded our plates at the buffet table they appeared.

Alan, charming as ever, was at my side in an instant to help me to the food.

'Caviar, darling?' he asked lifting a dish of what looked like miniature black ball-bearings.

'Oh no thank you, I don't like it,' I said.

He replaced the dish and tried another, 'Smoked salmon?'

'Oh no thank you, I don't like it,' I said again and at my other side Diana roared with laughter.

'It's no good, Alan. Doris and John only have cold chicken and a tomato!'

And I had to laugh because she was right. With all that rich food to choose from John and I invariably came away with just a bit of chicken and salad on our plates and possibly a bread roll to keep it company. The shame of it is that all this grand living has come too late for us. We'd never had the chance before to get used to caviar and smoked salmon and we're too old now to get started on that sort of thing. Apart from not liking the taste, we'd probably end up with dreadful indigestion!

Lunch was as merry as ever but for the first time I felt uneasy about Diana. She looked absolutely beautiful and yet something seemed to have happened to the figure she'd dieted so long to achieve. Her tummy looked enormous. Of course Diana enjoyed her food as much as the next woman but there was something about her shape that wasn't quite right. It didn't look as if she'd been on an eating spree, it seemed more serious than that.

As we moved away I said to John, 'There's something the matter with Di, I'm sure of it.'

Shortly afterwards we heard she'd gone into hospital with a stomach complaint. I was on tour at the time and dashing about from place to place with scarcely time to draw breath but between appointments I phoned the Lakes' home in Berkshire to find out where she was, and sent flowers to the hospital.

Then we were whirling off to the next town and by the time I caught up with the news, Diana was back home. Thank goodness, I thought to myself. It was a false alarm.

The weeks passed and then came the day I discovered I'd have to go into hospital again to have another lump removed. Of course I feared the worst the way you always do and I longed to talk to someone who'd understand. I didn't know if Diana was away or not but I rang her home on the off chance and she answered.

'Oh Diana, I'm so glad I caught you . . .' I said and soon I was pouring out all my troubles.

Diana was wonderful. She listened sympathetically to all my worries and when I'd finished she said, 'Oh sod it, kid. Just say you're not going to have it!'

And I couldn't help laughing. Thank goodness for the Sod It Club. And all the time I was moaning on to Di she knew that she herself was going to have to go back into hospital and the chances didn't look good – and she never said a word. What a wonderful lady.

My little operation was over quite quickly and I was up and on the road again when I picked up the paper one day and saw that Diana was back in hospital. I'd been feeling quite cheerful until that moment, but suddenly depression swept over me.

'Look at this, John,' I said pointing at the story, 'I think she's going to have a job to make it this time.'

There wasn't a moment to lose. I rang the hospital and after a short delay Alan came to the phone. They'd operated, he said but Di was too weak to talk at the moment. A cold feeling settled lower and lower in my stomach.

'We're thinking of you both, Alan, and praying for you,' I told him but as I put the receiver down I knew.

'I have an awful feeling about Di,' I told John, 'I don't think she's going to make it.'

A couple of days later we were having breakfast in our hotel room when the news came on the radio that Diana had passed. Even when you're expecting it the actual announcement is always a shock and my heart went out to poor Alan. I would miss Diana, of course, but I was relieved for her sake that it was over so quickly and she didn't have to suffer. She would be happy now with her family and her new life on the other side. It was Alan who needed help and sympathy. How was he going to manage without her, I wondered?

She had been his crutch in life. Would he find the strength to stand alone?

I can't honestly say that I was seriously afraid for Alan. I was worried about him of course and I felt desperately sorry for him but it didn't cross my mind that he might be suicidal. He and Diana were devoted to their fifteen-year-old son, Jason, and I never dreamed that Alan's despair would reach such a pitch that his need for Diana would over-ride his fatherly instincts. He was a good father and my first thought was thank goodness for Jason, he'll be the saving of his dad.

Not long after the announcement, Diana came through to me quite spontaneously, 'Tell Alan I'm only a whisper away,' she murmured in my ear, 'and that Minnie met me.'

Her voice was faint because she hadn't been over very long and it was difficult for her to communicate, but as always her concern for Alan was so great she felt she had to pass on some words of comfort.

I rang Alan immediately. There was a long pause. 'He's not taking any calls at the moment, he's too upset,' said the housekeeper, 'but seeing as it's you, Doris, I'll tell him you're on the line.'

The seconds ticked by and at last a distraught Alan came to the phone. 'Alan, I don't know what to say. There's nothing I can say to you,' I said gently, 'except, never forget, she's only a whisper away. I've spoken to her and she wanted you to know that Minnie met her.'

'Minnie's my mother,' he said brokenly, but he seemed relieved to know that Diana was all right and she hadn't been alone.

I didn't go to the funeral. I try to avoid conventional funerals whenever I can because spiritualists believe that a funeral should be, as far as possible, a happy occasion, when you celebrate the fact that the person who's passed on has taken his 'promotion' as we call it, and is free at last of all pain and suffering.

So I didn't go to the funeral but afterwards I phoned

Alan every week, on Sunday mornings when he came back from Mass, to give him what support I could. The months went by and my life became ever more hectic, yet somewhere at the back of my mind it registered that Alan wasn't recovering from his grief the way he should. He put on an act when he first picked up the phone, but good actor though he was you could tell. Then suddenly he'd break down and the phone would go dead.

To be honest I don't think anyone could have prevented the tragedy. A lot of Alan's friends blamed themselves for not realizing how ill he'd become and I felt guilty myself because the Sunday before it happened I hadn't phoned him. It was one of those things you regret for ever. I've already mentioned the bad back that plagued me that summer and by this stage it had reached such a pitch that the doctor decided to send me to hospital to have it looked at.

I was going in the next day and that Sunday I was in agony, but struggling to cook lunch, get my case packed and leave everything organized for John and Terry. All day I kept thinking I must ring Alan, I must ring Alan, but somehow I didn't get round to it. In hospital the next day it was the same. I'd taken the phone number with me and I fully intended to make the call but I was wheeled here, there and everywhere for tests. There were consultations with doctors, a stream of visitors and phone calls and all at once it was bedtime and I hadn't phoned Alan.

'Oh well, I'll definitely phone him tomorrow,' I said to myself. But Tuesday was the same.

Then on Wednesday, John switched on the television in my room just in case there was something on and then left it babbling to itself the way he often does. No one was taking much notice, when suddenly there came a news bulletin that stopped me in my tracks. Alan Lake had shot himself that morning at his Berkshire home.

I felt absolutely sick. If only I'd made that call —

perhaps things would have been different. Why hadn't I paid more attention to that nagging in my mind? It was so persistent I recognized it now as the spirit world's attempt to alert me to Alan's plight but I was so bogged down in my own problems I couldn't see it at the time. And what would happen to poor Jason? The more I thought of him the worse I felt. Poor boy to have lost both his parents so tragically and in such a short space of time.

It went round and round in my mind and by the end of the day I was in a right old tangle and inclined to blame myself. Fortunately, Ramanov came that night to talk some sense into me.

'Don't worry yourself, child, about things that can't be changed,' he said when I'd all but given up hope of getting to sleep. 'It is a waste of energy. There was nothing you could have done. It would have made no difference in the end, whether you made that phone call or not. Learn from this and go forward. Don't look back.'

And of course he was right, as I was to learn from Alan himself later.

It's strange how one chance meeting on a summer's day can lead to so many others. Just before Christmas I was invited by *Woman's Own* to their special Children of Courage service at Westminster Abbey and who should I bump into but Jason.

He was a beautiful child. Very like Diana but with light brown hair rather than blonde, yet when he moved you could see Alan in him.

After the service he came up to me and I noticed that his shirt collar was all frayed and I thought his mum would go mad if she saw it. But that's what kids are like. They have their favourite clothes and they won't stop wearing them.

'I'm going to America, Doris,' said Jason, 'what d'you think?' He had a stepbrother in America from an earlier marriage of Diana's.

'Well, love, you go,' I said, 'and see if you feel happy

71

living with Gary. But if you don't, come back because there are plenty of people here who'd like to give you a home.'

I was very impressed with Jason. The sadness was there at the back of his eyes but he was so brave and so mature you'd have thought he was nineteen rather than fifteen. He wasn't at all bitter against his father as some boys might have been.

'I was angry at first,' he admitted with that steady gaze so like Diana's, 'but I don't blame Dad now. He was hopeless without Mum.' And then he was a child again needing reassurance. 'They are still with me, aren't they, Doris?'

'They *are*,' I said firmly, 'and what's more your Mum in particular is watching over you and she's going to be helping you every step of the way.'

And suddenly over the hub-bub around us Diana's voice came chiming in. 'You'd better believe it.'

My contact with the Lake family didn't end when Jason went to America, however. Not long afterwards, to my amazement, I received a phone call from comedian Freddie Starr. Apparently Alan Lake had been his best friend and ever since the tragic suicide he'd been haunted by the feeling that Alan was trying to get in touch with him. Could I possibly help?

I looked through my diary doubtfully. It was booked up solid for months ahead. The only spaces occurred on Sundays, my day off. Now, as I've said, my Sundays off are precious to me. I can't do my job properly unless I have free time to recharge my batteries and of course I like some time at home with my family like everybody else.

Yet Alan and Diana were good friends to me. Diana in particular had always spared the time to listen and to cheer me up when I needed the support of the Sod It Club. If they were really trying to get through to Freddie and they needed my help then surely I owed it to them to see him. I picked up my pen.

'Well, Freddie,' I said, 'I'm afraid I only have Sundays free.'

'That's all right I can make Sundays,' said Freddie writing down the address. 'Now which garden can I land the helicopter in?'

I thought I was hearing things. 'Did you say helicopter?'

'Yes,' said Freddie, 'I was going to pop across in my helicopter.'

I laughed. 'Freddie, where d'you think I live? There's no room to land a helicopter in my pocket handkerchief garden. I'm afraid you'll have to come by car.'

But Freddie was so keen to set his mind at rest that the inconvenience didn't bother him. I'll let him explain for himself:

'Alan was my best friend and ever since he died I've had this feeling that he was still close to me. It was as if he'd left something unfinished between us and there was something he wanted to say to me. I had this feeling all the time but most strongly of all when I passed the graveyard where he was buried. It was like a magnet pulling me to the grave.

'Once I stopped the car at three o'clock in the morning and got out and went to the grave because it felt as if he was calling me. Yet no matter how hard I tried I couldn't hear what he was saying. It had been like that for months ever since the day he died, but after I found myself at the grave at three o'clock in the morning I knew I was going to have to do something.

'The next day I phoned Doris.'

Everyone thinks that Freddie Starr is just a zany comedian without a care in the world, but in fact he's a very sensitive, loving man. Just before he died Alan visited Freddie's home and when he left, he said goodbye and walked away through a garden gate. Freddie never saw him again and from that moment on he couldn't bear to look at that garden gate. It caused him so much pain that in the end he had it bricked up.

But, of course, before our first meeting I didn't know how nice Freddie was and I was a little apprehensive. I didn't know what to expect. Yet at four o'clock on that Sunday afternoon there was a knock at the door and in walked a compact, slimly built man with blond hair and the most beautiful blue eyes I've ever seen on a man. I've heard it said that some comedians are really very serious men and not at all funny off stage. Well I don't know whether that's true or not, but all I can say is that Freddie had us in stitches.

I didn't realize it then but he's a brilliant ventriloquist and hardly had he sat down when the bottles of drink we keep on the trolley for visitors began to talk. I glanced up in surprise and I distinctly heard a bottle of rum say:

'I don't need your ear, Doris, I'm a spirit!'

Well! It was definitely not a message from the other side, that was certain, but had I finally flipped as my mother always predicted? I looked round anxiously to see if the others had heard it too and then I noticed the mischief sparkling in Freddie's eyes.

'Freddie!' I gasped. 'It's you!'

'I'm a spirit, I'm a spirit!' insisted the rum while Freddie sat motionless, his lips not moving. But then he burst out laughing and gave the game away. Undaunted the other bottles started chattering too, and John and I laughed till we had to beg Freddie to stop because we were aching so much.

But of course Freddie had come for a sitting so the afternoon wasn't just confined to fun. There was work to be done too. Yet the work wasn't difficult because Alan was there immediately I tuned in. Freddie was right. Alan was anxious to talk to him. He wanted to explain to his old friend why he'd felt driven to take his own life and to reassure Freddie that nothing could have prevented it.

'It's Alan, darling!' he said straight away as soon as I began concentrating and his voice was as deep and rich as I remembered it. 'Tell Freddie about the black cravat. He was looking at the black cravat.'

I was puzzled but then I'm often puzzled by things the spirit people tell me so I just passed the message on to Freddie.

He looked blank at first but then he smiled. 'Last night I got Alan's photo album out and I was looking at a picture of me and Alan together,' he said. 'I noticed that Alan was wearing the black cravat that he wore all the time after Diana's death.'

'Well Alan must have been with you last night, love,' I said.

'Can he hear me now?' asked Freddie.

'Of course he can.'

'Right, Alan,' said Freddie to point over my shoulder. 'I was so mad at you for what you did. Did you know that? I was so bloody annoyed.'

'Look, Freddie, speak truthfully,' said Alan, 'if you'd been in the same boat and it had been Sandy you'd lost – could you have gone on?'

Tears sprang into Freddie's eyes and he looked at the floor. 'No, I don't think I could.'

'I hadn't planned to do it,' Alan went on, 'but I saw no future without Di. I never went back to the sauce (drink) but I'd started smoking again and I was so depressed.'

Then despite my protests he insisted on telling me what happened. Apparently out of the blue one morning he'd just decided he'd had enough. He didn't want to go on any longer. He just couldn't face it. He got his gun, rested the butt on the floor between his legs, leaned over, put the end of the barrel in his mouth and pulled the trigger.

'I felt a pain in my jaw, then blood came into my throat and that was it,' said Alan.

He told Freddie that since then the family Cadillac had been sold but the red car he used to drive was still there.

'We're together now,' he went on, 'but I got a

tongue-lashing from Diana when I first got here. She was furious about Jason.'

Then there was a weakening in the vibration and a woman's voice cut in. It was Diana.

'I was so angry,' she spluttered, 'I was livid. What was he thinking of leaving Jason like that? I told him he was a selfish bastard. After all I had no choice, but *he* did. But then I realized that Jason's probably better off this way. Alan's so weak he might have gone back on the drink and that would have been worse for Jason in the long run. Now at least he can remember his father as he was.'

And then she added, woman to woman, just the way she used to, 'I don't know. I'm still mothering him. I was mothering him then and I'm mothering him now, but mind, I love him.'

Other voices were crowding in now and I got an impression of a whole group of people jostling and eager to talk to Freddie.

'I'm Richard but everyone calls me Dick,' said a man loudly.

'That's my father,' said Freddie.

'Will you ask him to forgive me,' said Dick. 'He thought I didn't love him because I wasn't very demonstrative but I did. The trouble was I could never work out whether our Freddie was mental or whether he was a genius.'

Freddie laughed. 'Well I'll settle for half of that. I'm a mental genius!'

Dick went on to mention Jack, Freddie's stepfather and to say how pleased he was that Freddie's mother had married again and to tell her not to feel guilty about it because he wanted her to be happy. He also mentioned Muriel.

'That's my Auntie Muriel,' said Freddie in surprise, 'I've not seen Auntie Muriel for about twenty-five years.'

'Well Dick says that Muriel's been in hospital recently,' I said.

Freddie shook his head. 'I wouldn't know. I've not seen her for so long.'

But in fact Freddie checked with his mother the next day and it turned out that Auntie Muriel had had an operation only the month before to improve her hearing.

Dick also remarked that he enjoyed Freddie's shows and that he'd been with him to Barbados and to Canada.

'I hope he paid!' said Freddie.

Then, towards the end when the power was failing, Alan came back to say he was sorry for what he'd done and to thank Freddie for looking after Jason.

Afterwards, although it had been lovely to talk to Alan and Diana again, I felt drained. It had been an emotional sitting particularly since they were personal friends and Freddie seemed to sense my fatigue. He sat on the rug by the fire and talked quietly.

'What d'you think God is, Doris?' he asked suddenly.

It was a big question but he was quite sincere.

'Well I can't visualize God as a person,' I said. 'To me he is a divine power. That's the only way I can put it in words.'

Freddie was silent for a moment then he said. 'You know they spell it wrong. It shouldn't be G-O-D. It should be G-O-O-D because everything good is God.'

I thought that was beautiful.

In all Freddie stayed five hours. Although he arrived at four o'clock with the intention of staying half an hour or so, he didn't leave until nine o'clock at night. And being Freddie, the serious mood soon passed and it wasn't long before he had John and I in fits of laughter again. I don't think we've laughed so much in years. Freddie certainly did us more good than any medicine the doctor could prescribe.

As he was leaving, he put his arms round me and gave me a big hug.

'I'm going to give you a gift,' he said, blue eyes sparkling in that teasing way he has.

'Oh how lovely,' I said. I adore flowers and people often give me flowers after a sitting. Thanks to my sitters the house is always filled with the scent of fresh flowers.

'Yes,' Freddie went on, 'I'm going to give you a race horse.'

I nearly fell out of my chair, the placid response strangled somewhere in the back of my throat.

'A race horse?' I gasped half choking. 'Freddie, you're winding me up.'

'No I'm not,' said Freddie, his face going serious again. 'We've just had two foals born and I'd like to give you one. I'll keep it at my place for two years then you can choose your colours and put it with a trainer.'

I was overwhelmed and to tell the truth I couldn't believe he was serious. I mean whoever heard of an old lady in a London semi owning a race horse?

Yet Freddie meant it – as I discovered a few weeks later when he invited us over to see the foal.

It was a wet and windy Sunday morning, the sort of day when you look at the weather and wonder in a depressed way if spring is ever going to come. Yet for once the weather didn't bother me. I was as excited as a child on Christmas morning about meeting my foal. Although I must admit I was a little nervous too because I've always been a bit frightened of horses.

We splashed for miles through the dripping Berkshire lanes and at last turned in through a neat brick entrance. On either side all I could see were paddocks with horses and acres of lawn and trees. The drive seemed to go on for ever, and then suddenly there was a beautiful mansion in front of us and Freddie waving at the door.

He led us through into the hall and before I'd even unbuttoned my coat, two small blonde heads came charging towards me.

'Hello, Doris!' cried the little girl throwing her arms around me. This was Donna aged nine.

78

'Hello, Doris!' cried the little boy, Jodie aged five, doing the same.

They were lovely children. They'd just come back from a holiday in Spain so they had healthy brown faces and their father's bright blue eyes that shone even bluer against their tanned skin.

We sat down for a cup of tea, enlivened by Jodie's display of break dancing, then we all put on wellington boots and tramped up to the stables to meet my foal.

Jodie danced at my side as we squelched through the mud.

'I've got a horse too,' he told me, 'but not as big as yours, Doris.'

'Is my horse big?' I asked, alarmed. 'I thought it was only a baby.'

'Oh yes,' said Jodie. 'Bigger than mine.'

And in fact the horse *was* larger than I'd expected. When Freddie had said it was a foal, I'd imagined a tiny, fragile little creature staggering after its mother on matchstick legs, but the animal the groom led out into the stable yard was as tall as me. Nevertheless he was obviously very young, and nervous, and quite lovely. His coat was a beautiful reddish brown, he had a white diamond on his forehead and one white sock and when I stretched out my hand to stroke him, he put a nose into my palm that was as soft as velvet.

'Aren't you *lovely*!' I told him, 'I'm going to call you Stoksie.'

Freddie walked him round to calm him and then turned him loose into a paddock to play. He was a joy to watch. He galloped about revelling in the grass and the rain and kicking up his heels like a spring lamb.

'Freddie, he's the most beautiful gift,' I cried in delight. 'I love him.'

But the fun wasn't over. Freddie and his wife Sandy went to a great deal of trouble to give us a lovely day. I'd told Freddie not to bother about organizing a lunch.

'Sandy doesn't want to be working on a Sunday,' I said, 'a sandwich will do.'

But Sandy had laid out a delicious spread that included *vol-au-vents* and smoked salmon and must have involved as much work as a roast dinner.

Afterwards Freddie showed me the house. It was absolutely magnificent. The guest bedrooms alone were like hotel suites and one of them came complete with bed, bathroom, sofa, piano, TV and video. Freddie's own personal bathroom was all red and gold and columns and things like some impossibly luxurious picture in a glossy magazine, and his bedroom was lined in red pleated silk. I'd never seen anything like it. It really did take my breath away.

'You should have all this, the work you do, Doris,' said Freddie as he led me back downstairs again.

I shook my head. 'Freddie, it would scare me to death,' I told him and it would too. I'm grateful for my three-bedroom semi. I couldn't cope with a grand mansion.

Back in the sitting-room little Jodie was jumping about and exchanging meaningful glances with his father.

'Can we start now, Dad? Is it time?' he kept whispering.

Freddie evidently decided it was because we were requested to take seats and father and son disappeared to return a moment later with guitars. There they stood, father and son, Freddie with his guitar and beside him like a miniature replica, Jodie with his tiny guitar. Then Freddie started playing and singing and Jodie strummed away at one chord. Freddie went down on one knee and Jodie went down on one knee and all the time the little lad kept looking up at his father to check he was doing the right thing.

We all clapped heartily at the end of the performance, but Jodie hadn't finished yet. His tiny drum kit stood in the corner and when the applause died away there was an official announcement.

'Ladies and gentlemen, there will now be a cabaret in honour of Doris, performed by Jodie Starr.'

Grinning eagerly, Jodie bounded to his drums and gave us a very spirited rendering of something modern. I don't know what it was but it was very good and afterwards Jodie jumped down and gave a solemn bow and we all had to clap, then he ran off through the kitchen door and came back to take an encore. It was magic. Absolute magic.

We went home that evening, happy, full of food and convinced that the Starrs were one of the nicest, most unspoiled families you could wish to meet.

Chapter Six

At first there was nothing but a feeling of horror. Stark, terrifying, pure horror. Then a confused series of images. Bumping along in a car, then a dimly lit room and all the time the horror was growing until suddenly the impressions were shattered by a child's piercing scream. The pictures went blank and there was nothing but the terrible cry, 'I want my Mummy! I want my Mummy,' echoing round my head.

Cold and shaking, I lit a cigarette. A medium's job is not a cosy one. Every person who comes back to talk from the other side, describes the manner of their passing and not everyone is lucky enough to go gently in their sleep. I hear of illness and accidents, suicide and murder. I've spoken to young boys who've shot themselves and little children who've been stabbed to death, but nothing I've encountered so far, prepared me for the case of Lesley Anne Downey – one of the victims of the notorious Moors Murderers, Ian Brady and Myra Hindley.

No other case has left me with such a sick, cold feeling as if my tummy was filled up with ice. At the end of it I was mentally and physically exhausted and despite the central heating and the fire going full blast, it was hours before I felt really warm again.

I'd had no idea when I got up that morning, what I was letting myself in for. My diary said I had a sitting with a Mrs West who'd lost a child. Apparently a newspaper reporter had rung Laurie and asked if we could possibly see this lady because she was absolutely desperate. He gave us no other details and I was booked up for months ahead, but something told me it was important to see this mother. When the spirit world nudges me like that it's very unwise to ignore it so we did a bit of rearranging and juggling with dates and we made an appointment for Mrs West.

Just before she was due to arrive, I tuned in and immediately I heard the name Lesley, followed by a fleeting glimpse of a fragile, dark-haired little girl. A pretty little thing. Then the bell was ringing and I hurried out to the hall to open the front door.

Mrs West absolutely rushed in, there's no other way of describing it. She flew into the hall and gave me a big hug that spoke of years of pent up emotion.

'I can't believe it,' she said, 'I can't believe I'm actually here.'

You poor soul, I thought, my heart going out to her. You've been searching for a long time, and I prayed very hard that I'd be able to help.

She was an attractive woman was Anne West, with nice clothes, carefully blonded hair and beautiful eyes. Yet when you looked into those eyes you could see a great well of despair and emptiness. There was such a bleak quality to her unhappiness that I knew her daughter's passing had affected her very badly.

'Well come on in,' I said leading them into the sitting-room, 'and let's see what we can do.'

The reporter who'd brought Mrs West had a tape recorder and afterwards he very kindly gave me a transcript of the sitting. This is how it went:

DORIS: I can't promise you anything, my love. But I know you have come here with all this love in your heart and I only hope I can do something to help you. All I know is that your name is West and one of your little children passed over tragically. I started to tune in this morning and I got the name Lesley but her other name was not West.

MRS WEST: No, it was Downey. I married again.

DORIS: Where do I get the number ten from? Was it ten years ago when she passed?

83

MRS WEST: She was ten years old when she died.

DORIS: She will come back first as a child and later as the grown woman she is now. She tells me there's been four passings. She's telling me I'm not on my own because Mum has had other tragedies. Who's Terry?

MRS WEST: He's my son. My eldest son.

DORIS: She's talking to someone. I think it's Alice, Annie, Alan. She's telling me you haven't got it right, Doris. Listen. Yes, my love. It's Alan.

MRS WEST: Alan's my husband.

DORIS: She's talking about Alan. I thought she was talking to someone on the other side and she's told me to listen carefully. She's telling me he's very good to Mum. I love him for that. Who's Bill?

MRS WEST: My Dad.

DORIS: She's saying Bill's this side Doris. Try again love. Was that Millie. Molly. No it's Mary. Do you know a Mary on your side? No? We won't take it, love. We haven't got it right, love? Forgive me she's talking about Myra. She's saying don't upset yourself Mum over what you read in the papers about her being paroled. It's not going to happen because that woman will never reform. She's just play-acting. She's bad, Doris, really bad.

They were taking you where, love? They made you go with them? We were going for some fish and chips. Two of us went with them to show them where the chip shop was. We never went home again, Doris. Don't relive that, love. Your mum has had to live with this for years. Who is Vickie, love?

MRS WEST: My grand-daughter.

DORIS: Mum's got a red rose by my picture frame — thank you for that Mum. Alan thinks as much about me as my Mum, you know. Edward wants to say hello because no one ever talks to him. I'm ever so glad you came Mum because I wanted to tell you everything was all right.

I spend my time among the children Mum. The

children and the babies who have been taken back because no one wants them. But I love them and I spend all my time with them. I never had the chance to have babies of my own but I have lots of them to love here. Bill's here, Mum. And Jim wants to say hello.

MRS WEST: My brother.

DORIS: And Joe and Philip are here too.

MRS WEST: They're two old friends of mine. Brothers. They lived near us and died within two years of each other, about five years ago.

DORIS: She's grown into a beautiful girl, love. Auburn hair, or brown with touches of auburn. A beautiful woman. I have fulfilled my life, Mum. She's asking about a locket you wear with her picture in it.

MRS WEST: I usually wear it. I left it at home today.

DORIS: She's talking about Elsie.

MRS WEST: That's my sister.

DORIS: She's getting so excited and bubbling over. It's difficult love. John. He went over tragically. He should not have gone over.

MRS WEST: John was my nephew. He died three years after Lesley when a simple operation went wrong. They were devoted to each other.

DORIS: Are you all right, darling? Yes, I know it's difficult. No Lesley, you're talking to your Mum and I can't catch you. Mill Street?

MRS WEST: That's the police station where we first reported her missing. We went at four-thirty in the afternoon and they didn't want to know. Told us to go back later if she hadn't come home. It was ten-thirty before they started looking for her and there had been a fall of snow in between. That wrecked any chance they had of finding her.

DORIS: I met a man called Frank here. He used to be a policeman at Mill Street.

MRS WEST: Yes. Frank Rimmer. He was a sergeant.

DORIS: He helped when it happened to me and he is over now. I was able to say thank you to him for

85

trying to help. He said he only wished they had been able to stop it. But they did try, Mum, didn't they?

I see my Mum a lot, Doris. I was listening when they were talking about going to Spain.

MRS WEST: We were trying to work out whether we could afford a holiday in Spain because Alan is about to lose his job. That was only two nights ago in the kitchen at home. We haven't even mentioned it to anyone else.

DORIS: I was listening, Doris. I was saying go on Mum and Dad. Do it. Life is too short to miss anything. Look how short mine was.

She's talking about a caravan holiday she really enjoyed.

MRS WEST: Yes. She went away with the Sunday school to Wales, three months before she died.

DORIS: Best holiday I ever had. I did have a good time then this had to happen. Now I'm grown up I realize you must get through to kids they must never go off with strangers, but you just don't think when you are a child. You trust everyone.

Don't go on with that love. It's only upsetting your Mum and you as well.

What are you laughing at, love? A pub? The Green Man? Tell them I was with them in the Green Man, Doris. With Alan and Tony.

MRS WEST: Tony is Alan's brother. We had a night out with them when we came from Manchester to London to visit them.

DORIS: Don't worry Alan. Everything will work out. I can see from this side. Live your life, Mum, you've suffered enough. Be happy and do the things you want to do. I'm okay. I'm happy. When we came we were in hospital. They nursed us back. I had a spirit Mum for a while until I grew up and grand-dad came. So don't worry that no one looked after me. I know you were afraid I was on my own but we are not. Nothing hurts spirit

86

children. They are innocent so they are loved and taken care of.

I wish you'd stop laughing, lovey. I'll shake them. She's talking about a baby called Emma Louise.

MRS WEST: I don't know anyone like that.

DORIS: She's probably not born yet. Auntie Mo.

MRS WEST: That's Alan's sister.

DORIS: Well the baby's connected with Auntie Mo. She's talking about a stone in a graveyard. It's shaped like an open book.

MRS WEST: It's a grave by Lesley's. The book is open and the message of remembrance is carved into its pages.

DORIS: I often go and look at it when Mum's having a little weep over my grave, Doris. That's where they buried my body but of course I'm not there. I had a terrific funeral, Doris. There were so many people there. Mum gave me a big heart of flowers and she put a single red rose in the grave. It's been such a long time, Mum, but I've always wanted to say thank you for that. You gave it to me with love, Mum, and I brought it back with love. Mum has a single red rose by my picture at home, Doris. It's lovely.

MRS WEST: Yes it's a silk rose in a tiny rose glass by her framed picture in the lounge.

DORIS: She's really cheeky you know. She's talking about divorces in the family. Three of them.

MRS WEST: I can only think of two.

DORIS: Lesley says don't forget your own, Mum. Don't forget that one.

Bill's coming back. He's trying to tell me something, he's saying just say Rutland Street, love, and she'll know what I mean.

MRS WEST: Rutland Street was round the corner from where we lived when I was a child. My dad, Bill, used to drink at a pub called Joe Daleys' there.

I pray every night, Doris, that Lesley will one day appear to me. But it hasn't happened yet.

DORIS: You're trying too hard, lovey. Relax. It might happen. She says Mum still sees me as I was at the end. Wipe this out of your mind, Mum. We were cleaned up in hospital.

She says she played with someone called Claire. She lived next door. She's grown up now and is married. I used to play with Claire all the time, Doris. If I had been playing with Claire when it happened I would not be here now.

DORIS: What's that love? M what? You really loved her.

MRS WEST: Muriel, a Sunday school teacher on the caravan holiday. I was talking to her at Lesley's funeral and it was only then that she told me right through the holiday Lesley couldn't wait to get back home. She kept telling Muriel she loved me and missed me.

DORIS: She's talking about a tape. Something about a tape. No not those awful tapes at the trial. I mean the one Mum wishes she had kept. The one with me singing on it which got lost.

MRS WEST: It was a tape Lesley's brother Terry made of her singing her favourite song – *Bobby's Girl*. We had a stereo record player with a tape deck and he made the recording. Then he asked me if he could swap the set for a guitar and he gave the tape recording away as well. It didn't mean much at the time. But two months later Lesley was dead. And that was the only recording we had of her voice. It has broken my heart ever since that we didn't keep it.

DORIS: She's talking about someone called Edward. Edward is here and he wants to say hello. Because no one ever talks to him. He wants to say thank you. No one visits him.

MRS WEST: It's Edward Evans, another victim of Brady and Hindley. He is buried only a few feet from Lesley. It looks as if his grave has not been touched since he was buried. We try to keep it tidy. Tidying the grass and keeping the weeds down.

Lesley also mentioned the name Lillian, which Anne West couldn't place but afterwards it came back to her.

MRS WEST: What she was talking about was the day she had her waist length hair cut when she was about eight. She came home and Alan told her she looked like a boy and he was going to call her George. Lesley came right back at him and told Alan, if you're going to call me George, I'm going to call you Lillian!

There were a few things that Lesley told me which I didn't repeat out loud during the sitting for fear of upsetting her mother but I discovered afterwards that Anne West knew of them already. Most disturbing of all was the fact that rats had eaten the child's body before it was found. Anne confirmed that this was true and that she'd not even had a complete body to identify.

The story was a nightmare in every way. It was back in the early sixties when an apparently harmless young couple named Ian Brady and Myra Hindley began to look for victims on the streets of Manchester. To their family and neighbours they were a quiet, devoted pair. They worked together, lived together and were always in each other's company. They didn't seem to have many friends and they weren't interested in noisy parties or going dancing like so many people. Instead they were content to drive about in Myra's little van making frequent trips to the moors. Great country lovers were Ian and Myra.

What nobody ever suspected was that Ian and Myra buried bodies on the moors and then went back to picnic on the graves.

Three children were murdered before they were caught, John Kilbride, aged 12, Lesley Anne Downey aged 10 and Edward Evans aged 17. John and Lesley were both buried on the moors and Edward would have probably ended up there too, had the murderers not been arrested before they had the chance to move his body. Who knows how many children would have died if Myra's brother-in-law hadn't called the police when they tried to persuade him to help them move Edward Evans' body.

Poor little Lesley had been so happy before it happened. The last her mother saw of her was when she skipped out the door on Boxing Day 1964 with her two younger brothers and three little friends from up the road, for a trip to the special Christmas fun fair round the corner.

By all accounts they had a wonderful time. In fact Lesley enjoyed herself so much that when it was time to go she couldn't tear herself away. She asked her friend Linda to take her little brothers home while she went back for one last look at the roundabouts.

Her family never saw her alive again.

The world has become a more violent place since the early sixties and these days child murders seem to be getting ever more common, yet people still recall the Moors Murders with particular horror.

It wasn't just that the children had been killed, but that they'd been tortured before they were killed and Lesley Anne Downey's suffering was recorded on tape, presumably for the evil couple's gruesome enjoyment later. During the trial of Brady and Hindley the tapes were played to an appalled courtroom and afterwards the judge said:

'None of us are likely to forget them for a very long time.'

The memory of those anguished cries will probably haunt the listeners for the rest of their lives.

I don't believe in harbouring bitterness but I must say that I could understand how Anne West felt, particularly over the rumours that Myra Hindley was coming up for parole and might even be released from prison soon. If Lesley had been my child I would have found it almost impossible to put Ramanov's tolerant principles into action.

'It's the hate that keeps me going,' said Anne West quietly and with deadly sincerity. 'I will live until Myra Hindley dies.'

Her words made me shudder involuntarily. I believed her . . .

Chapter Seven

If I close my eyes and concentrate I can hear the music now. Da da, da da da da da da ... The distinctive opening bars of *Sunday Night At The London Palladium*. Every Sunday the sound of that familiar tune brought us hurrying from whatever we were doing, to our places in front of the television for a night of glamour, big names and good old fashioned entertainment.

Like millions of other families we sat glued to the set as Bruce Forsyth, or Norman Vaughan or even later I think, Jimmy Tarbuck, introduced act after act and the glittering Tiller Girls, all long legs and flashing head-dresses, high kicked their way round the famous revolving stage.

Sunday Night At The London Palladium was the highlight of our week and for the stars who appeared, it was the highlight of their careers.

I've lost count of the number of hours we must have spent watching those old variety shows and all I can say is thank goodness I'm not a fortune teller. If one night I'd glanced up and seen myself standing on that stage I'd have thought I was going mad. The idea that one day I might appear at the London Palladium would have seemed totally impossible and also quite terrifying. It was about as likely as John and I moving into Buckingham Palace.

Yet unknown to me, the years were gradually winding me towards that stage. Without realizing where I was going, I slowly progressed from draughty church halls to larger assembly rooms, from tiny provincial theatres to larger theatres, until at last in 1984 I was asked if I'd consider appearing at the Palladium.

The *Palladium*! Well I nearly had kittens.

'Oh, Laurie, I don't know,' I said. The very thought

brought me out in a cold sweat. 'It's one of the most famous theatres in the world. I mean the Beatles have been on there and just about every other big name . . .'

I mean Lewisham Town Hall was one thing, but the London Palladium . . .

'But Doris you've done the Dominion in Tottenham Court Road,' said Laurie at his most persuasive. 'That was no bother. The Palladium's very similar.'

Not in my mind it wasn't. I thought of all those plush balconies, the red velvet, the Royal Box. No, the Palladium was quite paralysingly different.

'We'd never fill it Laurie,' I said, stalling.

He grinned. 'Well let's give it a try and see.'

At that point I didn't really believe I'd actually do it. Even when Laurie said everything was fixed for December 16th I just nodded and humoured him. I didn't think it would really happen. You've still got the tickets to sell, my lad, I thought to myself. And when you can't shift them we'll have to cancel and forget all about it.

The day the tickets went on sale I was still convinced we'd have to call the whole thing off – until Laurie phoned that is.

'Doris, it's fantastic!' he cried, sounding so elated I thought he'd won the football pools.

'What is it, Laurie?'

'I've just heard from the Palladium. The tickets have sold out in an hour and a half. They say it's a record!'

I stared at the receiver blankly. 'Are you sure someone's not pulling your leg, Laurie?'

'Positive. They've gone. Everyone of them's gone in an hour and a half.'

I should have been beside myself with excitement, of course, but all I could think of was 'Oh heavens – that means I've got to do it. I've really got to go on at the Palladium!'

As December 16th drew near I hovered between excitement and panic. I tried on all my dresses, bought a couple more and still I couldn't make up my mind which one to wear. Worse still, my hair was a mess, I decided, and my nails were breaking up all over the place. But the fuss over details was only to cover the real panic going on inside. I was intending to get up on stage at the Palladium, in front of a sell-out audience without an act, without a script, without the ability to sing, dance or act, without anything definite at all and I was going to stand there and hope for the best. From thin air I was hoping the means would come to entertain the audience for two hours. Now this surely was madness.

My mother had always said I'd end up in a mental home. Was she proving right at last? Had I finally flipped? Supposing nothing happened? Supposing when I tuned in all I heard was the sound of my own thoughts? How on earth would I cope with those tiers and tiers of blank faces growing more hostile by the minute?

It was enough to give you nightmares.

'Trust,' Ramanov told me over and over again. 'Trust.'

And I pushed the doubts very firmly to the back of my mind. After all wasn't this the same problem I faced every time I did a sitting or appeared in any theatre? Yet while I was busy not thinking terrible thoughts, small decisions suddenly became overwhelmingly difficult. I swished through my wardrobe for the umpteenth time. Now should it be the pink, the blue or maybe the turquoise . . .?

At last on December 16th I was sitting in the wings in a pretty dress of soft peach, waiting to go on and trembling from head to foot.

John Avery, the manager, came past and smiled at me kindly. 'Don't be nervous, Doris,' he said, 'but then you wouldn't be a star if you weren't nervous. All the big stars that come here are just the same when they're waiting to go on.'

I wondered if Roy Castle could possibly feel as bad as I did. It was hard to believe. He always seems so relaxed when you see him on television. I was thinking of Roy because I'd been given his dressing-room. Six days a week he and Tommy Steele were appearing in *Singing in the Rain* and Sunday, their day off, I'd moved in. I hoped he didn't mind. I was very careful not to touch any of his things. There were good luck telegrams and cards all over the place and cuddly toy mascots and the dressing-room itself was beautiful. Lovely and warm, with soft carpets and the ceiling all draped in pleats like a dome. It was a far cry from the church halls where I started, where you changed into your dress in the toilet because the only room back stage was full of people drinking tea and gossiping.

I always try to relax quietly for a few minutes before I go on so that I can tune in and hopefully get a name or two to give me a start. So sitting there in Roy Castle's dressing-room I closed my eyes and concentrated. I was in luck. After a moment or two I heard a young boy's voice. He wasn't very old, no more than fourteen I'd have said.

'My mother's coming tonight,' he told me, 'her name's Rita.'

'And what's your name, lovey?' I asked him.

'I'm Stewart,' he said.

And that was it. But it was a start. Something to get my teeth into when I stood there in front of that audience.

Then all at once, the show had started. Tony Ortzen, the editor of *Psychic News*, had introduced me and I was walking out on to the stage at the Palladium. There were the tiers and tiers of balconies that I remembered from the television show, the chandeliers and the acres of red velvet and there on the stage, standing on a piece of carpet and flanked by flowers, were the chairs from the Royal Box. Nervous as I was, I couldn't help thinking goodness me, the Queen's probably sat in this as I sat down. It was a weird feeling.

I did my little gossip at the beginning, as I always do to relax people and reassure them that I'm just like

95

them and I'm not going to swing from the lights or wave my arms about or do any of the peculiar things that people unfortunately associate with mediums. Then I told them how I'd tuned in earlier.

'I got a little boy called Stewart who's looking for his mother,' I said. 'She's called Rita, or it could be Anita. They both sound similar to me. Is there a Rita or Anita here with a little boy called Stewart?'

There was an expectant silence, which grew and grew and my stomach started turning somersaults. Surely I hadn't mucked up my very first message?

And then, just as I was getting seriously worried, a woman stood up and walked, half-stunned to the microphone.

'I'm Rita and my son was Stewart,' she said faintly. We were under way.

After the weeks of anxiety, the evening seemed to fly past for me. Stewart talked about his family and the milkman, Philip. He was fond of Philip because he used to help him on the milkround. He raised a laugh when he said that a baby would be born and to ask Philip about it, and a few tears when he described how he was killed in a cycling accident.

Then there were various friends and family members who came to talk to Margaret who worked with mentally handicapped children and had the potential to be a medium herself. There was the mother who was worried because her son and his girlfriend were happily expecting a baby but had no plans to get married. Another tragic mother who had been buried with her dead baby and wanted to reassure her orphaned children that she was with them still and wanted them to enjoy their Christmas. There was the son looking for his mother, Jane Jones, and the father who'd been sent over without his teeth in. And so it went on and on.

Once or twice there were a couple of loud, unexplained bangs and out in the audience a light blew out for no apparent reason and I remembered that the

Palladium is supposed to be haunted. The resident ghost didn't put in an appearance though and I had enough on my plate with all the spirit people who wanted to talk to the audience without trying to contact anyone else.

Then, suddenly it was all over. We handed out the flowers I like to give to people who've had messages, there were cameras going off all over the place and at last I could escape to the dressing-room for a long cup of tea.

It was only when I sat down that I realized how exhausted I was. My hair and my back were wet with sweat and I felt too drained even to talk. Up the corridor in Tommy Steele's dressing-room they were having a party but I couldn't face it. Making conversation with all those people no matter how nice they were was too much of an effort. All I wanted was to get home to bed and so John and I crept out to the car and left them all to it.

'Hey, don't forget this, love,' said John as I stole away.

I looked back. It was the large box the doorman had brought in during the evening. It was marked 'fragile' and had been handed in for me at the stage door earlier. I make a point though of never looking at letters left at the theatre before I go on, and I was too tired now even to be curious.

'Oh. No. Could you bring it love, I've got my dress to carry.'

John picked it up. 'It's heavy,' he said in surprise. 'I wonder what it is?'

Back home he could contain himself no longer. Before he'd even got his coat off he was out in the kitchen with the box, sawing through the string with a knife.

From the sitting-room where I'd collapsed into my armchair I heard a low whistle.

'You'd better look at this, girl.'

I groaned to myself. 'Can you bring it in here, John?'

97

There was a pause and then out he came with the most enormous birthday cake tied in yellow ribbon, decorated with yellow roses and piped with the words, 'Happy Birthday Doris.'

I was so touched that tears sprang into my eyes. It was from a boy called Pat and he'd made it himself. Apparently he'd read in one of my books how John and Terry are apt to forget my birthday, coming as it does right after Christmas and how the spirit world once left me a gold rose outlined on the wall to cheer me up. This year he wanted to make sure my birthday wouldn't be forgotten so he'd sent me my very own birthday cake.

What's more the spirit world had even arranged a Christmas present for me through that same kind young man. The Palladium evening had come right at the end of a three week tour around the country and on top of moving house. Now here I was a week before Christmas and feeling so tired I could hardly move. I'd rashly invited a few friends over for Christmas dinner a day early on Christmas Eve. It had seemed like a good idea at the time. I could get all the cooking over with on Christmas Eve and relax on Christmas Day with nothing to worry about but a cold buffet. But now I was having second thoughts. I hadn't so much as unpacked my dinner service yet. It was still stashed away in a crate somewhere and frankly I didn't feel up to anything more strenuous than opening a tin.

This problem was still bobbing around in my mind the next day when I rang Pat to thank him for the lovely cake. We chatted for quite a while, and then the conversation got round to Christmas. What was I having for Christmas this year Patrick wondered.

'D'you know, Pat, I'm too tired to care,' I said. 'What I'd really like is for some caterers to come and do the whole thing for me. That would be better than any present.'

'I'll do it,' said Pat immediately.

'But Pat you're not a caterer are you?' I asked. I'd assumed that cakes were some sort of hobby for him.

'No I'm a chef,' he said.

'Well look it's very sweet of you,' I said, 'but I wasn't serious. It was only wishful thinking. I haven't even got my dinner service unpacked yet or anything.'

'Don't worry,' said Pat, 'I'll bring mine. Now don't you bother. I'll see to everything.'

And he was as good as his word. On Christmas Eve he arrived with a dinner service, coffee service and silverware. He even brought a candelabra. Then he sent me off to put up my feet while he cooked the turkey, vegetables and Christmas pudding. The meal was delicious and afterwards Patrick cleared away, and washed the dishes. I didn't have to lift a finger. It was the best Christmas present I could have had.

But the Palladium connection didn't finish there. Not long after Christmas, Rita Broadfield, whose son Stewart had come through right at the beginning and started the evening off, came for a private sitting. This time she brought her husband with her.

'Quite honestly I've come because I was afraid for my wife,' he told me sternly and I could see that he was deeply suspicious about the whole thing. He was probably afraid his wife was going to be taken in by some sort of weirdo.

'That's alright love,' I said. 'There's nothing to be afraid of. Just send out your love to Stewart and we'll see what we can do.'

As before, Stewart came along as soon as I tuned in. This time I could see him standing in my sitting-room beside his parents. He was a tall boy with fair hair and a lively face. It turned out that he was 13 and not 14 as I'd first thought.

He told me more about the accident.

'There were four of us at first,' he said, 'then two went off and there were just the two of us left. I was going up the bypass and then bang . . . It was the back of my head got hit . . .'

99

He talked of the heart of flowers his parents had given him at the funeral, the extension they were building at home and even Wilson School – the school he'd attended before the accident.

Then, right at the end, just as we were finishing sitting and the power was at its lowest ebb, Rita Broadfield said sadly, 'He never mentioned his sister.'

Stewart was at her side in an instant.

'Does she mean Caroline? I wouldn't forget Caroline.'

And that did it for his father. The pent up emotion he'd been supressing since the previous August when the tragedy happened came spilling out and he cried.

'Doris, there's no way you could have known all that,' he said afterwards. 'It was marvellous.'

Appearing at the Palladium has got to be the peak of anyone's career and once the big day was over I thought things would die down. Strangely enough though the reverse seemed to happen. If anything the fuss went on building.

Extraordinary news came from my home town of Grantham where tickets had just gone on sale for a show in a hall built over the exact spot where I was born. One Wong Row which in Chinese means Fresh Fields. Apparently there was a bit of a riot. The queue went right round the leisure centre where I was appearing, so that the end met the beginning and there were minor dust-ups over the number of tickets some people were allowed to buy. To add insult to injury ticket touts walked up and down selling tickets for £10 and £15 each.

Ticket touts! I thought in amazement. Anyone would think it was a pop concert. Perplexed, I put it down to the fact that it was my home town and probably a lot of people were curious to see what had become of the local girl.

But even stranger news came from SAGB, The Belgrave Square headquarters of the Spiritualist Association of Great Britain. I still try to give demonstrations there as often as I can, just as I used to in the early days when I first came to London and this particular week I had a free evening. The day the tickets went on sale however I had a desperate phone call from the chairman Tom Johannson.

'Doris, I don't know what I'm going to do,' he said, the panic rising in his voice. 'They've been sleeping out all night in sleeping bags. There's a thousand turned up and I've only got room for 180 and they're blocking the pavements so much I've had the police here.'

When I eventually arrived the place was like a refugee camp. There were people packed into every tiny space. They were sitting on boxes in the aisle, they were crammed standing, along the back wall, they were even overflowing on to the platform at my feet.

It was a daunting prospect and not for the first time I felt vaguely frightened. 'What do they want from me?' I wondered anxiously. 'What are they expecting? I can't perform miracles.'

Nevertheless it was a happy evening. There were a lot of animals. We had a dog called Barnaby back, a cat called Doodie and another cat called Candy. I thought at first they were talking about a girl, but no. Candy turned out to be a cat!

I also got two Andrews that night. The first belonged to a family from Wisbech near Cambridge.

'I've got a young man called Andrew,' I explained, 'and he's something to do with the police.'

'Yes,' said his father, 'he was a policeman.'

Then another man stood up. 'Our son's Andrew too. We've got an Andrew.'

And before he'd finished speaking the other Andrew came in loud and clear and it turned out that he too had a connection with the police. His father was a policeman.

I was so pleased, because it turned out that the parents had come all the way from Cheshire. They'd

101

left home at two o'clock in the morning, arrived in London at four o'clock and joined the queue.

We were in the depths of a very bad winter at this time and I'd cut my touring down to the barest minimum. I didn't have to be idle though, just because the weather was awful. I was able to use the time to do some private sittings – children wherever possible – and soon the sad cases were pouring through my door again.

There was something about one particular letter asking for a sitting that worried me and I asked the couple to come along. I'm very glad I did because during the sitting their son Alan told me that his father's hobby was shooting and that in moments of despair they'd talked of committing suicide. The father intended to shoot his wife and then turn the gun on himself. Alan of course was horrified by this idea. He begged them to promise that they'd never ever consider it again.

'Tell them I'm alright. I'm happy and I'll be there to meet them when their time comes,' he said. 'But that's not yet. They mustn't bring themselves over. They've got their lives to lead.'

Afterwards Laurie who'd organized the meeting received a lovely letter from them with a beautiful cameo enclosed, as a gift for me.

'Doris really helped Alan and I so much in bringing our son back to us,' wrote his mother. 'It was unbelievable. He was speaking to us nearly all afternoon.'

There were many other similar stories. There was the boy who'd suffered from a blood disease. Twice he thought he'd beaten it and then it started up again. He was only seventeen but he hadn't lost his sense of humour.

'Tell Roger I've seen Sue and I think she's a bit of alright,' he told me with a roguish wink.

Roger was his brother and Sue was Roger's new girlfriend. He also knew that Roger was wearing his ring, that his parents had planted a rose bush on his grave and that the old man in the end bed of his ward, old Walter, had since passed over and they'd met on the other side.

Then there was the young soldier only nineteen years old who was killed in Germany when the army vehicle in which he was travelling rolled over.

'There were three of us,' he said in disgust. 'And I was the only one who passed over. We were going home. Only forty-eight hours stood between the accident and when I should have gone home.'

He'd been bitter at first he told me. He was engaged, looking forward to getting married and then this had to happen.

'I've settled down now,' he said, 'but I was angry at first. I thought why did it have to happen to me.'

Then there was Sarah, an air hostess who went down too deep when she was scuba diving. She came and stood beside her mother as we were talking and I saw that she was the most beautiful girl with long blonde hair turned under and huge eyes.

'Yes I was attractive and I knew it,' she said. 'It was my own bloody fault. I was always a dare devil. I always had to go one better than anyone else.'

She struggled to give me an impression of what happened. Suddenly there was water all around me and she was putting something over my nose. I got an impression of swimming around looking at things, then there was a booming sound in my ears and nothing more.

'Yes she came to the surface too quickly and was incoherent,' said her mother. 'She was trying to pull off her mask. Her friend tried to pull her to the boat but she was too heavy and she was drowning him. He let her go and she slipped off the reef.'

But Sarah too could still laugh at herself.

'I'd just had all my dental work done. I had all my teeth crowned. If I'd known this was going to happen I'd have saved my money. It cost me a bomb!'

Afterwards Sarah's mother confessed that she'd been living with the fear of losing a child for a long time.

'I've always known I was going to lose one of them,' she said. 'I kept thinking it was a wicked thing to think but somehow I just knew. And I thought if it had to happen, let it be quick.'

Well it had been very quick. Sarah was enjoying herself, then suddenly she lost consciousness and knew nothing more about it until she woke up on the other side. That was one small comfort I could offer her poor mother. Sarah didn't suffer at all.

After sittings like these it's difficult not to feel sad. When you meet the grieving parents and speak to the young people, lovely children every one, it's hard not to feel a sense of waste. Yet I know that young as they are, they've done their time on earth and now they are happy and fulfilled in new lives on the other side.

We shouldn't weep for them because nothing can hurt them now.

Chapter Eight

They were making a valiant effort at the estate agents'. There was a big board nailed over the window and the neat rows of photographs of houses for sale had been taken down, but the name of the shop was still boldly outlined over the top and inside it was business as usual.

Set in a comfortable, suburban area amongst newsagents and grocery shops you'd have thought that the owner, doing particularly well, was simply having the place smartened up. In fact this ordinary looking estate agents, apparently no different from any other, was reputed to be haunted.

A number of disturbing events had worried the staff and the strange goings on had already attracted the attention of the local paper.

From what I could make out, there had been a series of unusual accidents, interspersed by small, but inexplicable incidents. First, during a spell when the electricity supply was off, workmen had come to install mobile gas heaters, and in a freak accident, one of the gas cylinders blew up, injuring one of the men. Not long afterwards a water pipe burst, flooding the shop and no sooner had they got the place dry than there was a terrible commotion outside and a car careered across the road, mounted the pavement and crashed straight through the estate agents window, missing the owner by inches.

As if this wasn't bad enough, less dramatic but equally worrying things were happening almost every day. There was a room at the back of the shop where there was a definite atmosphere – almost as if an unseen presence was watching and a dog belonging to one of the staff refused point blank to enter this room.

One day the owner was sitting there attempting to work when the strange atmosphere suddenly built up around her. She ignored it for as long as she could but in the end it became so oppressive that she had to run out of the room and slam the door behind her. So shaken was she by the experience that she couldn't bring herself to cross the threshold again until the next day.

In the outer shop objects were frequently moved about, the closed sign on the front door was often mysteriously turned around to read 'Open' when the shop was shut and one morning the staff walked in to find a house brick in the middle of the floor. It had not been there when they'd locked up the night before, no one else had been in the shop and there was no sign of forced entry and yet, somehow, the brick had found its way into the centre of the carpet.

It was the sort of story that papers love to print and readers love to read but not nearly so fascinating for the people involved. By the time the Thames News picked it up and decided it might make an amusing little item for the tea time show, the people in the shop were beginning to feel desperate. Most of all they wanted to know what was going on.

The first I heard of it was at 2.00 one afternoon when Thames News rang to ask if I could do an urgent job for them.

'Well when did you have in mind?' I asked uncertainly. The photographer from the publishers' had arrived and we were in the middle of doing the pictures for the cover of my new book.

'Straight away,' they said. 'We'll send a car for you.'

'I'm sorry but I don't think I can.' I explained, 'I've got the photographer here and we're doing a photo session.'

There was a hurried exchange at the other end of the phone, then the researcher came back. 'How long will you be?'

'I don't know, just a minute I'll ask.' I put my hand

106

over the mouthpiece, 'How much longer will it take?' I called out to the photographer.

It had already taken longer than I'd thought because I'd had to change. I'd worked so hard to make myself look nice. I'd put on a new navy blue dress with spots, navy blue stockings and navy blue shoes and I thought I looked marvellous, a real thoroughly modern Millie. And the first thing the photographer said when I opened the door was, 'Oh. Haven't you got anything lighter?'

So we trouped upstairs and looked through my wardrobe and he picked out an old pink dress that I've worn dozens of times before! So much for thoroughly modern Millie!

Anyway, by the time I'd changed and tidied my hair again we could have taken a whole roll of film.

Fortunately the photographer was a good-natured man and he didn't mind being rushed. 'Seeing as it's you Doris we'll get it done in an hour,' he promised.

I told the television people to collect us just after three o'clock and we galloped through the picture, then I dashed upstairs to change again, because the photographer had put me in a long dress and the viewers might think it strange to see me gallivanting round an estate agents' in evening dress at tea-time.

By now I was feeling distinctly breathless. What I didn't realize was that the peculiar jinx affecting the estate agents had now extended to include the TV story as well. And if you think jinx is too strong a word for it look what happened.

First of all, the driver the company used happened to be at home in Essex when the call came through and it took him some time to reach us. By the time he arrived the rush hour traffic was building up and ahead of us was one of the worst journeys you can make in London. I live in South East London and the shop was in North West London and separating us was a whole city of jammed, exhaust-fogged streets where the cars crawled at walking pace. Not surprisingly the journey seemed to last hours and by the time we arrived, the producer was getting rather anxious about his chances of finishing in time for the programme that evening.

'I don't like to rush you Doris,' he said, 'but we really do need to start filming at once.'

'That's alright love. You start and I'll do my best.'

But the cameras had hardly started rolling, when they stopped again.

'Sorry, Doris. The batteries have gone down on the sound.'

We took a break while the batteries were changed then we were off again, but a few minutes later the same thing happened. By now the producer was quietly distraught. The situation was practically unheard of he told me as he hurried off to phone the studios and get fresh batteries sent out by messenger.

In all three lots of batteries went down before we managed to start filming and then the crew announced that they finished at 6.30 and they were going home. I thought the poor producer would have a stroke but instead he looked resigned.

'Well we've no chance of catching the news now,' he said. 'There's no point in panicking.'

We sat down to wait for the new crew to arrive but when they turned up, our driver, who had been hanging around throughout all the disasters, suddenly told us that he had a date and he couldn't wait any longer. He was off. He climbed into his car, accelerated away up the road and that was the last we saw of him. John and I looked at each other and burst out laughing. You had to see the funny side or you'd go mad.

Fortunately the sitting went better than the filming. When we'd first arrived the owner took me into the room where the atmosphere was sometimes oppressive. She believed the trouble stemmed from this room and I felt she was probably right. I walked carefully round, checking for a presence. This must look rather strange to people who don't realize what I'm doing but in fact you can tell if there's an entity present by the cold spot. This is a place in an otherwise warm room which is freezing cold for no apparent reason. It's a strange sort of cold which creeps up from the floor and chills you to the bone. Once you've felt it, you'd never mistake a cold spot for an ordinary draught again. The sensation is quite different.

Well I walked around, pacing every bit of that room and nothing happened. The warmth was uniformly spread over the floor.

'He's not here at the moment,' I said at last, but as things turned out we had plenty of time.

When filming eventually started I went back to the room and this time I felt it straight away. Walking past the desk a stream of icy air suddenly flowed up from the floor freezing my right side. I stopped and as I did so the room shifted, swung before my eyes and somehow rearranged itself. The desk was different. I saw a dictaphone, two telephones and an in tray on the top and beside it a big swivel chair.

'This is how it used to be when it was my office,' said a man's voice.

The image held for a moment longer, then it disolved and I was back with the camera crew. I described what I'd seen and the new owner gasped.

'That's right. We've got a photo of it like that,' she said.

We were in business. The man wanted to talk. Apparently he'd run the estate agents some years before and got himself in a bit of a mess. Eventually he'd taken his own life.

'I went into the garage and did it in the car,' he said.

Now his main concern was for his wife. He hadn't been married very long and he wanted his wife to know how sorry he was for the misery he'd caused.

'There were two children,' he said, 'my wife had one and I had one. I'm afraid I treated her quite badly because I was worried.'

He had been moving things about at the shop he

admitted because he was trying to attract attention. He wanted to warn the new owner about a possible business problem and most of all he wanted a message passed on to his wife. Could they buy her some flowers as a token of his love and tell her he was sorry?

As further proof that he really had been one of the previous owners of the shop, he told me that he used to keep the keys in a very unusual place.

'I'll say,' said the new owner, 'he kept them behind the radiator.'

The one thing he wouldn't do, however, was claim responsibility for the accidents that plagued the shop. They were simply accidents, he insisted, and the fact there had been so many was unfortunate coincidence.

'And as for the last one, the car coming through the window, I'll tell you what happened there. The woman was pulling into the side of the road, went to put her foot on the brake and hit the accelerator instead. She lost control of the car and it shot across the pavement straight through the window. But don't let them blame me. I wouldn't do a thing like that. Someone could have been killed.'

By the end of our chat the man seemed much happier. We promised that the message would go to his wife and he said he'd leave the shop in peace.

At last filming finished. We'd long ago missed the early evening news but the producer said they'd keep the story and use it another night. It had been a very long day. By the time we got home it was nine o'clock and I hadn't even started the dinner. I just hoped I'd been of some help at the estate agents because a medium can't always put a stop to such 'hauntings'. I can't force a spirit person to do something against his will. I can only find out what's troubling him, attempt to put it right and endeavour to persuade him that it's time he accepted that his earth life is over and it's time he moved on to higher things. But spirit people don't have to take my advice any more than people here do.

People have some very funny ideas about 'ghosts'

and 'hauntings'. In fact 'ghosts' never 'haunt' a place in order to scare people – or at least I've never come across one like that. They tend to cling to places they have known either because they refuse to accept that their earth life is finished, or because they are desperately trying to communicate with someone and can't rest until they've done so. They very seldom drift about for nothing.

One of the most extraordinary and poignant 'hauntings' I've come across in recent years was brought to my attention by journalist Michael Hellicar. He had written an article about life after death for the *Daily Mirror* and afterwards one of his readers rung him in desperation. This poor man thought he was going mad because he kept seeing his wife who'd died only a few days before. Michael phoned me and asked if I could help save his sanity.

Well I did a sitting and I remember I picked up the wife very easily because she was hovering so close to her distraught husband. It seemed to go well but as far as I was concerned there was nothing particularly remarkable about the case. It was a tragic affair, but sadly I seem to hear so many similar stories these days. It wasn't until long afterwards that I heard the whole story from Michael Hellicar and then I realized I'd been involved in something very unusual indeed. I'll let Michael explain it to you the way he explained it to me.

Michael Hellicar: 'I had quite a big response to my story on life after death but the strangest of all was a phone call from a man whose wife had committed suicide the week before by jumping off a tower block near their home. Apparently her death wasn't entirely unexpected because she'd had a history of mental illness, but she was only twenty-seven, had left a young family and he was very upset.

'The reason he was phoning me was that he feared he was going mad. Apparently after he'd talked to the police, identified the body and gone through all the gruesome formalities, he went home, walked into the bathroom and there she was. Solid and real wearing the dress he liked her in and her usual perfume. He reached out and touched her and his hand didn't go straight through. Her flesh was warm and real and what's more she talked to him. She said how sorry she was for what she'd done, but that she couldn't explain why she'd done it. Then she went on to give him advice about how to bring up the children.

'The man was totally confused. His senses told him one thing and his mind told him it wasn't possible. Could this really have happened, or was he mad?

'Now I must admit at this point I thought he'd been temporarily deranged by grief. But I've been a journalist for 30 years and by now I can tell whether I'm talking to a crank or not. The peculiar thing was that this man seemed completely sane. What's more as he continued his story, it became stranger and yet oddly more plausible.

'The next day he'd woken convinced that he'd dreamed the whole thing and that grief had made the dream particularly vivid. He put it out of his mind and set out to break the news to his family. On the way though, he bumped into a neighbour and stopped to tell her that his wife had died the morning before.

' "Oh no," said the neighbour when she'd got over the shock, "it couldn't have been the morning. You must be mistaken. I saw her at the window yesterday afternoon watching for you to come home the way she always did."

'Puzzled the man assured her that his wife had definitely died in the morning. Later at his parents' home he was sitting at the table breaking the dreadful news when he saw his younger brother pass the window. His brother waved and a few minutes afterwards put his head round the door.

' "Hello," he said. "Where's Jan?"

'Everybody winced and the parents gently told him that Jan was dead.

112

' "Don't be silly," he said, "I just saw her sitting with you when I looked through the window," and he described the dress she was wearing. It was the dress she'd been wearing in the bathroom the night before.

'More confused than ever the husband went home to find his wife's perfume filled the house and the dog refused to go upstairs. He walked into the bathroom and there she was again. This time she begged him not to brood about why she'd done it but to get on with his life and marry again.

'Shortly afterwards the phone rang. It was his in-laws. "You won't believe this," they said, "but we saw Jan last night. She came to the house and sort of melted through the wall."

'It was at this stage the man phoned me. After reading my article he thought I must be an expert on such things. Was he going out of his mind he wanted to know, and if he wasn't, what had happened to his wife? He didn't like to think of her just floating around.

'Well I met him and I was very impressed by how straightforward and normal he seemed. His story was incredible but he didn't seem to be unbalanced or lying. The only problem was that I couldn't answer his questions and I felt that if the situation went on much longer he'd have a breakdown under the strain. In the end I phoned Doris and asked if she could help. I didn't give her all the details. I just told her this man had lost his wife and thought he'd seen her after her death . . .'

Well, although I hadn't heard this extraordinary story it was quite obvious that this man's wife was anxious to talk to him. She was there the moment I tuned in and she told me her name was Jan and that she'd jumped off a roof.

'He's quite right when he feels that I'm close to him,' she said. 'Last night he was very clumsy and broke a teapot and today he went out and bought another one. It's a pretty yellow one. I like it.'

The astonished husband agreed that this was quite true.

Jan went on to say that she felt better now than she had when she'd first gone over. She was still full of guilt for leaving her family but she felt easier in her mind.

'At first I didn't want to tell him why I did it. I didn't want to cause trouble,' she said, 'but now I know that he needs to know and he won't rest until he finds out.'

And she went on to explain that there'd been a row with her mother and sister. Apparently in the heat of the moment they'd told her that she wasn't bringing up her children properly because she was always in and out of mental hospitals.

'They'd be better off without you,' they'd said. And Jan, in her disturbed state, promptly went out the next day and threw herself off a roof.

'But please don't blame them,' she begged her husband. 'It wasn't their fault. I was sick in the mind. I would have done it sooner or later anyway.'

She gave a great many family names, thanked her husband for removing the ear-rings in which she died and replacing them with her favourite pair and finally she mentioned a little surprise she'd been planning.

'I'd saved £15 to take the kids out to the seaside for a treat,' she said, 'it's hidden under a pillow in the cupboard over the wardrobe. Please give them a good day with my love.'

The husband promised that if he found the money he would. By now the power was growing weak. Few people realize that it's as difficult and tiring for spirit people to contact a medium as it is for a medium to contact them, especially when the spirit person has not long passed over. Jan was getting very tired and her voice faded.

'Tell him not to feel guilty if he meets someone else,' she said. 'I want him to be happy,' and then she was gone.

The sitting was over. Michael and the husband

stayed on a little longer, drinking coffee and I was pleased to see that the man looked much happier.

'So I'm not going mad, Doris,' he said, 'I really did see her?'

'I'm sure you did love,' I answered him, 'She's very close to you. It's only her old overcoat in that coffin.'

And of course it's not unusual for people to see loved ones who've passed over. It depends how psychic they are and how hard they are trying. Children are more psychic than adults and they see spirit people much more frequently but either they don't say anything for fear of ridicule or their parents don't believe them. As for adults I'm sure it's no coincidence that we see spirit people when we least expect it. Time and time again bereaved mothers or widows will tell me they keep trying to see their husband or child but nothing happens. I can only conclude that it doesn't work when you try too hard. Perhaps your conscious mind swamps the psychic part and drowns any psychic messages struggling to get through. I know that when I'm trying desperately hard to do well at my work I've often been disappointed with the results and yet at other times when my mind's not fully on it for some reason, if I'm not feeling too good or I'm thinking about something else – I've been astonished how clearly the messages have come through.

Anyway, Michael Hellicar and his reader eventually left and that was the last I thought of the matter. Michael Hellicar however, had become very interested in the case. He gave the husband a lift home and out of curiosity went inside with the man to see if the message I'd given them about the money hidden in the wardrobe was correct.

'We went into the bedroom and I saw that there was a bridging unit between two wardrobes,' Michael told me. 'The husband opened the unit and inside was a pillow. He lifted the pillow and underneath was £15 just as you told him. It was amazing.

'But that wasn't quite the end of the story. A couple

115

of weeks later I rang him again to see if the sitting had done the trick. He sound much better.

'Apparently after the sitting he'd found a note in his wife's handwriting on the dressing-table, yet it had not been there before. It read: "I'm sorry but now at least you understand." And since then she'd not been back and the dog was quite happy to go upstairs again.

'I'm quite happy now,' he said. 'I know my wife's alright and that she wants me to get on with my life.'

And as far as we know, that's exactly what he did.

Chapter Nine

'Doris,' said the woman at the microphone, 'can you help me?'

It was question time at Fairfield Halls, Croydon and she'd been patiently waiting her turn in the queue. A fragile little woman but she held her head high and she spoke out bravely.

'I'm living in agony because I know I'm not long for this world. I'm not frightened of death but I'm frightened of waiting for it,' she paused and swallowed hard. 'And . . . and I don't want to leave my family behind.'

My heart went out to her. Poor woman. She had cancer, of that I was sure and I knew how she must be suffering. I've been there myself. I've been lucky so far but I've had a glimpse of what it must be like for those poor souls who can't be helped by modern medicine. What could I say, in just a few moments, to comfort her?

'Well, darling,' I said gently, 'you can't take your family with you, can you? But remember you're only going into the next room. You are only a whisper away. To me death is nothing to be afraid of. I don't want to go just now I admit because I've only just got my house and I'd like to have time to enjoy it. It would be just my luck to pop my clogs just when everything's going well!'

The atmosphere lightened and the woman smiled.

'But seriously, death is a great adventure,' I went on, 'I just hope you don't have any pain . . . Besides, how do you know how long you've got? Miracles do happen. Until the time comes I don't believe I'm going. Why don't you join our Sod It Club? Whenever

117

I'm going in for tests I say sod it, I'm not going to have it!'

Little by little the tension went out of the woman and after a few minutes she was laughing. Afterwards I got Laurie to give her my telephone number so that she could telephone me for moral support whenever she felt down, and that's how I got to know Ros quite well. It turned out we were both going into hospital for tests at the same time and afterwards I rang her to see how she'd got on. It was bad news. The cancer had spread and there didn't seem to be much hope.

'What about you, Doris,' she asked, 'have you had your results yet?'

And the words stuck in my throat. How could I tell her I was all right after she'd had such bad luck.

'Ros, I don't know how to say it. I feel dreadful after your news. But I've got the all clear.'

'Oh Doris, I'm so pleased,' she said warmly and the relief in her voice was so sincere it brought tears to my eyes. In spite of her own turmoil and tragedy she could still feel glad for me.

She was such a brave lady. That morning she said, she'd been talking to her young window cleaner whose wife had gone off and left him with a three-year-old son.

'Doris, I thought what's the matter with the world,' she said. 'There's that girl with everything to live for, a nice husband and little child and she goes away and leaves them. And here's us, such a close family and I'm being forced to leave them.'

And yet, she could still feel for that boy and sympathize with his unhappiness. That's what happens when you're getting near the spirit world. You seem to find acceptance of your own fate and a new understanding and compassion for other people.

I didn't know what I could do to help Ros so in the end I sent her a poem which had been sent to me, in the hope it would give her strength:

He Walks The Wards

If Christ came to this world again
Would He sit with those in pain?
Would he walk the hospitals at night
With tender steps so soft and light
Would he pause by each bed and pray
Hoping that He might hear you say:
'My pain is easier to bear, Christ
Now that I know you're here.'

Well, Christ is there my friend with you
He walks the ward the whole night through
He pauses by each bed to pray
So if you can, I beg you say
Your pain is easier to bear
Because you know that He is there.

Do you think that He who suffered so
Would stand aside and let you go
Through all those hours that you have passed
Pain-racked and faint yet holding fast
To life with all your bravery?
Why Christ is always there

He knows the fight you've had to wage
He alone your heart can gauge
He knows those moments when you feel
That nothing but your pain is real
He knows and lends His hands to you
To hold on till you get through

So don't give in, you mean so much
Don't ever feel you're out of touch
With life and all the folk outside
For none of them are satisfied
Unless they too can with you say
Christ passed along my life today

And in your ward and by your bed
Those words are very truly said
For Christ will ever linger near
All those who live close to a tear
And He will dry your eyes and give His Strength
    to you
So you may live within His Heart
And living there will make your pain much less to
    bear.

It makes me cry to read that poem. I think it's so
beautiful. In fact I'm sent a lot of lovely poems. The
most inarticulate people are suddenly touched by the
spirit world and words pour out of them. Here are
some of my favourites:

Mother

You always used to watch us
Anxious if we were late
In Winter by the window
In Summer by the gate.
And though we mocked you tenderly
Who took such loving care
The long road home would seem more safe
Because she waited there.
Her thoughts were all for us
She never could forget
And so I think that where she is
She must be waiting yet
Waiting till we come to her
Anxious if we're late
Watching from Heaven's window,
Leaning on Heaven's gate.

L. Lawler.

Age

Age is a quality of mind
If you have left your dreams behind
If hope is cold
If you no longer plan ahead
If your ambitions all are dead
Then you are old.

But if you make of life the best
And in your life you still have zest
If love you hold
No matter how the years go by
No matter how the birthdays fly
You are not old.

It doesn't seem so long ago
We came to say goodbye,
We held your hand and kissed your face
And had our private cry.

You looked so peaceful lying there
It was hard to realize
That when you left us here on earth
You simply closed your eyes.

So if it's true what people say
We have no cause to fear
For God will take you by the hand
And ever keep you near.

We wouldn't wish for you to stay
And suffer day by day
So when God took your hand in his
It was as if to say
No need to suffer any more
So let's quietly slip away.

Mrs Blanche Lloyd

Send Them To Bed With A Kiss

To Mothers so often discouraged,
Worn out by the toils of the day,
You often grow weary and cross and impatient,
Complain of the noise and the play,
For the play brings so many vexations,
But Mothers, whatever may vex you,
Send the children to bed with a kiss.

The dear little feet wander often,
Perhaps from the pathway of right,
The dear little hands find new mischief,
To try you from morning till night,
But think of the desolate mothers,
Who would give all the world for your bliss,
And as thanks for your infinite blessing,
Send the children to bed with a kiss.

For some day the noise will not vex you,
The silence will hurt you far more,
You will long for the sweet childish voices
For a sweet child's face at your door
And to press a child's face to your bosom,
You'd give all the world for just this,
For the comfort 'twill bring you in sorrow,
Send the children to bed with a kiss.

Shado's Poem

So small was he, so fat and round
His tummy nearly touched the ground
He stood on my hand with room to spare
Regarded me with brown eyes so aware,
Sized me up, then adopted me this special pup.

He grew in size, in wisdom too
Always seeking things to do,
The children were his special babes

122

None dare touch them, they were his
Love and licks and always a kiss.

Football was his special love,
Be it on the beach, on grass or on TV
He knew it all, but oh the referee
Never knew the furore he caused
When the ball was held more than a pause!

He knew his Dad was ill and tired
So kept a vigil at his side,
Those wise brown eyes so more than we
Who waited for the inevitability.

He stayed by me throughout the time
That dragged on endlessly,
Then suddenly he needed his rest,
His time had come, my special chum,
He deserved the best.

I can still see him now on that lovely plain
He'll yawn and stretch, find no more pain
That well loved voice will say to him
'Well done my son – where's Daddy's boy?'

Enjoy your new life my lovely lad,
Go walks, play games with beloved Dad,
You gave so much love to everyone,
For you the best is yet to come.

When my time to roam is over
My heart will be so happy to discover
The two of you there to wait—
One wagging his tail, one leaning on the gate!

My lovely poems may not be worthy of Shakespeare
but they bring tears to my eyes just the same. You can
tell that every one is written from the heart and springs
from the suffering and courage of personal experience.

Shado's Poem was accompanied by a moving letter from Cathie Cluff:

Dear Doris,

Thank you for all the comfort your books have brought to me ever since my beloved husband David passed over last year.

I was one of the many who were lucky enough to have a contact through you at the Usher Hall in November 1984. David was the cheeky one, in RAF Bomber Command. You were puzzled at the connection with Guy Gibson until I explained that David had flown on that Squadron. As you said 'I was Guy Gibson's driver so I know you have no connection with him – yet there is a connection!' How right you were. Right away you said 'Lancasters'.

Well, Doris, I know you occasionally like poems so hope you like this one. You see Shado adored David, never left his side towards the end and was distraught when David passed over. I had to get the vet in to him. The vet to the dog and the doctor to me – you can imagine what it was like!

I was convinced that Shado was left with me this past year to help me, too, in fact he kept my sanity. The years of nursing were taking their toll. In January of this year Shado was telling me his time had come. Arthritis had taken his rear quarters badly. So I was there too when Shado passed over. A strange thing this, Doris, don't ask me how but I know David and Shado are together again. They are company for each other and to that end, two days after Shado died, I found myself writing Shado's Poem. Thought you might like to see it.

Hope John is keeping well. I understand what hell he went through at Arnhem.

Love

Cathie Cluff.
Edinburgh.

People who sneer that a pet is 'only an animal' obviously have no idea how much comfort and love they bring, and how much sorrow the owners feel when they pass. I think a lot of readers must have been surprised to discover from my past books that animals too live on, because I get a lot of letters on this subject.

Chatham,
Kent

Dear Mrs Stokes,

I was given one of your books recently – A Host of Voices – following the death of my dog three weeks ago. Although he was only an animal, to me he was more a member of my family – a child almost, and it was a great loss when I had to have him put to sleep through throat cancer.

Reading your book gave me great comfort, not only for this loss but also for the loss of a very dear friend who committed suicide last year – and for other deaths which I must surely come up against in the future. I feel confident now that one day I will see them both again and that in the meantime my dog has got all the fields to run in he could ever want. I still say goodnight each evening because after reading your book I know he is still around.

Once again, many thanks for your help and comfort in your books. I realize that my grief must be small compared with most people's losses, but I'm glad to have found the opportunity to discover Spiritualism.

Good luck in your work and may God bless you.

Mrs B. Edwards.

Dear Mrs Stokes,

A little note to say a very big thank you. I went to the City Hall, Sheffield, on 27th November last year with many friends, and you have changed my whole life.

On 4th March our darling Rupert (cross fox terrier/poodle) passed over. I just thank God that although he was nearly 15 years of age he had had a wonderful life with quality. He was so very much loved and I long to put my arms round him and cuddle him. He loved his cuddle. I know he is only a whisper away.

Yours sincerely

Mrs V. Kembery

She is absolutely right of course. Our pets do live on and it was proved to me yet again only a couple of weeks ago.

I've already mentioned Patrick who baked the beautiful birthday cake for me and then cooked my Christmas dinner – well Patrick and I have become great friends. He pops in regularly and when he does, he always brings a little gift – a plant for the garden or some flowers for my spirit children or sometimes another cake.

'Patrick you mustn't feel you have to bring something every time you come love,' I said after a whole string of gifts had arrived. 'It's just nice to see you.'

But he insisted it gives him pleasure. He lost his mother not long ago and he likes to think of me as a substitute mum. Anyway, one particular Saturday while he was visiting me his mother came through with news that was going to be difficult to break. Apparently Patrick's beloved dog Sally was about to pass over. Oh dear, I thought. How am I going to tell him that. He loves that dog like a child.

'Patrick, love,' I said gently, 'you've got to be very brave. Your Mum's just come through and she's told me she's waiting to welcome Sally into the spirit world.'

The colour drained from Patrick's face. 'Oh no, surely not. She doesn't seem too bad.'

Sally was after all sixteen-and-a-half years old and her health was variable.

'I'm sorry Pat but that's what your mum says and if they're preparing a place for Sally it must be right. I think she'll pass over either tomorrow or Monday.'

Poor Patrick didn't know what to say. He'd known for a long time that Sally was a great age for a pekinese and couldn't last much longer, but he'd tried to pretend it wouldn't happen.

Well that night, he told me later, Sally didn't seem too bad, but the following morning she was obviously ill and by the afternoon Patrick realized she was going. Distraught he phoned me.

I tuned in straight away and his mother was there, all ready to collect the dog.

'It's her time to come to us,' she explained.

'Now Patrick be brave. You've got to let her go,' I said. 'Your Mum's come for her and it's only your love that's holding Sally back.'

Naturally Patrick was upset but he realized the poor dog was ill and it wasn't fair to try to keep her any longer.

'Pick her up in your arms,' I said, 'and say, "here you are Mum. Take her with love."'

There were some muffled sounds as Patrick put down the phone and reluctantly did as I suggested. Nothing happened at first but then he whispered, 'Go on Sally. Go to Mum.' And as he said the words Sally went limp in his arms and I had a sudden mental picture of a little honey brown dog bounding away

127

across a sunlit meadow towards a woman who was standing with open arms.

'It's all right, Patrick,' I said when he returned speechlessly to the phone. 'She's safely over. I've seen her. She's racing around, happy and as lively as a puppy.'

The saddest letters, of course, are from parents who've lost children and it gives me special pleasure to know that I've been able to give them a little comfort in their grief.

East Lothian
Scotland

Dear Doris,

I hope you don't mind if I just call you Doris but you don't feel like a stranger to me, more like a trusted friend.

Our beautiful wee boy Craig passed over. I and my husband knew our wee boy was very ill, only we kept hoping and praying that it was all a bad dream and we could wake up and take him home to us, away from the hospital and just love him and look after him. Craig was only nine days old but we treasure all the beautiful memories of him and the happiness he brought to everybody.

I've always believed that when we die there is something more, that someone is looking after us. I was given your book and it seemed to lift me and reassure me in a way I can't explain very well.

The poems are beautiful and I try to remember them when the awful black despair closes in.

We love our wee boy so much. I pray we can meet him again, cuddle him and never have to part again.

You have given me the strength to really believe this.

Mrs T. Johnston.

Dear Doris,

I expect you receive many letter like this, but I would like to say thank you so very much for making life easier for my Mum and I after having lost our little Jessica of three months in a cot death. Even though she was so young we found there was a great hole in our hearts. Twelve months have now passed but it seems like yesterday.

Until I read your books death frightened me even though I am a committed Christian. Many friends have told me it is wrong for Mum and I to believe in what you do and stand for – yet you were the one who brought comfort to our grief stricken family, knowing Jessica was being well looked after.

May God bless you both, thank you once again for being such a comfort and friend.

C Ruttey

Yarmouth
Isle of Wight

Dear Doris,

Today I listened to your Desert Island Discs programme which has very much moved me.

Forty-three years ago today, my husband of 24 years was shot down and died over Germany, flying with Bomber Command.

The child I was carrying was born in July '42 and brought all who knew and cared for her much joy, and to me much comfort. She was taken into spirit two days before her 11th birthday, 1953 after falling into an empty lift-shaft. Although I had by then other children and a fine husband I prayed to die, we had been *so* close, and I loved her *so* much.

Since then, but not at the time, I've learned much

129

and truly believe her short life was completed and she is with her dear father.

But for years, before my eyes I saw that white coffin going into another deep black hole.

I have passed your books to my sister who is Catholic and whose life has been transformed. Also to friends in hospital.

I can hardly see to write, having two cataracts, not to mention tears! God bless you, my dear, and give you the strength you need for your glorious mission.

Mrs B. Pense

The bulk of my letters though, are about grief in all its different forms, because of course there is not one of us who escapes grief.

Tintagel,
Cornwall

Dear Mrs Stokes,

I feel I have to write to you after seeing and hearing you on the Wogan Show last evening. Having read your books, your thoughts and experiences have given me the extra courage to face the world since my beloved husband slipped quietly away from me two years ago.

When you said you and your friend belonged to the Sod It Club how could you know that for the past 20 years or so it was my beloved's favourite expression. Oh how through the years it has relieved the tension over so many traumatic times.

Even our vicar uses it now! As indeed do all my friends.

Yours sincerely

E. Keness

Dear Doris,

Until I saw you on TV last year I'd never heard of Doris Stokes. I was overwhelmed with what I saw and very soon after I bought one of your books, read it and quickly bought and read the other three. I can't put into words the impact they had on me. You took away any fear I had of death, you explained so beautifully the continuation of life when we pass over and the more I read the more you became a personal friend.

Shortly after this wonderful happening, my mother passed over and immediately I knew she was with her loved ones who she'd earlier lost. When I left the cemetery I knew I wasn't leaving mum behind, and in the visits to her grave since, they have only been out of respect, for I know she's not there. Mum's with me whenever I want her to be, she's in my home, she's any beautiful flower, she's the brightest shining star in the sky.

You've given so much love and happiness to so many people that it makes me so happy just to write and tell you so.

Paul Russo

Bolton,
Lancs

Dear Doris (please forgive familiarity!),

I feel I must write to you after hearing your selection on Desert Island Discs yesterday morning. It was my birthday and my dear husband passed on two years ago last February and I miss him so much, especially on such anniversaries.

I was very weepy but I cannot tell you how your record selection touched me so much, for each record you picked Doris (with the exception of your own lovely verse) had a very special place for Tom and me.

I wrote them all down when you started with Lena Martell's One Day At A Time – a *special* favourite of Tom's – and then I could hardly believe my ears at all the rest of your choice. It was wonderful. Just as if dear Tom was sending me a birthday message through you.

Thank you so much. I've been so unhappy since he went but my heart was lifted for a best ever birthday present.

Yours sincerely

Mrs J. Norris

I also receive letters from children and I find it very touching to think they've struggled through my books and understood them. This is the letter from the little girl I was hoping to meet in Liverpool:

Withington
Manchester

Dear Mrs Doris Stokes,

I am writing to you because my Daddy has just died I am age 10 one time I watched television and my mummy said that you were very good and Mummy said that she would take me to see you at your house if you would let me becouse I love my Daddy ever so much and I would like to know if he is happy or sad becouse I keep on crying all the time for my Daddys love

All my love

Gale

Finally there are my 'tonic' letters. Like everybody else I get tired and fed up from time to time and when it's bitterly cold and I've got to struggle into my dress and travel miles to some theatre instead of sinking into my armchair by the fire for the night, I think to myself what are you doing Doris? You must be mad.

Well I'm lucky. Because when I feel like that I've only got to read a few of my tonic letters and I know that the effort is all worthwhile.

Perranporth
Cornwall

Dear Mrs Stokes,

I felt I just had to write and thank you for such a wonderful evening last Saturday at St Austell. Having read all your books and any magazine article I could find, it became an ambition of mine to see you 'live' at one of your meetings. I found the reassurance and comfort you gave to those fortunate enough to have a sitting with you so marvellous and I'm sure most people like myself sat there spellbound!

My husband came with me on Saturday and beforehand was quite sceptical and so sure he would be able to 'see through' you. However he came away a total believer!

So thank you once again for a wonderful evening and for all the marvellous work you do.

With best wishes

Jayne Moon

A Midlands vicarage

Dear Mrs Stokes,

I am an Anglican priest and had almost lost my faith when I read your books earlier this year. You have helped me greatly and given me much more confidence in the realities of the spiritual world.

With all good wishes
(I will not embarrass him by
publishing his name)

Kingsbridge
Devon

Dear Mrs Stokes,

I have just been listening to Desert Island Discs and I feel so strongly to say what a comforting feeling it gave to me. I do so staunchly believe in a better life to come but, Doris, you made it all so clear, bless you.

My eyes aren't so good now but I read two of your books a few years ago and now, to hear you in the flesh is something I will never forget.

Yours most sincerely

Mary Winterburn

Dormansland
Surrey

Dear Doris,

I came to your evening at Croydon and I can't stop thinking or talking about it. You gave so many messages which brought so much relief, comfort and happiness not only to those to whom you were talking, but to many others present as well. The evening was a very happy one despite all the tragedies we heard about.

I have never been to a more packed theatre and the audience on leaving were very animated – hundreds of people were converging on to the car park – all talking at once.

Something happened to me during the day prior to coming to see your show. I was convinced that it was my mother's doing. Almost towards the end of your show you were talking to another spirit called Bert – you said, 'Just a minute Bert, I have a Violet coming in.' Nobody claimed Violet. Violet is my mother's name. You carried on speaking to Bert for a minute or two. Then you said, 'I have a Violet looking for Pat.'

I am Pat. I was so overcome that I just couldn't

134

move to speak or come down. You carried on talking to Bert again. Then you said. 'I have someone here who died of cancer of the lung.' So did my mother. Someone did claim that their father died of cancer of the lung and this message may have been for them but it did seem a coincidence.

I said to a friend that if something else happened the following day – which did seem very unlikely to both of us – then I would be convinced that the Violet you heard was my mother. This did happen so I am convinced.

Thank you Doris for all the comfort you have given in your books and also for giving us the experience of sharing in your incredible gift. It was a truly marvellous evening last Monday and one I shall never forget.

Yours sincerely

Pat Hearn

Chapter Ten

Half way through the sitting Terry put his head round the door.

'Sorry to interrupt but I'm looking for that letter from Lincoln. It's very important. Have you seen it?'

I looked at the shelving unit beside me, every surface overflowing with mail. 'Yes – well it's here somewhere.'

And I was just rummaging through when a voice from the spirit world said: 'No. It's back here,' and my hand was pushed back to the shelf behind my chair.

'Oh. No it's not,' I corrected myself. 'They've just told me it's on this shelf back here.'

I reached back and sure enough, the first letter I put my hand on was the important one from Lincoln.

'By God that's useful,' said Pat Coombs, my sitter, 'I wish I could do that. I've lost a photo album and I'm very sad about it. I wish my mother could tell me where it is.'

Her mother had been talking to us before Terry came so I tuned into the same vibration and asked. Back came a message about a garage and a chest that used to be kept there.

Pat shook her head. 'No, I've looked in the garage and it's not there.'

But her mother was insistent.

'She's really certain, Pat,' I said. 'It's in a chest that belonged to your grandparents and it was always kept in the garage. You're not to worry about it because you're going to find it very soon.'

I could see Pat was a bit sceptical about this but the sitting went on and more and more evidence came through. Her mother brought back Pat's old cat, Pip, and then she kept going on about Tiddy. I thought this must be another pet, but no, it turned out that Pat's mother's nickname was Tiddy May. She mentioned other members of the family and then suddenly a man's voice cut in. A very domineering voice.

'I was in the army,' he said.

'Oh, what rank?' I asked.

'Well you would have had to call me sir,' he chuckled. 'I was a major.'

'Yes, Tom's with me.' Tiddy May confirmed in case Pat was in any doubt that her father had arrived.

'I was always very strict and military,' he said, 'but I went peculiar towards the end. I'm glad I came over before I got incontinent. I didn't approve of Pat going into acting at first,' he added, 'but afterwards I was so proud of her. I used to say Coombs is my name. Pat Coombs' father.'

By now a great many of Pat's family and friends had come to say hello. Some of the names, however, she couldn't place. I kept getting the name Lillian which meant absolutely nothing to Pat. Back it came again and again and I was getting myself into a bit of a mess, when Ramanov took pity on me.

'It's not Lillian,' he said, 'it's Lally.'

Pat recognized it at once. 'Lally Bowers! An old actress friend of mine.'

There was also an answer to a tragic mystery. A young man called Nicholas joined us, bringing with him a feeling of confusion.

'My nephew,' said Pat.

He mentioned Kings Cross in Sydney, Australia, where he'd lived and also talked of Brighton. Brighton, Australia? I queried. 'No. Brighton-on-Sea, England,' he said.

'That's quite right,' said Pat, 'we used to live there and he came to visit us.'

Nicholas should not have passed over when he did he kept telling me. It shouldn't have happened. There was a great deal of confusion surrounding his last hours on earth. There was something about a car.

'I was thrown,' he said, 'that's the last thing I remember. I was thrown.'

'Nobody knows what happened,' said Pat. 'His body was found beside a road in Australia. He had head injuries but apart from that there wasn't a mark on him.'

From what Nicholas said it sounded as if it wasn't an accident. The poor boy was an epileptic and it may have been that he started to have a fit and the occupants of the car, thinking he was turning violent, opened the door and pushed him out.

By the end of the sitting Pat was even more fascinated than she'd been when she arrived and she stayed on chatting for most of the afternoon. She was particularly pleased by something that sounded almost like a prediction from the other side, although I always stress that I don't tell fortunes.

I heard the name Agatha Christie very strongly and at the same time I got a very clear impression of Pat moving away from comedy.

'Pat, people associate you with comedy,' I said, 'but from what they're telling me, you could do much meatier roles. I'm getting the name Agatha Christie.'

'Oh God, I'd love to do Agatha Christie,' Pat agreed.

'Who's Michael?' I asked suddenly.

'He's a writer friend. He adapts things.'

'Well I think Michael might have something to do with you appearing in Agatha Christie. You'd make a wonderful Miss Marple,' and as I said it a vivid picture of Pat as Miss Marple with a battered hat, a bicycle and a cat round her ankles flashed into my mind.

'Let's hope you're right, Doris,' said Pat, 'I'd love to play Miss Marple. I really would.'

Most extraordinary of all the things she'd heard from the spirit world as far as Pat was concerned though was the affair of the photo album.

When she got home that afternoon she phoned her sister to tell her what happened.

'But when I got to the part about the photo album she went very quiet,' Pat told me afterwards. 'It turned out she'd found the album that very morning in a sort of treasure chest that belonged to our grandmother. The chest was under her bed but before it passed to her it probably had been stored in the garage for years.'

People are often astonished by the accuracy of the spirit world, even more so where figures are involved. I'm not quite sure why. After all, all the messages that I hear quite distinctly are correct, so why some truths should seem more impressive than others I don't know. I remember once at a public demonstration the spirit world remarked that a woman in the audience had just bought a new oven and she'd got £130 off the recommended price. The audience were amazed when this turned out to be absolutely correct. Yet when another woman was told that a relative had just had a baby and was given the correct name, the audience seemed almost to take it for granted. I couldn't help feeling puzzled. Surely both pieces of evidence were equally good?

Something similar happened recently. A couple who'd lost their much loved daughter, Sarah, came for a sitting. The wife seemed very keen but the husband was highly sceptical and I got the impression he was only there on sufferance to please his wife. Throughout the conversation with Sarah, he sat there looking perplexed, as if he knew there was a catch somewhere but he couldn't work out where. Then towards the end, Sarah said that she'd left £28 behind to buy her brother, Chris, a present.

'Well we can soon settle that,' said her mother, 'I've got her pay packet here. I've not opened it yet.'

And she opened her handbag, brought out a battered envelope, tore off the top and shook out the contents. Onto her knee fell several notes and some

139

loose change. She counted it. There was exactly £28.20.

At this the father shook his head in wonder.

'There was just no way you could have known,' he said. 'Even we didn't know . . .'

Even Laurie, who sees these things happen all the time, is sometimes shaken. Not long ago we were talking about Marc Bolan. I'd once contacted Marc on the other side during a sitting and it turned out that Laurie knew Marc on this side and that his brother used to work with him.

'He was such a nice guy,' said Laurie, 'd'you know he even left Alphi £5,000 in his will. Unfortunately when it came to it there wasn't enough money in the estate to pay out so Alphi didn't get anything, but it didn't matter. He was really touched to know that Marc remembered him.'

I was just about to agree what a nice thoughtful boy Marc was, when suddenly Marc himself arrived.

'He's had the money now, Doris,' Marc assured me, 'and he got £6,000 not £5,000.'

'Laurie, Marc's just told me Alphi's had the money,' I said quickly, 'and it was £6,000.'

Laurie shook his head. 'No, love. You're wrong somewhere. This was years ago and there wasn't enough money to pay Alphi. He didn't get a thing.'

Well I didn't pursue it. It wasn't important and Alphi's affairs were none of my business. I didn't even give it another thought until a couple of days later, Laurie phoned me in great excitement.

'You'll never guess, Doris, I've just had a call from Alphi. He wants to take my wife and I out to celebrate. The money from Marc Bolan's come through and he did get £6,000. Marc left him £5,000 but the interest has been building up all these years and it's £6,000 now.'

Laurie himself has never had a sitting with me. Night after night at theatre demonstrations he meets so many people desperate for a sitting that he feels it would be wrong to ask me to use up my psychic energy to satisfy curiosity when there are more urgent cases out there than I could ever hope to get through in a lifetime. Nevertheless I sometimes come out with little bits without realizing it.

One morning when he called in, I asked him if he'd mind taking a bundle of clothes we no longer wear down to the Oxfam Shop or the Salvation Army for the old folk. Laurie didn't mind at all and we were just stuffing them into large carrier bags, when a woman's voice suddenly said: 'Tell him to take them round to Issy's.'

'You're to take them round to Issy's, Laurie,' I repeated out loud.

Laurie stopped dead, a pair of trousers poised in mid-air.

'What did you say?'

'It's your Mum, love,' I explained, 'she's just come over and said you're to take the clothes round to Issy's. What's Issy's?'

Laurie looked flabbergasted. 'I can't believe it. When we were kids in the East End my Mum used to take us to Issy Goodyear's in the Roman Road to buy second-hand clothes. I've not even thought about Issy's for years. The place must have been knocked down thirty years ago!'

He was so thrilled to hear from his mother that he phoned his wife, Iris, straight away to tell her the news.

'I couldn't have better proof that my old Mum was there,' he said. 'No one else would ever have known of Issy's.'

Yes, it's certainly true that occasionally the spirit world can help you find things or give you information that you want, which as Pat Coombes said, is very useful, and it's for this reason I'm sometimes asked to work on police cases. When I was in New Zealand last, I was asked to help find a missing girl. She gave her name, Susan, and she described the

141

landscape she remembered in her last moments, but it was wintertime and the whole area was covered by snow. Later when the snows had cleared the police went back and searched the place and sure enough they found the body. I had pinpointed within 500 yards, the motorway where she was picked up and last seen alive.

But I must stress that it doesn't always work. Sometimes the messages are too confused, sometimes the significance of the information doesn't dawn until after the case is solved – like the time I was given the name Sutcliffe during a sitting with the parents of Jayne MacDonald, one of the victims of the Yorkshire Ripper. Mrs McDonald said it was an old family name and we thought no more about it until the Ripper was caught and he turned out to be a man called Peter Sutcliffe – and sometimes the spirit world deliberately withholds information if it would do more harm than good.

I remember recently the police brought a man to see me whose seventeen-year-old daughter had been raped and murdered. Naturally they were after any clues they could get to the identity of the killer but I just couldn't help. The distraught father sat there on the sofa willing me to come up with a name and all I could feel was hate and the desire for revenge. The poor child came back and tried to talk to her father.

'I was a good girl, you know,' she kept saying. 'Tell him I was a good girl.'

But I didn't feel he was properly listening. He didn't so much want contact with his daughter as a name to pin on his hatred.

The violence of the atmosphere washed over me in wave after wave until I eventually faltered.

'Ask her who did it. Ask his name,' insisted the father, knuckles white, teeth clenched. 'Who did it, who did it?'

But from the spirit world there was only silence.

'It's no good,' I said at last, 'they're not going to

give me his name because if I tell you I know what you'd do. You'd get up from that sofa, get in the car, find that boy and kill him.'

'Yes, that's right. I would,' said the father.

Many fathers in similar situations must have threatened the same thing but this man really meant it. These were no empty words.

'Well,' I said, 'the spirit world won't help you do it. What good would it do? What would happen to your wife and children with you in prison? Because that's what would happen to you.'

He wouldn't listen. 'I'll worry about that,' he said. 'Just give me his name.'

But his relatives on the other side had more sense. They refused to be a party to his plans and although they probably knew the answer, they said not a word.

'I'm sorry,' I apologized to the policeman at the end of the sitting, 'I can't help you. It might work with another member of the family but I'm afraid the father's blocking it.'

In desperate circumstances of course I try to help because there's always the chance that the tiniest scrap of information might lead to the capture of a killer and prevent another murder, but I stress strongly that I can't guarantee anything.

Not long ago I received a telephone call from the *Sevenoaks Chronicle* asking if I could help find a missing person. I explained the problems but they were still keen to try. I didn't know the details and I didn't want to but I gathered the case was something of a mystery and the normal channels had failed. I was a last resort. We could well be dealing with a murder, I realized, so I agreed to do what I could.

The reporter came along with a tiny, nervous looking middle-aged lady who was clearly at her wits' end with trying to solve the puzzle. They set up a tape recorder, the reporter got out her notebook and once we were all settled in armchairs with a cup of coffee close by, I tuned in.

143

At once my head was full of German voices. I don't understand German but I knew instinctively that German was the language I was hearing.

'I hear German being spoken,' I began uncertainly.

'That's right,' said my sitter, 'I'm German.'

And in fact she did have a faint trace of an accent but her English was so good it was impossible to say where she originated from.

Oh well, I thought, I suppose I'll have to ask Ramanov to translate the whole thing for me, but to my surprise the atmosphere changed and the rest of the evidence came spontaneously in English.

Now I could understand what was said but it didn't seem to make any sense.

'Yugoslavia,' said a distant voice and I got a confused image of mountains. Now why, when we'd just established the German connection, was I getting information about Yugoslavia, I wondered.

'I'm hearing something about Yugoslavia, mountains and things,' I said, 'so there must be a connection there.'

'Yes, that's right,' said the woman.

Then I was surrounded by darkness and I didn't know what was going on. Out of the black the man's voice came again.

'Anna,' he said.

'That's me,' said the woman eagerly.

'And who's Willie?'

'That's my husband.'

Instinctively I understood that it was her husband who was missing and I was pretty sure it was Willie I was talking to on the other side, although he hadn't said so in so many words. I was very reluctant to come right out and say that he'd definitely passed over, however – I always am in cases like these. I will never forget the war years when John was missing, presumed dead and a medium had told me that he was definitely on the other side, when in fact he was wounded and lying in hospital in a prisoner-of-war camp.

We can all make mistakes and sometimes the voices are muddled and indistinct. There are times when you might think you've made contact with a particular person when in fact you're tuned in to a member of their family who's talking about them.

I find it best to keep an open mind, repeat what I'm hearing and leave it to the sitter to decide if it sounds like the person they've lost.

'Anneliesse,' said the voice in my ear.

'Who's Anneliesse?' I asked.

'That's my full name,' said the woman, 'but everyone calls me Anna.'

It was sounding more and more as if it was indeed her husband I was talking to.

'I feel there's a great mystery and a lot of confusion,' I went on. 'I feel as if I'm falling. I feel as if he was walking in the mountains and you weren't with him.'

Willie was getting agitated. 'I left everything behind in the hotel,' he said. 'Some people say it must have been planned, but how could it? I left everything behind. My clothes, everything.'

Once more there was an impression of darkness and then a drop. I struggled to keep hold of the vibration. It was really frustrating. The impressions were so confused I could hardly make head or tail of what was coming through. From somewhere a long way off came a hard 'k' sound. A name.

'Carl . . . Kurt . . .' I tried.

'Kurt,' said the woman, 'he lives in Sevenoaks. He's worked very hard to try to find Willie.'

But I hardly heard her voice. Suddenly I was on a rocky path and very loud I could hear the sound of rushing water. Not far away there was a waterfall.

Now at last we were getting somewhere. This, I felt sure, was significant.

'I can hear water rushing,' I explained out loud, 'and there's a drop close by and a waterfall. And this man who's talking to me, he has a very loving voice. He isn't the type to just disappear. He says he had only been there three days and if he'd wanted to disappear he would have gone on the first day. He just went out and never returned.'

'Katarina,' said the man emphatically.

'Who's Katarina?' I asked.

'She's a Yugoslav girl who was there,' said the woman.

She too was important. The man was obviously anxious to prove that he hadn't planned to run away, neither had he been suicidal.

'Ask Katarina,' he said, 'she will tell you I was perfectly all right. I wasn't depressed.'

And then there was the rushing water again. The sound was in the background the whole time. If I closed my eyes it would have been difficult to believe I was sitting in my own armchair in my own sitting-room. I felt as if I was high on a mountainside beside a stream. And there was the waterfall again. There was something about that waterfall . . .

'He's saying you go up the path before the fall, then there's a drop,' I said slowly. 'And it's a big fall . . .'

But my contact couldn't seem to hold the impression steady. I was getting the sounds all right but the pictures kept going. The rocky path disappeared and instead I got a name.

'Wolfgang.'

The woman gave a little gasp. 'That's Willie's real name – but nobody knew. Everybody called him Willie.'

The man was getting agitated again. He had a very orderly mind and he seemed to feel that the search hadn't been thorough enough.

'He gets very impatient,' I explained. 'He can't understand why they are so lax. He says they only have to go five paces and they would find him. He seems to think they've stopped bothering in Yugoslavia.'

146

Another impression flickered before my eyes. I was bending down to look at something interesting, some plant I think and then something hit me on the back of the head. The sound of running water continued but in addition I got a fleeting glimpse of caves.

'He was climbing just before the waterfall and stopped to look at something that interested him,' I said out loud. 'Further up the mountain there are caves . . . I don't think the caves have been searched properly.'

The sitting went on. There were more names. The man mentioned Derek, his son, and Jenny the cat and he even asked about his white car. I was pretty certain from the way he was talking that he was the missing husband and he'd been killed in suspicious circumstances. I couldn't think why but there seemed to be some sort of cover-up somewhere.

'Well, what do you think, love?' I asked Anneliesse when the power eventually faded. 'D'you think we've been talking to your husband.'

'Oh yes,' she said. 'It sounded just like him.'

Afterwards the reporter filled me in on the story. Apparently the couple were called Mr and Mrs Bleyberg and they had been going to Yugoslavia on walking holidays for the past twenty years or so. They always went to the same area and they knew the hotel and locals quite well. They could even speak some of the language.

Willie was a respected science teacher in Sevenoaks, Kent, and the couple lived a quiet, ordinary life. Then in July 1984 when the time for their holiday came round again, Anneliesse's mother was ill and she had to stay behind to look after her. Anneliesse wasn't keen on her husband going away alone but he seemed to have his heart set on this holiday so reluctantly she agreed.

The morning he disappeared was fine and bright and Willie breakfasted at the hotel and set out for his walk straight afterwards. He left his personal belongings behind in his room and gave every indication that he would be returning for dinner.

Later in the day two locals saw him on the mountain alone but cheerful, and an hour or two afterwards they bumped into him again. He'd tried one particular path he told them but it was too difficult so he was going to set out in a different direction. Off he went with a good-natured wave and was never seen again.

The extraordinary part of the story was that Anneliesse wasn't informed that her husband was missing until five days later. The area was searched but nothing was found, and to add to her distress, Anneliesse realized that without a body she couldn't prove that her husband was dead and all his financial affairs would be frozen until a death certificate was issued – which couldn't be done, of course, without a body.

The muddle and the uncertainty, added to her natural grief, was proving almost too much for the poor woman. The only consolation was that the evidence from the sitting might be enough to persuade the authorities to reopen the case and call for another search.

Yes, the spirit world does often help us find things – but it's not a one-way affair. Sometimes they want us to help them!

I was doing a couple of demonstrations in Bridlington not long ago and I had been looking forward to it. After the long cold winter and several doses of 'flu, a breath of sea air was just what I needed. We were staying in a nice seaside hotel and that first night I was hoping for a long refreshing sleep.

Well I had the refreshing sleep all right, but it wasn't very long! Early in the morning, just as the dawn chorus was starting up, I heard a voice talking to me.

'It's Paul. I hung myself,' he said.

Half asleep, I thought I was having a nightmare. I peeped out through slits in my eyelids and saw that

I was quite safe in my comfortable hotel room. I'm dreaming I said to myself and turned over for another hour or two.

'I hung myself,' said the sad voice again. And this time I realized it was no use. I couldn't pretend. I wasn't asleep and I wasn't dreaming. The voice was real.

I sat up. 'You what, love? What did you say?'

'I hung myself,' said the boy. 'Can you tell my Mum I'm sorry? She's so upset.'

'Well how am I going to find your Mum, love?' I asked. There was no telling where he came from or anything.

From the other side I could feel a great effort being made. The lad couldn't have been over very long and he was having difficulty keeping the power going.

'Paul,' I heard again. Then, 'Plane Street.'

There was silence for a long time and then just when I thought he'd gone there came the name 'Hewson', very faint.

'I was twenty,' he added. 'Shane's got my things.'

That was it. Well it wasn't much to go on. How on earth was I going to find Paul's Mum. I had part of an address but Plane Street on its own wasn't much use without a town to go with it.

Luckily later that day I had an interview booked with a reporter from the Hull *Daily Mail*. Perhaps she might have heard something. After all if it had happened recently it might have been in the paper.

When she arrived I explained what had happened.

'I got the name Paul, and Hewson and Plane Street,' I said. 'He said he hanged himself and that he was only twenty. Does that ring any bells? D'you think Plane Street could be in your area?'

She shook her head. 'No, it doesn't mean anything to me, Doris. I don't remember a story like that, but I'll check with the paper if you like.'

She rang through to her office and we waited while they flicked through back copies of the paper. Then

149

ten minutes later they found the item. On the previous Saturday a boy named Paul Hewson hanged himself. He lived in Plane Street. They couldn't confirm whether there was anybody in the family called Shane, but Paul was only twenty years old. Now all I needed was the Hewsons to be present at my demonstration that night and I could do as Paul had asked.

Well it didn't work out quite as neatly as that but it wasn't bad. Mrs Hewson wasn't in the audience that night but her cousin was. I gave her some flowers to take home to Paul's Mum and I explained that if Mrs Hewson would like to come to the demonstration the following night, we'd arrange it. Thank goodness we were doing two nights in Bridlington!

Sure enough, Mrs Hewson wanted to come and during the second half of the demonstration Paul came back, clear and strong. His practise the morning before had obviously helped him get the hang of communicating.

Mrs Hewson came to the microphone as the message began and gradually she was joined by more and more people.

'He's still talking about Shane,' I said as we began.

'Yes, Shane's his brother,' said Mrs Hewson.

'And he tells me he's being buried at three o'clock on Friday.'

'That's right.'

'Who's Donna?'

'His girlfriend.'

Dabbing quickly at her eyes, a very young girl came to the microphone. 'Donna and I were going to get engaged you know,' Paul said proudly.

'Yes, we were,' she sobbed.

Then Paul spotted someone else he knew. 'There's Dave. There's my mate!' he cried in delight. 'He's in my group.'

It turned out Paul was a drummer in a pop group and his friend Dave had been very close to him.

Dave stepped forward to join Mrs Hewson and Donna.

'We were doing so well with the group and Donna and I were going to get engaged. I must have been mad. I must have been off my trolley to do it,' Paul went on.

'Apparently he had words with someone, Dave, about a gig,' I explained. 'He was a very likeable boy but very sensitive and someone upset him.'

But Paul didn't want to dwell on the unhappiness. 'My guvnor's here tonight as well,' he confided, 'Frank.'

Sure enough, Frank was there and grinning bashfully he came out of the audience to join the little crowd round the mike.

'I'll always be with Frank in the car,' said Paul. 'When he's out in the motor tell him to think of me and I'll be there.'

'Yes we were often together in the car,' said Frank, 'I used to run him around.'

Most of all though, Paul was concerned about his brother Shane. I couldn't quite work out what he meant. He seemed to want Shane to have something that belonged to him but I couldn't catch what it was and Mrs Hewson couldn't think of anything that seemed likely.

'Well I don't know quite what he means,' I admitted, 'but I know he's very concerned about Shane. He says it frightened Shane badly.'

Mrs Hewson nodded. 'Shane hasn't broken down yet, you see,' she said. This was a bad sign. When people don't cry it means the pain and bitterness turns inwards and can make them ill. No wonder Paul was worried.

'Well give him something of Paul's and tell him that Paul wants him to have it with his love,' I said. 'It might help.'

And, finally, right at the end Paul told me that they were having a beautiful set of drums made in flowers for his funeral.

'Thank them for that, I shall enjoy it,' he said, 'but tell Mum not to spend too much money.'

I couldn't devote the whole evening to Paul's people, of course, because it wasn't a private sitting and other families wanted a turn too. I had to move on. But at least Paul had been able to prove to his mother that he wasn't dead, that he was still taking an interest in the family and above all that he was sorry for the heartache he caused.

Chapter Eleven

It was spring, though you'd never have guessed it from the weather, and there we were back on our travels, gliding down the motorway in our posh limousine heading for Cornwall.

The rain was streaming down the windows, the wipers slapping like mad but our voices drowned out the storm as we sang along lustily to *Sing Something Simple*.

Maybe it was the flat countryside we were passing through or maybe it was the tune I was croaking, but suddenly my memory did a backward somersault – the years rolled away and I was bowling along in the battered old Morris E with running boards on the side that we'd bought for £32. Terry couldn't have been more than four in those days and we couldn't afford holidays, but it didn't matter.

On fine summer Sundays we used to get up at the crack of dawn, load the Morris and head off to Skegness, our nearest seaside resort – sixty miles away. We'd drive as far as our empty stomachs would allow, and then when we couldn't stand it any longer, we'd pull up in a pretty spot, get out the little spirit stove and I'd cook breakfast at the side of the road. Later, on the beach, we paddled with Terry, and John took him in swimming. Then at the end of a long happy day we'd drive back, singing along to *Sing Something Simple* at the top of our voices.

I sighed and wiped condensation from the window. Here we were forty years on swanning round in a Daimler and staying at the best hotels, yet we'd never been so happy as those days when we rattled off to the seaside in our £32 Morris and had to stop and think

153

twice about whether we could afford to buy an ice cream for Terry.

There's something about travelling that sparks off memories and when I'm anywhere near Lincolnshire, the floodgates really open. Grantham, of course, is my home town and although it's changed a lot since I was a girl it's still like stepping into a time machine when I go back.

The last time I was there I met my long lost cousin Ron Sutton and when he walked in my stomach did a sudden flip, because these days he looks so much like my father it was as if Dad had come into the room. You can certainly tell Ron's a Sutton all right.

He's a great character is Ron. Everyone in Grantham knows him. Sixty-nine years old, he jumps fences like a two-year-old and races around on his moped in his leather jacket and crash helmet. The effect is a bit spoiled by the fact that Ron doesn't wear any teeth, but when people ask where they are he says: 'I left them in a jam jar when we lived in Norton Street. I suppose they were still there when they pulled the houses down.'

He's not at all bothered. 'I can eat whatever I like. Pickled onions, anything,' he insists and he can as well. He must have very tough gums.

In his time Ron has been known to do a bit of poaching – just like my father. When I was a little girl my father once disappeared for a week and I was told he'd gone to Lincoln. This was quite true, but I didn't find out until I was older that he'd actually been sent to Lincoln prison for poaching.

In those days we were very poor and it was quite common for people to do a bit of poaching to make ends meet. My father was quite open about it.

'Yes and I'd go to prison for 7 days again rather than see my family go hungry when Lord Brownlow's got all those rabbits running wild on his land,' he used to say.

It all came back as Ron stood grinning in the

154

reception of the George Hotel, his crash helmet dangling from his hand.

'I've just been to the sales,' he told me. 'By – there was some good stuff going for little or nothing.'

And once again it could have been my father talking. Dad loved auctions and what we called 'the stones' in the market. Grantham is an old market town and on Saturday the farmers used to bring all their produce in. There was cattle one side, then all the pets, puppies and kittens and caged birds, then the big furniture and then the small stuff laid out 'on the stones' – small areas enclosed by railings with tables full of boxes in the centre.

Dad used to gravitate towards the stones and what he was after was clocks. He had a thing about clocks. We had so many clocks in our house it was incredible. You must have heard the place ticking like a time bomb from right up the street. When I look back now I think why on earth didn't we keep them? They'd be worth a fortune now. There were chiming clocks and grandfather clocks, you name it and we'd got it. Dad used to get them cheap if they didn't go. He fiddled until he got them working and then, as often as not, if someone admired a particular clock he said, 'Well you can have it.'

He gave them all away.

But no matter how many clocks we had, Dad just couldn't resist the market. In fact he loved it so much that he carried on visiting from the other side, as I happen to know.

Like everyone else in Grantham, John and I used to do our shopping in the market on Saturday. There was an old saying in Grantham that if you wanted to meet any of your old pals you haven't seen for years, go down to Grantham market on a Saturday and sure enough, somewhere or other you'll bump into them.

Well John and I with Terry in tow used to shop and chat then we'd wander up to the auctions on the stones for a look round. One particular day we were standing

155

peering through the railings when I noticed a large cardboard box standing on the table inside. You weren't allowed to examine it, you were expected to bid and hope for the best. It seemed crazy. I mean who'd bid for a cardboard box without knowing what was inside?

I was just shaking my head at such madness when I heard my father's voice clear as clear.

'Bid for that box, Dol,' he said firmly.

And I didn't hesitate. When my Dad used that tone of voice you did as you were told – even if it was over thirty years since he'd passed.

'I'm going to bid for that box, John,' I announced loudly.

John stared at me as if I'd been out in the sun too long. 'Don't be a fool. You don't know what's in it.'

'I know, but I'm going to bid for it,' I insisted, and I went right ahead.

There were obviously quite a few people as reckless as me because the bidding went up and up and eventually it reached ten shillings, which was a lot of money in those days. Ten shillings! I thought with the first pang of anxiety. But Dad had told me to do it and he must have seen something in that box that was a bargain.

I shot my hand up. 'Yes ten shillings!' I called in case they hadn't noticed my hand.

And miraculously everyone else dropped out and the box was mine. John shook his head in disbelief, quite speechless at such extravagance, and I must admit I had a few qualms myself.

'Suppose it's full of old clothes or plaster ornaments,' I thought in horror. But I held my head high and handed over my ten shillings as confidently as if I knew for a fact that the box was full of treasure. All the way home I had a nasty fluttery feeling in my stomach and I raced inside as soon as John opened the door.

Down went the box on the kitchen table and rapidly I tore open the top and ripped out the newspaper packing. Then I relaxed and a great big grin spread over my face. Good old Dad. He hadn't let me down.

'John, look at this!' I called and I pulled out of the box a silver Queen Anne tea service, followed by a set of silver cutlery with beautiful carved ivory handles.

That box was a godsend. It went under my bed and whenever we were really hard up I rummaged through for a piece of silver to sell. My silver got us through quite a few difficult times.

I'm sure Dad continued to go to the sales with us because a year or so later the same thing happened again, only this time it wasn't a cardboard box but a sealed jewellery box he told me to bid for. When I got it home I discovered it was filled with pretty pieces of jewellery.

I don't suppose they were worth a fortune but they brought in a shilling or two when I was at my wits' end and didn't know how we'd manage till the end of the week.

Ron and I had a wonderful time catching up on the old days. There was a time when his house had been like a second home to me and Ron's mum, Aunt Aggie, was very good to me when I was a little girl. She had a thing about lace did Aunt Aggie and she had lace draped over her pictures and mirrors and lace draped along the mantelshelf. In fact anywhere you could drape lace, Aunt Aggie draped it.

She was very kind. The first thing she said when you crossed the threshold was, 'Are you hungry? Have you eaten girl?' And there was always something to eat even if it was only a piece of bread and dripping. And when I was fourteen and just started work and came home with my hands all chapped and bleeding from scrubbing floors, it was Aunt Aggie who rubbed them with vaseline and bandaged them up for me.

So I was astonished when I came out of the hotel, climbed into the Daimler and waved goodbye to Ron one day, when a lady said to me, 'How on earth did you get a relative like Ron Sutton?'

I just stared at her in amazement. I come from a poor background and I'm not ashamed to admit it. I'm proud of being a Sutton, just like Ron. It's made me hard-working and self-reliant. Years ago when he came home from Arnhem with a head wound, John found he couldn't work in the factory. The noise of the machines was driving him mad. He needed peace and quiet and the open air, so he took a job as a gardener at a private school just outside Stamford.

Accommodation was provided and I was to do a bit of everything – cleaning, standing in for matron, a little cooking now and again. At the interview we'd been shown a pleasant little flat inside the main building, but when we arrived with our furniture, having given up the house we'd been renting, the owner announced that she couldn't allow a man in the place with the girls, so she was putting us in the coach house.

Well we couldn't believe our eyes. The place had previously been used as a stable. There were rats as big as cats and no proper cooking facilities. Another woman might have turned right round and gone straight back to Grantham and who could blame her – but I was a Sutton and Suttons, I decided, stuck it out. We'd burned our boats in Grantham. Factory work was making John ill. We'd just have to make the best of it.

I scrubbed the place from the top to bottom. I made do and I learned how to make Yorkshire puddings in a frying pan on an upturned electric fire. We survived and we stuck it out for six months until John found something better.

That was the way I was brought up and Ron too and no matter what material things we collect along the years we're still the same people. So why on earth shouldn't I have a cousin like Ron Sutton?

Yes travel does send me off down memory lane but that's not to say that the present isn't every bit as interesting as the past. Cornwall turned out to be just

158

as pretty as people told me it would be. The hedgerows were full of buttery primroses, there were daffodils in every garden and the little thatched cottages really did look like chocolate box lids come to life. It was a pity about the rain but through the flowing windows you could tell it would be beautiful when the sun came out.

There had been a bit of difficulty booking a hotel. Laurie had found a conveniently situated place but when he phoned they sounded doubtful.

'Are you a group?' asked the receptionist.

'I suppose so,' said Laurie, 'there are four of us.'

The receptionist wasn't sure this counted. 'You'll have to ask the manager,' she said.

The manager wasn't too encouraging either.

'Doris Stokes,' he said. 'Never heard of her.'

Nevertheless, he agreed that if Laurie sent in written confirmation it would be all right. Well Laurie wrote his letter but just before we left some niggling doubt made him phone the hotel again, just to make sure.

It was a good thing he did, because the rooms had been let to other people.

Perhaps it was a simple mistake, but I got the feeling that the manager didn't want the likes of us staying there. Maybe he thought I'd bring ghosts into the hotel, or hold weird seances in my room!

Undaunted Laurie found us another place in Newquay, but I was a little anxious about the reception we'd receive. Perhaps we wouldn't be welcome in Cornwall.

It just shows how wrong you can be. They couldn't have been nicer at the hotel in Newquay. The manageress herself came to greet us, apologizing profusely because her hands were grubby.

'I've just been potting up some plants in the greenhouse,' she explained. Then she peered at our tired faces, bleary from the seven hour journey. 'You look as if you could do with some tea,' she said. 'Come and get settled and I'll bring you a pot. I've put Mr and Mrs

159

Stokes in the villa because we've got a wedding tonight and it'll be quieter away from the main building,' and she led us outside, chatting as if we were old friends come to stay.

The villa turned out to be a pleasant little house in the grounds and we'd hardly put down our suitcases before the manageress was back with a tray of tea.

'Now don't forget. If there's anything you want just call.'

It was a hectic visit. We'd travelled to Cornwall to do a charity show in aid of the Save the Children Fund at a school hall in St Austell, where we were also to be presented with a cheque for the same cause. There were a frantic few moments when Laurie found that the man who'd organized the whole thing and made all the arrangements couldn't be reached at the telephone number we'd been given. We had panicky visions of having come all this way for nothing, when Ramanov stepped in with some sensible advice.

'Get in touch with the radio station. They will find him.'

'Brilliant,' said Laurie and sure enough little more than an hour after the SOS went out over the local radio, the organizer phoned us.

While we were in Cornwall there was one sitting I had to do. Apparently there was a girl who'd been trying every way she could think of to get a sitting. She'd even written to *Jim'll Fix It*. I didn't feel I could turn her away after that, particularly as I was going to be in the area, so I invited her to come and see me.

Well three of them turned up, Phyllis, who'd written the letter, and two other girls, Pat and Nicola. It was a right old mix up, with spirit people wanting to talk to all of them, but we managed to sort most of it out. It turned out that Phyllis' husband, Peter, had died suddenly of a heart attack while he was playing badminton and Peter was related to Pat.

'That's my sister,' he told me.

160

Peter's parents, Bertram and Ivy, came back too, to say hello and then I kept hearing a strange word. It sounded very like 'Catshole'. I tried to ignore it but they kept sending it back to me. Well I didn't know what to make of it. It sounded a bit rude to me but they were so insistent, I decided to risk it.

'Look I don't know what to make of this,' I admitted, 'but I'm hearing something like Catshole. I don't know what it means . . .'

'Yes Catshole!' exclaimed Pat in delight. 'It's a place. We used to live there!'

They seemed quite pleased with the sitting but there was no time to hang around, we had to be off to St Austell. I changed into my long dress, climbed back into the car and we set off down tiny lanes with steep green banks on either side. It was still raining. If it carries on like this I'll need flippers not a long dress, I said to myself. I'd long since given up worrying about my hair. In damp weather it goes just like a gollywog and I must have looked like something the cat dragged in. But in St Austell it didn't matter a bit. We had such a wonderful evening, there was so much love generated in that school building that if you could have connected it to the national grid we'd have lit up Cornwall!

They'd gone to a great deal of trouble with the stage and it looked magnificent. They must have emptied six flower shops. There were tubs and tubs of daffodils and great baskets of flowers for me to give away. It glowed bright gold even with the lights turned down and when the spotlights came on it was radiant.

Nobody was left out. As the audience came in they were presented with white carnations and I was given a beautiful spray of yellow roses.

The atmosphere was wonderful from the start and the voices flowed. One in particular stands out in my mind because it was a lesson for all of us.

A boy named Richard came through, very distressed because he'd taken his own life. He was looking for Lynne he said and Stephen went with Lynne.

161

A woman came forward at once.

'I'm Lynne,' she said, 'Stephen's my son and Richard's my son in spirit.'

'Richard's very distressed,' I began tactfully.

'Yes, Doris,' said the woman, 'he shot himself.'

She seemed quite composed so I went on.

'He's got a girl with him.'

'Yes that'll be my daughter, she drowned.'

I paused unable to quite believe all the tragedy I was hearing. 'And there's another young person just joined them who's just gone over and . . . Oh dear, don't say he took himself over as well . . .'

'Yes,' said the woman, 'that's my nephew, Kevin. He took his own life three days ago.'

The horror grew. More and more names came through and the woman recognized them all, reeling off their sad stories one by one, 'Oh yes he took himself over, she did it . . .' Until in the end I was almost speechless. What tragedy some people suffer, I thought, and yet this lady's face was serene and she managed to smile.

'Well like you, Doris, I take one day at a time,' she said, 'there must be a reason for it.'

I had to admire such courage. What a marvellous attitude. She was absolutely right of course, but in the same situation I don't know if I would have had the strength just to trust and believe that everything happened for a reason.

There was great love and unselfishness that night. Later I got the name Maria.

'Who's Maria?' I asked.

'I am,' said an Italian woman walking down to the microphone.

I got her son back and as I was talking to him I felt something cool and knobbly put into my hand. It was a rosary.

'He's put a rosary into my hand,' I said, 'so I know you must have put one in with him.'

Maria broke down. 'That's it, it's all I wanted to

162

know,' she sobbed in relief, quite content to move aside and let someone else have a turn now she'd got the one piece of evidence that proved to her her son was still close.

The same unselfish attitude touched everyone. They held a raffle for a beautiful doll during the evening and later when I was having a cup of tea in one of the classrooms, the winner asked if she could come and see me. She came in, tears streaming down her face, the magnificent doll in her arms.

'Doris, my little girl's only sixteen months old, too young for this,' she said, 'I'd like you to have it for the Save the Children Fund.'

The doll was exquisite, all done up in silver organzine but, I thought, a child would sooner have a doll she can undress. So when we got home I asked a clever friend to make a set of clothes and underwear that could be taken off and put on again, so that I could give the doll to the bone marrow unit at Westminster Hospital for some frightened little girl to play with.

There were more lovely surprises at St Austell. When the demonstration was over, two little children came on stage carrying a giant £2,000 cheque between them, just like the giant pools cheques you see on television. They presented it to me for the Save the Children Fund, then off they went, only to return with Tracey, the little girl staggering under the weight of a huge box of Cornish goodies and Stephen the little boy, carrying a breakfast set of Cornish pottery. Gifts from Cornwall for me to keep.

Then a man stood up and said he'd written a poem specially for me. His name was Basil Thorne and he came on stage to read it. It went like this:

Cornwall's mystic and magical charms,
Welcome you Doris with wide open arms,
We need your gift to strengthen those,
Within whose breast, doubts still repose.

163

We wish to know more of the power from within,
That you can receive from our kith and kin,
We believe very strongly and know that it's true,
That Spirit transmits their thoughts through you.

Our gifts are many, varied and free,
All different branches of the very same tree,
We must all make the most of the gifts that we
    have,
And use them to strengthen the weak and the sad.

One thing is certain, we don't always choose,
The right road to take – our gifts best to use,
We hope that your visit will help in some way,
To clarify things for our people today.

And now dear Doris, let's hasten to say,
It's lovely to have you with us today,
We've waited so long so listen we pray,
We hope the next time you come here to stay.

Then he presented me with a copy, all beautifully
written on thick creamy yellow paper. But that wasn't
the end. When Basil left the stage two young girls,
Karen Retallick and Norma Arthur came on to sing me
a song they'd written and composed themselves. It
was a special welcome song and the chorus went:
'Welcome from us Cornish folk to the land of pasties
and cream.'

By the time they finished, my eyes were so full of
tears I could hardly see the stage. I felt quite overwhelmed. The journey had been long and tiring but
the love they'd shown me in St Austell made it worth
every mile.

And just as I was walking out of the hall, a man
leaned over from the audience and said, 'How about
the *Don Lane Show*, Doris?'

I stopped in surprise. The *Don Lane Show* was so
far from my thoughts I felt sure I'd misheard.

'I beg your pardon?'

'The *Don Lane Show*,' the man repeated, 'the last time I saw you Doris was in Australia!'

I couldn't help smiling. What a small world. I'd come all the way to Cornwall to be reminded of the day all the fuss began – when I appeared on the *Don Lane Show* in Australia.

When we got back to our hotel the manageress had seen that the lights were on in the villa, the table was laid up with cold meats and salad and there were hot water bottles warming our beds. It was the perfect end to a perfect evening.

To cap it all, the next morning as we were leaving, the rain actually stopped and the sun came out. The bay was all blue and glistening as we drove away and I could see what looked like little black and white penguins bobbing about in the water.

Penguins? I thought, In Cornwall! But when we got closer they turned out to be little lads in black and white wet suits surfing!

We seemed to spend a lot of time on the road that spring and I dread to think how many miles we covered. We crossed and recrossed from one end of the country to the other and as well as the charity evening in St Austell, I was asked to speak at a literary dinner in Yorkshire.

We drove up and up into the moors until our ears were popping and I hardly dared look out of the window because I'm scared of heights.

'When you said Yorkshire, Laurie,' I said as we passed another sheer drop, 'I thought you meant a town somewhere.'

'So did I,' said Laurie.

But we ended up at a beautiful old world hotel deep in the moors. It was a lovely place, all beams and great log fires and there was time for a nap in our rooms before dinner.

At seven forty-five we went downstairs to the bar where everybody was meeting and we couldn't believe our eyes. The people were crammed in, shoulder to shoulder and extra tables were being carried into the dining-room. How they squeezed so many people in I don't know, but Robbie who drives our Daimler was wedged in so tightly he could only use his left hand! He was able to trap a carrot or two as they went by he told us later, but that was about all!

Johnny Morris was the other guest that night. We'd expected him to tell some animal stories but instead he sang the *Floral Dance* which certainly made a change. You don't associate Johnny Morris with singing.

Then it was my turn. Earlier as I was getting ready I'd heard the name Cocklin and though I didn't know what the literary dinner people were going to make of me, I asked if there was anybody present who knew the name.

'Yes that's me,' called a woman in surprise. 'I'm Mrs Cocklin.'

She was there with her husband who apparently had come with the greatest reluctance.

'Well I'll go for an evening out,' he'd said, 'but it's a load of old balderdash.'

Well I was chatting away to Mrs Cocklin when suddenly a woman's voice interrupted us.

'Oh by the way,' I said, 'I've got a lady here called Lizzie and she wants your husband.'

The man beside her, a little flushed from the wine and the heat all those people had generated, stood up, a bemused expression on his face.

'I just don't believe this. I said to my wife on the way here, if there's any chance of my mother coming back she'd come back, but there isn't. And here you are getting through to her. Nobody ever called her Elizabeth. It was always Lizzie.'

We were under way. A boy called Ashley came back to his mother. Then there was a Mrs Turner.

'Who's Ronnie, living?' I asked.

'Ronnie's my husband,' she said in such a surprised

voice I think she suspected Ronnie of passing me a note under the table or something.

It went on and on and it was nearly midnight before we were able to slip away to our room. I'd hardly taken my shoes off though when there was a knock at the door. It was the organizer.

'I'm sorry Mrs Stokes but you're supposed to be signing books. There's a long queue.'

So back I went and signed books till one o'clock in the morning. It was the longest dinner I've ever had!

A month or two later there was another lovely trip in the diary, this time to Portsmouth. Unfortunately I was very tired by the time we got there – but it was my own fault.

The Portsmouth visit happened to coincide with the *Psychic News* dinner dance. Now as a rule, apart from work, John and I hardly ever go out. We do so much travelling and attend so many functions in the line of duty as it were, that we like to spend our free time flopping at home. The last thing we want to do on our nights off is climb into our fancy clothes and go out on the town!

The *Psychic News* dinner dance though is the one exception of the year. It's the chance to meet up with our old friends, have a good gossip and let our hair down if we feel like it and we never miss it. This year in particular was going to be fun I knew, because Russell Grant was going and Derek Jameson was guest of honour and would be making the speech and knowing Derek's sense of humour, it was bound to be hysterical.

Well we had a marvellous time. I danced every dance and we didn't leave till the end, even though we were driving straight down to Portsmouth afterwards. My feet were killing me by the time we came away. It was my own fault entirely, of course, but as I told the audience the next day, when handsome young men come and ask you to dance at my age, you have to get in when you can!

Had we been able to set off there and then though, it wouldn't have been too bad, but it was at that point I discovered I'd left my pills behind. My pills are vital. I have to take them every day of my life because my thyroid gland was removed after I was injured by a patient when I was a mental nurse.

For a moment we thought we'd have to go all the way back home to fetch them, but then Laurie had a brainwave.

'Let's call in at the hospital. They'll let you have some, Doris.'

The hospital was just round the corner and they said yes, it would be quite all right, but I would need to see the doctor. So in we went in all our finery, me in my long dress and John in his smart suit and we sat in casualty for half an hour. It was long past midnight by now but we were so exhilarated by the dancing we were wide awake.

At last the doctor called me in.

'Actually I didn't really need to see you,' she confessed, 'but I've heard you on the radio and on TV and I wanted to meet you!' But she organized the drugs for us and at last we were off.

Oh well, I thought, another one and a half hours and we'll be tucked up snug and warm in our hotel. Which just goes to show how wrong you can be even if you're psychic! Not far out of London we came upon a bad accident on the road and we sat there for over an hour while we waited for ambulances and breakdown lorries to clear it up.

Oh dear some poor soul's got it tonight, I thought. You couldn't grumble. You just sat there thankful to be safe.

We eventually got to our hotel at four in the morning. Almost staggering with tiredness John and I let ourselves into our room to be greeted by a great welcoming basket of fruit and a letter addressed to Doris Stokes.

'Heavens above who knows I'm here?' I said to John. 'We're only here two nights.'

But it wasn't a heartrending letter imploring me for

168

a sitting, it was just a little note from the Chief Accountant thanking me for the books because he'd enjoyed them so much.

As expected we paid for our adventurous night by feeling particularly sluggish when we got up. Well it serves you right, Doris, I told myself. If you will go dancing all night like an eighteen-year-old what do you expect! But as the show drew nearer it stopped being funny.

I just don't know how I'm going to do it, I thought as I went off reluctantly to get ready. But when I started to tune in, in the bathroom as I always do in the hope of a few scraps to get the ball rolling at the theatre, a little boy walked in. He was about ten years old, fairish, and he was wearing a t-shirt with writing across the front.

'Hello, love,' I said drying my face.

'Kittiwick,' said the boy, and, 'Sylvia,' and a bit later, just as he was going, 'Brent.'

I couldn't make out if it was a place or a name but when he vanished I put my head round the bathroom door and called John.

'Can you help me remember, love? It's for tonight. Kittiwick, Sylvia and Brent.'

'Kittiwick, Sylvia and Brent,' repeated John. 'It doesn't sound like much.'

'No I know, but it was a little boy and I bet his Mum's in the audience tonight.'

Driving to the theatre that evening we pulled up at traffic lights and a red car drew alongside us. There were four youngsters inside and when they noticed us, they started shouting 'Hello Doris!' and waving their tickets at us.

The lights changed, the red car shot ahead and suddenly in the back window appeared a big sheet of paper saying:

'We love you, Doris!' and still waving and shouting, the kids led us to the theatre.

After such a warm welcome I was surprised to find the theatre manager a little cool. I couldn't understand it. I'd been to Portsmouth before and everything had gone well then but this particular manager hadn't been there at the time so perhaps he didn't know. Or perhaps he was simply annoyed at having to work on a Sunday. Whatever it was I felt he didn't seem all that pleased to see us.

Fortunately the audience didn't seem to share his feelings. When I walked on stage they didn't just clap, they stamped their feet and cheered. What's more, Sylvia was in the audience and the meaning of the little boy's visit became clear.

Sylvia lived in Kittiwake Close, she'd lost her ten-year-old son, Matthew, and his friend was called Brent. I got Matthew back again when I tuned in and the whole tragic story came out.

Sylvia had been going shopping and Matthew begged to be allowed to stay behind to play with his friend. Some time after his mother had gone, Matthew decided he wanted something from the house, and impulsively tried to climb through one of the small open windows at the top of the main window.

'Oh I was so naughty. So naughty,' said Matthew, repentant now. Somehow he'd slipped with his head caught in the window and broke his neck.

'Mum's not been back home since,' Matthew told me, 'but she's got all my pictures up.'

I didn't understand how this could be, but Sylvia confirmed it was true.

'Oh yes. A friend went and fetched them for me,' she said.

When I came off after the first half the manager was a changed man. He put his arms round me and gave me a big hug.

'That was marvellous,' he said, 'the last time we had anyone like you here it was embarrassing and I thought tonight would be the same, but what a difference. That was marvellous.'

And out came the silver tea service for my intermission cup of tea and everything was all right. I was in.

170

The rest of the evening went just as well. Throughout I'd been rather puzzled because I kept hearing the name Daisy but no one claimed it. Then during question time a little old lady came up to the microphone to ask a question about her sister Maisie.

Instantly I got it.

'That wasn't Daisy, I was getting, it was Maisie!' I exclaimed and immediately Maisie was back.

'I came over with a brain tumour,' she said, 'and now my sister's got the same thing.'

The sister was worried about the suffering she might have to go through but Maisie soothed her fears.

'Don't worry, it's as easy as slipping on butter coming over here,' she assured her, 'and I will be there to take your hand.'

The little old lady's face lit up. 'I'm not worried now. Not if Maisie's with me.'

The other nice surprise was that Joan Scott Alan was in the audience, unknown to me. I'd never met Joan but I'd given a message to her daughter during a demonstration in Nottingham last year. I'd given the daughter Joan's full name, the fact that she nursed the mentally ill and that she wrote beautiful poetry inspired by the spirit people.

Her daughter Pauline was so impressed she phoned her mother the next day and Joan wrote to me enclosing a tape of some of her poems. They were certainly beautiful and I printed one of my favourites in my last book.

Somewhere in the back of my mind I suppose it had registered that Joan lived near Portsmouth but I hadn't heard from her for some time and I never gave her a thought when I walked on the stage. I was absolutely delighted though when a message came through for her and she walked to the microphone and we were able to meet for the first time.

'Joan they're telling me you've retired now from nursing,' I said.

'Yes, Doris, I have.'

'But you're still writing the poems.'

Joan smiled. 'Yes I am, in fact I've brought some with me tonight to give to you. There's a special one I've dedicated to you.'

But the spirit people weren't finished.

'They tell me you must concentrate on the poetry but forget the music,' I repeated. It seemed rather a shame because Joan had previously set her poems to music but perhaps she was using vital energy on the music when the important part of her work was the words.

'Oh, I see,' said Joan, perhaps a little disappointed.

Nevertheless afterwards she left me a whole sheaf of poems and as ever they were absolutely beautiful.

This is the one she dedicated to me:

The Interlude

My brief encounter on the earth
Was bitter sweet – I had to search
I could not bear the grief and pain
I knew I'd give but not in vain.

The sacrifice I had to make
To help this soul her path to take
The wretched pain the silent grief
So many souls through her would speak.

I made my journey to the earth
All alone she gave me birth
I clung in love against her breast
In sweet serenity to rest

Her mother love engulfed the air
She washed and tended me with care
No greater love could ever be given
To a tiny soul sent from heaven.

172

She proudly put me on display
My Gran would laugh – then walk away
You'll spoil that child she would often scold
Mum's reply was a tighter hold.

Her love emitted from her soul
The mother love you can't control
I knew the pain she'd have to bear
When I was taken from her care.

She sang me lullabies at night
I clung to her with all my might.
I knew the interlude was brief
Forgive me Mum – I kiss your feet.

For many months she walked alone
With heavy eyes and heart of stone
Her anguished soul cried out in pain
John Michael please come back again.

Her cries were heard her sorrows shared
The people here did really care
But they all knew that one day soon
The gifts she had would fully bloom.

I met her in her dreams at night
To show her that I was all right
I crept beside her, watched her sleep
Her lovely face made me weep.

Dear Mother I'm so proud of you
All the loving things you do
So many souls you comfort bring
The heavenly choirs for you do sing.

So please may I be forgiven
For leaving you to go to heaven
The Father's works we have to do
And some are the specially chosen few.

173

When your earthly job is done
You're more than welcome to my home
You'll have the time to stand and stare
And understand just what we shared.

Until that day dear friend, dear mother
I watch and guard you like no other
Your earthly life will always be
A path of love and serenity.

Before I go I feel so sad
For I have not included Dad
The part he plays and love he shares.
Is not forgotten over there.

My Mother you will always be
A true companion to me
The love you gave in my interlude
Is being repaid back to you

And now my story has been told
Go in peace till you are old
You have helped the Kingdom come
And I am proud to be your son.

I wish I could tell Joan how much that poem means to me. I read it over and over again till the tears streamed down my face. It's the story of the loss of my baby John Michael, told from John Michael's point of view and if I can live up to the words of that poem then I'll be very pleased with myself. Joan has captured perfectly the way I try to live my life, so that my family on the other side will not be ashamed of me when I arrive. I often fail of course but at least I try.

One of my other favourites in the batch she handed me shows great compassion for the parents of handicapped children:

A Parent's Lament

Ring out the bells
Aloud from the hills
A child is born
Our hearts are filled

With love and pride and joys untold
What perfect beauty to behold

We watch her grow
With hearts so full
Of love and caring
But she's no fool

The moment we both creep away
From that nice cradle where she lay
A cry rings out

An icy hand grips both our hearts
That cry is something quite apart
A different ring – what can it be?
Our little child is almost three

We watch her play
Why can't she walk?
All other children seem to talk.

With heavy hearts we take advice
And find this soul will pay the price
For we are told in gentle tones
This child can never be left alone.

Oh God our hearts cry out in pain
What did we do to upset you
That we should rear a child in vain?

The dear Lord heard our cry and said
Hush now, take your child to bed
Then listen to what I say – let me explain
These children are my precious gifts
It's not meant to bring you pain.

If you just stop and think it through
My special gift I've sent to you
To teach you simple things of life
And most of all she's saved from strife.

The world is such a greedy place
Where man fights man
And hate meets hate.

Our worldly goods we proudly show
But when we pass where do they go?
To be passed down?
And so it goes
NO that is mine NOT for Aunt Rose.

Have you heard all this before?
Well now I knock upon your door

My special gift to you I give
That you may learn from her to live.

A life that's full and very sweet
With face upturned sat at your feet
With love that melts the hardest heart
Take this child set apart
Watch her try to talk and sing
And then, thank God for everything.

Jean's poems are always a great joy to read and they
brought a lovely evening to a close for me. As the
demonstration ended the audience went mad. There
was so much clapping and stamping and waving of

handkerchiefs they almost pulled me off the stage. I looked up at the swaying rows of cheering faces, all 2,000 of them, and it didn't matter how fagged out I'd been earlier I knew I was doing the right thing. I was on the right track, doing the work I'd been made for.

Chapter Twelve

I couldn't believe my eyes when I opened the paper.
BATTLE OF THE PSYCHIC SUPERSTARS said the
giant headline strung across two pages and beneath it
was a report of demonstrations given by myself and
medium Doris Collins as if we were arch rivals fighting
for supremacy.

It was annoying because it's so untrue. Doris Collins
and I have known each other for years. We once even
shared the *Psychic News* award for Spiritualist of the
Year. Doris is a very good medium and I respect her.
Our styles are different just as any two people working
in the same field will bring their own different person-
alities to the job, but there's certainly no need for us to
'battle'. There's more than enough work around to
keep us, and goodness knows how many other mediums as well, fully occupied for the rest of our lives.

More than anything the story was a disappointment.
The reporter had come along to a public meeting at
Fairfield Halls, Croydon and we'd had some marvellous
evidence. I got two lots of twins back including a pair
who'd gone over after a premature birth. The poor
mother had gone into labour unexpectedly on holiday
in Greece and she'd lost both babies.

'You're grieving, love, because you left them in
Greece,' I said. 'You came home and you left your
babies there.'

'That's right,' she sobbed.

'Well, you didn't leave them, love, because they're
here with you now. Two little girls and I'm getting the
names Amy and Donna.'

'That's what I called them!' she cried and her whole
face became radiant.

Not long afterwards I heard the name Stephen.

178

'I want a little boy named Stephen,' I said. 'Our side of life.'

And to my surprise a little boy, no more than eight or nine years old came racing down to the stage.

'I'm Stephen,' he cried, while behind him, his mother struggled to catch up.

It was a young man I was talking to and since the woman didn't look old enough to have a grown up son I felt sure it must be Stephen's father.

'It's a man's voice, love,' I told her, 'a young voice.'

'Yes, that's right. I lost my husband when Stephen was only six months old,' she said.

'Does my Daddy know me, does my Daddy know I'm here?' asked Stephen bouncing up and down.

'Yes he does, darling,' I assured him and to prove it his father said, 'Tell him I know about Simon. He's a big bully.'

'Yes he is,' Stephen agreed. 'Actually he gave me a black eye last week.'

'Well stand up to him, son,' said his father, 'and if you can't hit him, kick him. You only have to stand up to a bully once.'

Stephen stood there taking it all in, his head on one side. He was a dear little soul, very old-fashioned and well spoken.

'He likes Tim, though,' the father went on.

'Do you know a Timothy?' I asked. 'Your father says you get on well with him.'

'Oh yes he's a good chap,' said Stephen.

Then the father began to talk about other members of the family. He mentioned Kitty, but before Stephen's mother could answer Stephen jumped in again. 'He's talking about Auntie Kit, Mummy.'

'Kitty's very good to him,' said the father.

'Well actually I don't see her very often,' said Stephen 'but when I do see her she's very good to me.'

At the end of the message I said to Stephen, 'Because it's a very special occasion because you've never seen your Daddy, I'm going to give you the big centre piece of flowers to take home. Your Daddy tells me your Mummy's got a car so she'll be able to manage it.'

So Stephen came up on to the stage and staggered off with the flower arrangement that was nearly as big as he was.

I thought that was last I'd seen of Stephen but after the demonstration was finished, when I was relaxing in the dressing-room, there came a knock on the door. It was Stephen bringing me a single flower from the spray.

'This is to tell you I love you,' he said.

I put my arms round him. 'And I love you too,' I said. And suddenly there was a great flash and I looked up to find the photographer for the newspaper was still there, taking pictures.

'There's a photographer taking pictures of us,' Stephen whispered.

'Yes I know,' I said, 'we're going to be in the *Sunday Mirror*.'

Stephen's eyes widened. 'Oh really. Are we? How spiffing!'

He was thrilled by the idea and so looking forward to the day the paper came out. I too waited eagerly to see the pictures of the two of us and the single flower.

But when the day came there was no mention of Stephen and no photograph. Instead just this battle of the psychic superstars nonsense. It was such a shame and I could imagine how disappointed Stephen must have been.

Mind you, to be fair, the newspapers are mostly very kind to me and I've had some lovely write ups. It's odd to see yourself as others see you and some of the descriptions make me laugh. John Slim from the *Birmingham Evening Post*, was very nice and he had an amusing turn of phrase . . .

'She emits a sudden, chesty laugh which hits her hotel room like a quick half hundred weight of bucketed gravel . . .' he wrote, 'Doris Stokes . . . is a motherly mixture of humility and good humour who carries her ample poundage with the implacability of a benevolent battleship . . .'

John and I were in stitches over that one.

'When people start describing you as a battleship, it really is time to go on a diet!' I sighed.

One interview I'd been anxious about was with Jean Rook of the *Daily Express*. She'd seemed very friendly on the phone but I'd heard she can be very sharp about people in print, and I couldn't imagine what she'd say about me. If you wanted to I suppose it would be quite easy to do a mickey-taking piece about spooks and ghosties.

Jean had a very tight schedule and what with one thing and another she ended up coming to interview me in my hospital bed. I'd had to go into hospital for a couple of days for tests – as I have to regularly since I had cancer and Jean obviously didn't think much of my chances because she wrote afterwards . . .

'Mrs Stokes was lying in bed, pale as her cream satin négligée. And looking too close for my comfort to the Threshold she professes to cross as casually as most of us move from room to room.'

The one thing Jean didn't want was a sitting. She put up a great barrier and was most emphatic that she didn't want to talk to anyone. It was strictly an interview. Nevertheless she was a great friend of Diana Dors and while she was there Diana popped in.

'Jean's very good at tennis you know,' she said.

That shook Jean a bit I think. It turned out that Diana had never known Jean played tennis and in fact has become so keen on the game that she's having a tennis court built at her home.

After that I stuck mainly to the questions, but sometimes things happened that I couldn't help. Jean stayed a long time and she even waited while I went off for one particular test. On the way back to the ward I sensed Diana with me.

'Oh Di – could you go and look at the results for

me?' I asked because this was the test I'd been worried about.

She zipped off and a few moments later she was back. 'It's all right, kid. You're clear,' she said.

Back in my room I smiled at Jean. 'It's all right. I can relax and have a cup of tea now. I'm clear. Diana's just told me.'

Jean looked rather doubtful and made no comment but later on the doctor looked in.

'It's all right, doctor, I know the results already,' I told him cheerfully, 'I'm clear.'

He grinned. 'Yes you are.'

Then just as she was leaving, I did it again. Earlier I'd heard the name Eileen, and it came back suddenly connected with a man who passed very quickly with a heart attack.

It meant nothing to Jean, but the photographer turned pale.

'My mother's name is Eileen and my father died of a heart attack seven months ago,' he said shakily.

'Well tell your Mum your Dad's fine now, love,' I told him.

After that I couldn't think what Jean would write and I was a bit jittery until the paper came out. But I needn't have worried.

This is what she wrote:

Medium rare

I make a pig's ear of it when the spirits are all trying to talk to me at once, says Doris Stokes

Even for sceptics, Mrs Doris Stokes is the ultimate psychic phenomenon.

Few people in this world – even with one foot in the next – can pack the London Palladium with its capacity

2,000 audience, plus standing room. And not a dry eye in the sobbing, cheering, rapturous house.

Mrs Stokes is a built-in telephone exchange to the Other World. She claims to speak to the dead. She plugs them in to their living relatives. Takes messages from the Great Unknown like an answering service.

For grieving multitudes, this 65-year-old spiritualist is the antidote to death's sting. She is Victory, in a £100 beaded evening dress, over the grave.

Whether or not you believe a word she claims the dead tell her, her delivery is stunning. She dismisses all candlelit hocus and gloomy pocus. All the audience gets is a well-lit, plump, grey, permed housewife, talking on an imaginary phone to their loved ones who are not lost.

She gives the distraught parents of a 17-year-old, who died of a heart attack, all the chat they want to hear: – 'Change that coloured photograph you keep of him, lovey – he doesn't like it, he says his hair doesn't look right.'

Stokes is the thoroughly modern medium. She will appear for three Sunday Nights at the Palladium this summer – already sold out.

Comfort

Even Frankie Goes to Hollywood causes no more stampede for tickets than Doris Goes to the Other Side and Back.

When we met last week in London's Guy's Hospital for a rare 'private sitting', Mrs Stokes was lying in bed, pale as her cream satin negligee. And looking too close for my comfort to the Threshold she professes to cross as casually as most of us move from room to room.

She has survived 13 cancer operations. 'When I told Dick Emery I'd lost a breast, my thyroid, my womb, a large chunk of intestine and my right ovary, he joked: "Doris, they want you over the Other Side but you've too much work to do so they're taking you across bit by bit".'

183

She added: 'I'm not worried about today's tests. I took Diana Dors down to the X-ray unit with me, and she's already checked on the results and told me I'm clear. So we can have a ciggy now, and relax,' she said, lighting her Menthol.

Did Mrs Stokes know it was the eve of the anniversary of Diana Dors' own death from cancer? (my first slip – don't feed the medium information). Did she know I'd come to ask her to raise Diana (slip two – don't show the medium your hand and give her something to grasp at).

Right out of the blue she claims is heaven, Mrs Stokes fixed me with her unnaturally huge, cloud-grey eyes and said: 'Diana says you're a terrifically good tennis player.'

Diana, though the closest friend in life, didn't even know I played tennis. And nobody but my family and the building firm knows I've just paid a deposit on a hard tennis court.

Game to Miss Dors and Mrs Stokes.

May I see Diana? 'No and I can't,' said the clairaudient (as opposed to voyant) who can only hear the dead. 'I can hear her in this room as clearly as the evening she died, when I didn't even know she was in hospital.'

How did Di take the news of her death?

'She was angry when she first got there, like Noele Gordon two weeks ago – they'd fought so hard to stay down here. Diana was angry too when Alan committed suicide (Diana Dors's husband Alan Lake shot himself five months after her death).

Laughed

'They came together to me and she told me how he did it – put the shotgun between his knees and balanced it under his chin. She kept saying: "How could you leave our baby? (their son Jason, now 16). Why didn't you have the guts to stay with him?" You know how straight out with everything she was.

184

'When he told her "I was like a bird without wings without you it was hopeless," she forgave him everything.'

What do you wear on the Other Side? 'Anything you fancy. You certainly don't wear wings or a white sheet and go "oooh!" and frighten folk to death.'

'To WHAT?' I said cunningly. A slip of the psyche, laughed this Grantham-born daughter of a Romany who 'lived across the road from the Prime Minister.'

'Margaret got awfully upset one night because she heard some kids outside church whisper: "There goes Creeping Jesus" – she thought they meant her Dad, who was a lay preacher. I told her not to worry, as they meant me.

'I worried though. I tried to hide what I could hear *and* see – because when I was young I could do both. I can still see spirit children – because I've lost four and love them so much.'

When her longest surviving child, John Michael, died at five months, she and her healer husband, John, accepted her unwanted gift. 'I really DIDN'T want to know, I wanted to be normal and ordinary. Sometimes I still tell the spirits to "push off" if they start whispering to me at a party.'

Do the blue lights which is all she can see of the spirits flickering above her audience, ever glow angry?

'Oh, they do, dear, they tell me to "get on with it, woman" when I get my wires crossed, and I do make mistakes when they're all trying to talk at once,' said the psychic whose greatest strength is admitting weakness, even to desperate parents, with: 'No, I'm guessing. Don't take that. I'm making a pig's ear, don't believe what I'm saying.'

'And they sometimes get cross with This Side. The nastiest case I had was a widow all in black, sobbing "that's my husband Jim, he only passed over last week." and Jim yelling in my other ear: "The bloody hypocrite, she's sitting next to the boyfriend she was carrying on with when I was in hospital." '

Chatting

Six years ago, she began to raise huge audiences from her soirees with the spirits and massive money from her four autobiographical books. 'I like the money. I just bought a new house,' she said.

I grabbed at her grasping flesh. Nothing materialized but a modest £50,000 semi-detached.

Her much talked-about limousine is hired: 'Because I have to stretch out my body to ease the pains.' Her £1,000 cut of an expensively staged Evening with Doris Stokes goes to charity.

'Who's Pepe?' she said. 'There's a dog barking!' 'Peri,' I said. My long-lost poodle, dead 15 years. 'No not dead, dear, jumping about all over the place.'

She had now been chatting, almost non-stop, for two hours. And not always to me and the photographer, alone with her in the room.

'Who's Eileen?' she'd asked, an hour before. Now she said: 'I've got someone here who died very suddenly of a heart attack. He's connected with the Eileen I asked about earlier.'

My photographer, Barry Gomer's father, died of a heart attack seven months ago. His mother's name is Eileen. Even I didn't know until 10 minutes before we left the office, which photographer would be going with me. Or his mother's name.

'Well, tell your mother he's fine, lovely,' she said There was a long silence. For startled Barry it wasn't dead.

My spirits sank. Which is where I intended them to remain. 'You've a barrier built up against me, lovey,' said the woman who, in one of her rare sightings, alleges she watched Tommy Cooper rise from his body when he slumped, dying, on live TV.

I have an electrified fence, I thought silently (maybe she reads your mind, like a palm). When my beloved father died, 16 years ago, he made me swear on everything but the Bible I'd never try to contact him.

'Why do I get a conservatory?' she suddenly said.

She knew she'd cracked it. How many journalists have a 'conservatory' as opposed to a greenhouse, or cloche?

And why did my mother pick this week, after 40 years in our Yorkshire family home, to have my father's treasured, but now disintegrating Victorian conservatory restored?

'I'm sure I could make contact at a sitting at home,' beamed Mrs Stokes, now lit up like the sun shining through glass, brightly. 'But I'm only the bridge, I can't do it if you're not willing and he's not willing.'

'We're not,' I said, speaking up before Pa weakened and had a word with Mrs Stokes.

I'd prefer to speak to him quietly, myself. And much as I still adore him, at some later date.

Daily Express
Monday May 6 1985

Yes, generally I can't complain. The papers have been very fair with me. Only one article has made me really angry and that wasn't about me at all. It was about Diana Dors and Alan Lake. It was a very nasty piece full of insinuations that Diana and Alan didn't love each other. That Alan was off with other women and Diana was having an affair in the last year of her life.

I was furious when I read it. How could they say such terrible things about two lovely people who weren't here to defend themselves. And what about Jason? Hadn't he suffered enough without reading such terrible things about his parents?

The more I thought about it the angrier I became. I couldn't believe it. Diana was far too ill in the last year of her life to be interested in an affair and as for Alan – he was a flirt, that's the way he was made, but he didn't mean anything by it. He worshipped Diana.

I got so upset by the whole thing that I couldn't eat

187

for two days and in the end Ramanov gave me a talking to.

'Child, this won't do,' he said sternly. 'You are wasting your energy and making yourself ill. You have work to do and others that depend on you.'

He was right, of course, but then Ramanov always is.

He has been spending quite a lot of time with me lately. We've been going through a difficult patch with Terry and though the crowds wouldn't think it from my smiling face on stage, life at home has been very hard at times.

Last year Terry had a dreadful accident. He could have been killed but he was lucky and escaped with severe concussion. He seemed to get over it very well, but then just after Christmas he began to look ill. He developed violent headaches, he had no energy and suddenly for no reason, he'd fly into terrible tempers.

There were quite a few unhappy scenes at home before we discovered the problem. The shock of the accident had brought on sugar diabetes and his body was completely out of balance. In the meantime though, my nerves got very bad and I sometimes fled to my room in tears. But I wasn't alone. Ramanov was always there.

'Why does this have to happen now?' I sobbed one night. 'Just when everything's lovely and we've got this beautiful house. Why does it have to be spoiled?'

'I never promised you sunshine all the way did I?' said Ramanov. 'Learn from it. There are many lessons here.'

Well I tried and I think I've learned to be more tolerant. I've tried to understand why Terry gets these violent moods and bit by bit we've guided him through. As long as he sticks to his diet he should be all right.

I don't want it to sound as if Ramanov runs my life for me because he doesn't. The spirit world won't do that. If you have a problem you have to try to solve it yourself, but if you've tried everything you can think of and nothing's worked, then a prayer to the spirit world will usually be answered.

Many times I've turned to Ramanov in despair and said it's no good, I've tried and tried and I'm at my wits' end. Can you help? And the next morning I've woken up with a new idea in my mind that turns out to be the solution to the problem. But you do have to help yourself. It's no good saying 'I need £1,000. Please God work a miracle.' They will only help if they can see you've genuinely done your best.

Mind you, although he doesn't run my life, Ramanov certainly lets me know if I'm straying from the path. If I start to get too materialistic he steers me back and shows me where I'm going wrong.

Now I have got a little money for the first time in my life it would be so easy to go wrong. I used to be a great idealist. I used to say that material things don't matter – and they don't really – but in spite of that, it is nice to have a beautiful bedroom to relax in and a lovely house to come home to and I'm not going to pretend it's not.

I'd be telling a lie if I didn't say it's nice to have a house with nice gardens and to be able to look out of the window and say this belongs to us.

People at the mobile home park say they can't understand it. Why on earth are we saddling ourselves with all this at our ages. But I say, you've already had it love. You've had your beautiful house, you know what it's like. I never have. I've always lived in ex-servicemen's flats or prefabs or rented houses where I've had to ask permission to hold sittings or have people in. Now I can do what I like. Maybe it's late in life but at least I can say I've done it.

One thing I thought was lovely was that when the article about my house appeared in *Woman's Own*, I didn't have one letter begrudging my good fortune. Everybody wrote to say how beautiful it was and that I deserved it. I think I do too! I've worked very hard

189

and I've known what it's like not to have two pennies to rub together. I think I deserve a little comfort now.

Of course it's no good being the richest body in the cemetery, as Ramanov keeps reminding me, so I do a lot of charity appearances and give away as much as I can and it gives me great pleasure to do so. It's so nice to be able to help people out in a practical way at last.

I do get tired and fed up with work at times and wonder if I'm mad gallivanting around the country at my age, but Ramanov finds lessons for me in the smallest things.

One day in early spring the builders cleared away a pile of rubbish beside the drive of our house and when I went to look I saw a group of tiny crocuses that had been buried by the bricks. They were bruised and battered but they'd struggled up through all the rubbish and were flowering bravely. And as I admired them I heard Ramanov's voice in my ear.

'See what I've been telling you for so long,' he said. 'As long as you keep the spark alive, no matter how bruised and battered you may be you can survive, just as these fragile little flowers have managed to struggle through the bricks to give beauty to the world.'

His words often come back to me when I'm moaning about being tired, and also when I'm talking to someone who is stricken by grief. The human spirit is battered and bruised by grief just as the crocuses were battered by bricks, yet if we can just keep that spark of love alive we'll come through it. And you know grief isn't a bad thing. It's God's healing gift to us, because it enables us to cry. Without crying the bitterness would stay inside and make you ill.

I know it's easy for me to say, but truly no one can escape grief – not even a medium who knows that loved ones live on and talks to them every day. The tears flow because you can't touch them any more. It's the physical presence we miss.

Although I know with certainty that there's another world, if anything happened to John I would go through exactly the same thing. I would weep and weep because I couldn't put my arms round him any more. That's grief and nobody can bear that cross for us. But if we know that God or our guide is there to hold our hand, we can get through it.

Ramanov comes along at the most unlikely moments. On May 8th 1985 we were celebrating the 40th anniversary of VE day and it was an extra special occasion for John and I because it was also the day he came home from the prisoner-of-war camp. He got a beautiful new leather jacket out of that!

Anyway there we were toasting each other in tea, when Ramanov interrupted.

'This is all very well,' he said, 'but while you are celebrating peace, there are wars going on all over the world. Until you learn to live as brothers and love one another you won't have peace.'

It made me stop and think. I mean people are always saying, if there is a spirit world why don't they do more to stop wars and violence, but my Mum and Dad couldn't run the country when they lived here, so why should they be able to run the country now, just because they've been to the spirit world. And after all, it's the people here now, who're making wars.

As Ramanov's said before. 'God gave you a beautiful world to live in and look what you're doing with it.'

It's no good us complaining. We've made the problems and we must solve them.

When I came back from St Austell I brought a poster with me which reads: 'Any act of kindness no matter how small, is never wasted!' and I've got it up on my wall. It's so true. If everyone followed that advice, the small acts of kindness would lead to greater acts of kindness and we'd be well on the way towards loving each other.

I know that it is true – just as the reverse is true. Small acts of unkindness can have a ripple effect and do far more damage than the original mean act.

I remember doing a demonstration at SAGB not long

ago and as soon as I walked onto the stage I could feel there was something wrong. Well it was a terrible night. I gave the wrong messages to the wrong people and I couldn't understand it. I've not had a night as bad as that for years.

This happened about the time we were having difficulty with Terry and I wondered if the traumas at home might be affecting me. Whatever it was, I knew I'd been dreadful and I apologized to the people there. They were very sweet and said it was fine, but I knew they were just being kind. It was not fine and I knew it.

Then two days later I had a note from a woman who'd been in the audience. She said how sorry she was that I was unhappy with the evening. We weren't hostile to you, it was the man on the door, she said. Apparently the doors had opened at five-forty-five even though the demonstration didn't start till seven and this man was shouting at people and telling them to shut-up and refusing to let them leave their seats to go to the loo or get a drink. Naturally they didn't like it, the hostility and anger built up and the evening was spoiled for everyone.

That one small act of unkindness ruined things for over one hundred and fifty people and many of them probably lost the chance of making contact with loved ones – a chance they'd been waiting for for months.

I've been doing a lot of public demonstrations lately and at most of them, I'm happy to say, the atmosphere's been marvellous. It makes such a difference. It's the love in the air that brings the spirit people close and the more love that's generated, the more contacts we get.

Some extraordinary things have come through. One night at Woolwich I was talking to a mother on the other side who was trying to comfort her husband and daughter who were grief stricken. She gave me a number of names and family details and then the

192

daughter explained how they came to be attending the meeting that night.

Her mother had been to see me last year at a demonstration in London and had obviously been impressed.

'The Saturday before she died, she said if I'm going to come back through anybody it will be Doris Stokes,' said the daughter. 'She made me promise to buy tickets for this show and to come with Dad.'

'We bought the tickets for her,' said the bemused father, 'and she's come.'

On a lighter note, I was talking to a young boy who'd been killed in an accident. He was chatting away to his sister who was quite happy and regarded it all as perfectly natural.

'And there was a Mr Barns or Burns,' said the boy, 'he was a right pig.'

The sister laughed, 'Oh that'll be the coroner. Yes he was!'

But his next words were drowned out by the squawking of a parrot.

'Good boy Joey. Good boy Joey. Who's a pretty boy then?' it screeched and I couldn't hear a word anybody else was saying.

'Could you keep the parrot quite a minute?' I begged the spirit people. Then I turned to the audience.

'Does anyone recognize a parrot called Joey?'

A young girl came forward at once. 'It's my mother's parrot.'

'Well she's brought it back with her, love.'

'Have a Guinness, have a Guinness,' muttered the parrot into my ear and I burst out laughing.

'Oh they never taught him to say that! He's saying have Guinness, have a Guinness!'

The girl nodded. 'That's right. Dad used to come in drunk and that's what the parrot would say.'

The audience, of course, loved it.

I must say my theatre visits have been much more enjoyable for me lately because of a marvellous shop I heard about in Forest Hill, London. Some years ago, as I tell everybody, I had a masectomy and until you have something like that you don't realize the problems it causes.

For instance, you're like a bird with one wing, particularly when you're my size and it's very easy to over balance if you're not careful because your weight is no longer evenly distributed. You have to think twice about all kinds of everyday things, like climbing into the bath. Climb in from the wrong side and you're likely to go flying – as I did a few months ago. To make matters worse we didn't have any grab bars on the sides of our bath, so I couldn't get out again. I just lay there with my legs in the air not sure whether to laugh or cry!

Going on stage was another problem. The false boob they'd given me at the hospital weighed a ton and was very hot to wear, particularly under spotlights. When I got home my muscles would be aching and I found I'd perspired so much it was soaking wet.

I'd more or less resigned myself to the fact that I'd got to learn to live with it, when someone told me about this girl in Forest Hill who was going to have to close down her shop because she couldn't make a living wage. Apparently she stocked special bras for ladies like me and she has special lambswool pads to go inside them.

She sounded just the person I was looking for and I discovered she runs a wonderful service as well. Sometimes she tries on as many as seventy bras to make sure she gets the fit absolutely right. She measured every little part of me and if it fitted in one place and not another, she'd take it off and try another. She spent ages, altering a piece here and a piece there. What a difference from the hospital where they simply put a tape measure round you and give you a bra, a bag and a piece of foam filled stuff to put inside, and that's it.

What's more this girl doesn't charge for the service,

only for the articles she sells. And when any of her ladies are going to a wedding or a special function, they take all their clothes to the shop, dress, shoes and everything and they try it all on with the bra to make sure it looks right.

Now that's what I call doing God's work and it'll be a tragedy if she has to give it up for lack of money.

Chapter Thirteen

'Doris,' said the young man at the microphone, 'just before my grandad died seven years ago, we had a blazing row. I told him to drop dead. And he did. It's been playing on my mind ever since. Do you think he blames me?'

It was question time. The short spot that opens the second half of my public demonstrations, and this lad had obviously been waiting all evening to ask the question that had been worrying him for seven years.

'Oh you poor soul,' I said. 'Of course he wouldn't blame you. He wouldn't bear any malice. We all say it when we're young don't we. He's just come through and he says, "I was a bit of a nagger." But he's watched over you ever since and he says you've been right down on the floor and he's picked you up and you're doing all right now. That row doesn't make a bit of difference. He still loves you.'

I get asked all sorts of things at question time but the same subjects do occur again and again, so I thought it might be helpful to collect a few examples of questions and answers from recent demonstrations. These are the sort of things people want to know:

Q. My friend's still got her Dad's ashes and she doesn't know where she should put them. What should she do?

A. We've been asked some rum things before! He says, 'I don't care a damn, love, I'm here.' If it'll make you happy I think he liked rivers, you could spread them on water. But let him go free with love and he will come back with love.

Q. My question is about senility. If people are senile before they pass, do they remember what happened to them when they get to the other side?

A. No, because they are not responsible for their actions. When they get to the other side they go into hospital and are nursed back with love. They don't remember the details of their passing. When they come back they usually say: 'I got very difficult towards the end.'

Q. If a murderer goes on to a different plane on the other side what happens to someone who commits suicide?

A. They are sick in the mind so they go into a special hospital where they are nursed until they're well. The person you're talking about was in a car wasn't he love?

Q. Yes

A. He's here and he just told me: 'I was in the car under some trees and I was found,' he said. He'd had words with someone and wanted to frighten them.

A. Well he's here now love and he's better. He's fine now. He's not in hellfire or anything like that.

Q. My little girl died when she was two. Who looks after her? Does she still play?

A. Yes. She's happy, love. They don't let anything hurt the spirit children. They even keep them away from our grief. A spirit mother looks after them. You have a grandmother over there and she is looking after your little girl. When there are no close relatives on the other side a girl who's gone over without knowing the joys of motherhood will be given the child to look after.

Q. Is it possible to see someone if they have died? I did several times and I was told I was imagining it. I think I upset him because I told him I couldn't take any more and I haven't seen him since. Did I do the wrong thing?

A. If it was wrong, love, they'd have left me years ago because when I was young I used to get so fed up with the spirit people I used to say, oh push off – leave me alone. I think they are giving you time to adjust and if you have psychic ability you must use it, love. If it happens again say: Hello, how are you doing?

Q. My friend lost her husband in 1983. He died from a rare disease. Now they want to open him up. Is it the right thing to do?

A. He's just come in. I think it was something to do with the brain wasn't it because he says, 'I went like a baby'.

Q. Yes that's right.

A. He says it doesn't matter a bit what they do with his body and if it will help someone else let them get on with it.

Q. I lost my little boy about two years ago. I moved from that flat but people say the little girl who moved in keeps pointing when there's nothing there and things are being moved. Could it be my little boy?

A. Yes. The little girl will see him. Children are psychic until ten or eleven. He just wanders in and out to see what's happening in his old home.

Q. Last year my sister went over. Just before she died she had a row with my brother and we wonder whether she's forgiven him.

A. Of course she has. She went very tragically, very quickly didn't she? It was a virus and it was all over in 48 hours she tells me. Don't cry she says because she's all right and of course she doesn't bear any malice. We all fall out now and then but it doesn't mean anything.

Q. You seem to pick up people who haven't passed long ago. Does that mean it's harder for people to come back if they passed a long time ago?

A. It's not harder love it's just that when someone has just passed their relatives are still grieving and they want to reassure them. They stay close to comfort them. But the other night I had a girl whose mother passed over when she was three and she came back to talk to her daughter twenty-seven years on!

Q. If you carry a kidney donor card and leave parts of your body to someone on earth, does it hinder your progression into spirit?

A. Oh no, love. Blimey I hope they've got my parts parcelled and labelled! I've had so many bits and pieces taken away, love. Whether I'll be any good to anyone now I don't know but John and I have put in our will that anything that can be used, can be used. It doesn't make any difference to us over there. My mother only had one eye. She lost it at birth but when I saw my mother on the other side I couldn't understand what was different about her at first – then I realized she had two eyes.
They can put me in the dustbin when I've gone for all the difference it'll make to me. I'll be away.

Q. You never seem to talk to foreign people in public meetings why's that?

A. I do. The other night I had a woman from Cyprus, but I agree I talk to more British people in public demonstrations. I think it's because I have trouble getting my name round foreign names and it takes up so much time, it's better to save them for private sittings when I have longer.

Q. If a child is not born on earth what age does it grow up to in the spirit world?

A. The age it should have been had it lived here. It will grow up and be brought back to see its mother and when she goes over she will recognize him or her immediately, even though she never saw her child on earth.

Q. If you lose a baby what happens when the person looking after it gets too old to look after it?

A. They don't, love. There's always someone there to take care of them and when you've reached the age you were meant to reach you don't grow any older.

Q. I was waiting to adopt a baby when my nan passed over. Does she know I've got my son now?

A. Of course she does. She comes to see you regularly.

Q. The evening my grandmother died I was in the bedroom and she said there was someone else in the room and she didn't want them there. Who was it?

A. Someone from the spirit world come to get her. The minute you see that you know you're about to pop your clogs! Your gran probably would say take him away, because she didn't want to go just then.

Q. If you have more than one husband, who do you end up with?

A. If you loved them both equally you'd go to both because there is no jealousy. But if you didn't get on on earth you probably wouldn't want to see each other again so you wouldn't. You go where the love is.

Q. How do you develop psychic power?

A. Everyone has a psychic spark but in some it's stronger than in others. Sometimes it is inherited and sometimes you get interested in psychic things and it just happens. Join a good developing circle — you'll hear of one through your nearest spiritualist church. Or if that doesn't suit you sit with two or three friends in love and harmony and offer yourself in service.

Q. If you have an animal put down, are you held responsible even if it was for the good of the animal?

A. No, love. I hope someone would do the same for me if I was suffering and never going to get well. But animals live on too and they are fit and healthy on the other side. You will meet your pets again.

Q. Do they celebrate birthdays on the other side.

A. Yes. They are lucky. They have two celebrations, the day they were born on earth and the day they arrived in the spirit world.

Q. Can I put in a request now to work with animals over there?

A. Oh yes, love. There are always poor animals that are put down because they're unwanted or are killed in accidents and they are nursed back on the other side too. They tell me you've got a dog called Sammy now.

Q. Yes and I love him to bits!

Q. If they watch you from the other side, do they come into the room or do they watch you from somewhere else?

A. Are you worried about your privacy, love? There wouldn't be any babies born if everyone thought like that. No, they respect our privacy. They come when you send out love. If you think, isn't this lovely I wish so and so could be here to see it – they come.

Q. If we are all here to learn, what have the people in Ethiopia got to learn?

A. I'm afraid I can't answer that, love. I've often wondered myself. It's the people at the top who're to blame. But the rest of us can learn from the suffering people in Ethiopia. Look at Bob Geldoff. He went there and was touched by what he saw. It will have changed him for the better.

Q. Have we all got a spirit guide?
A. Yes, every single one of us. Someone on the other side volunteers to give up their progression in the spirit world to guide us even before our bodies are conceived. They are waiting and our spirit is waiting to come to earth and when we go back the guide goes back. You might call it your conscience or your instinct or a hunch, but it is your spirit guide trying to lead you onto the right path.

Q. I lost my daughter last year and I want to know if I live to be ninety, will she still be there when I go over or will she have gone on?
A. No darling it takes hundreds of years. It doesn't matter how old you are she'll still know you are her mother. It doesn't matter how long we have to wait, we'll see our kids again. The love link is eternal.

Q. I have been grieving badly for eleven months now and I wonder if that grief will stop the person from progressing in the spirit world?
A. Well yes, I'm sorry to say it'll make it more difficult. You have to let them go free with love so that they can come back with love. We all have to go through a grieving period, but it makes them sad to see us unhappy.

Q. Is healing hereditary?
A. Well I inherited my gift from my father who was a Romany Gypsy so I should think healing might be inherited too. You only have to want to help people and if the gift is there, it will come.

202

Q. My mum didn't have a very happy life but I have a very very happy life and I want to share it with her a bit more but I'm frightened.

A. Well it scared me at first, love, but really there's nothing to be afraid of. It's as natural as breathing. Your mum will be close to you, just say hello to her and put a flower by her picture with your love.

Q. I lost five relatives recently and I wonder if they are together. Also does it hurt my dad because I love him so much?

A. They will be together and it hurts your dad to see you unhappy. You can't live with your daddy in the spirit world can you, love? You've got your own life to lead and your own family to think of. You mustn't send all your love with your daddy. He's happy in his new life but your grief is making him sad.

As you can see, the questions come in all shapes and sizes and every question time is slightly different but these are the types of questions I'm most often asked. Perhaps yours is amongst them.

Chapter Fourteen

The other day I was going through the mail as I do first thing every morning when I shook one envelope and out fell a faded snapshot. People often send me pictures of their spirit children for my wall, but I knew immediately that this was something different. It was old and blurry, not a bit like the glossy colour photographs we take today.

Curiously I picked up the magnifying glass to have a good look and suddenly the face of my dear old Mum leapt out at me. I gazed at the picture in delight. It showed three ladies dressed in the style of the twenties or thirties walking along a street in Skegness and I knew them all; Winifred Webb, Florrie Hodson and Mum. Mum and two of her friends were obviously enjoying a holiday, or possibly a day trip at our nearest seaside resort.

People often ask me why I've printed pictures of my father in previous books but not my mother. Well it's not that I loved mum any less – it's just that there are hardly any pictures of her in existence. You see Mum had only one eye, she lost the other at birth during a forceps delivery and she went through life wearing an ugly old shade. She was always a bit self conscious of it and consequently when anyone got a camera out, Mum would head off in the opposite direction. She was extremely reluctant to have her picture taken to say the least and now there are hardly any photographs to remind us of her. That's why I was so thrilled to receive the Skegness snapshot and since then we've had it blown up and I've included it in this book.

You can tell just by looking at the way Mum's hat is pulled down low on her forehead how much she hated that eye shade and tried to hide it. Yet when I saw her in the spirit world she had two eyes, good as new. We lose all our infirmities over there and Mum had got rid of that patch for good.

Memories of my family have been crowding in lately because I've just come back from Lincoln which is very nearly home ground. Actually it should have been home ground proper, but we had such difficulty over the arrangements for a demonstration at Grantham that we moved the whole thing down the road to Lincoln. I mentioned earlier the trouble there was over ticket touts and some people getting twenty tickets while others had none. Well in the end there was so much bad feeling I felt I couldn't work in that sort of atmosphere, so we laid on coaches and ferried all those who wanted to go to Lincoln and back, and the proceeds of the evening went to the mentally handicapped.

We had a lovely room in Lincoln overlooking the cathedral which is floodlit at night – a very beautiful sight. The only trouble was people kept climbing the fire escape next to our room to take pictures of it. The first morning there I woke up in alarm, convinced a crowd of people had come into the room. Fortunately the room was empty, but when I drew back the curtain I hastily let it fall again. Some particularly enterprising tourists had climbed over the fire escape onto the flat roof outside our window and were clicking away at the cathedral from there! I had to creep about with the curtains closed until they'd gone!

After all the kerfufle with tickets and coaches and change of venue I was a bit apprehensive about the evening but the spirit world didn't let me down. When you're worried about something they always come up trumps. In the bathroom – where I always go for a bit of privacy! – I heard the name Maisie Bolton from The Pastures, Barrowby. It was Maisie's Mum.

'I was a medium like you, Doris,' she said. 'My guide was called Topsy.' She wanted to wish her daughter happy birthday she said, because it was her birthday the following week.

Well when I got on stage and tried to find Maisie Bolton from The Pastures, Barrowby, I discovered her Mum had miscalculated Maisie – or Mavis as her name turned out to be, I'd misheard – wasn't there. She'd fallen ill and given the tickets to a close friend.

Her mother was quite put out. She told me her name was Doris like mine and she folded her arms and settled down for a good chat and wouldn't let anyone else in for some time. In the end she agreed to let other spirit people have a turn on condition that Mavis' friend took some flowers to her for her birthday.

'And tell her it's true what I used to say about the after life,' she added as a parting shot, 'I'm here now and it's just as I said.'

Once Doris cleared the line they all came through; a husband who'd left a trilby hat in the wardrobe and was complaining because he'd splashed out on a new suit just before he passed, the mother who knew that her daughter had got a new car and £250 knocked off the price and who worried about her grandson, a lovely boy who 'wouldn't apply himself', a young girl who passed with leukaemia and knew that her sister was wearing her favourite blue sweater but hadn't managed to get into her shoes because they were too small, a mother who complained her family had put artificial flowers beside her picture instead of fresh ones, a little boy who'd left behind £4.75 in his building society account and so it went on . . .

At one point I got a contact for the Richardson family. They were all sitting there in a row, about twelve of them, and I got practically all their names; Donna, Diana, Deborah, Peggy, Alan . . .

It was marvellous. A wonderful evening for me and for the mentally handicapped.

The next day we set off for Bridlington where we were doing two shows and a very lively time we had!

The weather had changed at last and we glided through the Lincolnshire countryside, bathed in warm sunshine. I'd forgotten how pretty Lincolnshire can be. We passed whole fields of shining gold which I took to be mustard, but later Tony Ortzen who was introducing me on stage said, 'Did you see all those fields of rape?'

'Of what?' I asked, horrified.

'Rape,' he grinned, 'that's what it's called.'

'Well we always called it mustard,' I told him, 'I think that's much nicer.'

And as we skimmed through the country lanes I suddenly saw a name that sent the years rolling back. Scampton. My very first station when I was in the WAAFs.

'Oh Robbie, slow down a minute,' I said to the driver. 'There's my old station. I wonder whether they'd let us have a look round and drive down to dispersal.'

This was the place where one cold dawn long ago I'd heard a young airman whistling *The Lord's My Shepherd* as he climbed into his plane and I'd known with absolute certainty that he wasn't coming back. Yes Scampton was the place where I'd come to terms with my psychic power for the first time. It made my heart beat faster just to look at it.

It had been modernized, of course, but the old married quarters where we'd been billeted were still there. We slept under canvas in those days but we used to go to the married quarters to get undressed and get ready to go out and to wait for the buses that took us to our tents for the night.

Robbie stopped the car. 'I'll go and ask them if we can look round,' he said and strode away to the guardroom but sadly it wasn't to be. Apparently you had to write in and make an appointment. I often wonder if I'd thought to ask myself whether it would have made any difference. After all having been in the forces myself I know how to put the question and who to ask for. But there you are I didn't think of it at the time and when I did it was too late.

Disappointed we continued on our way, but the magnificent Humber bridge almost made up for it. It was such a wonderful sight, rolling out and out across the brown water. An incredible feat of engineering.

At our seafront hotel in Bridlington, the lady on the desk was thrown into confusion by our arrival.

'What terms do you want?' she asked.

'Terms?' said Laurie. 'What do you mean?'

'Well, do you want dinner or just bed and breakfast?'

'Oh I don't think we'll want dinner tomorrow night,' I explained. 'We'll be at the theatre, but tonight . . .'

'Surely Doris Stokes can order what she wants,' Laurie interrupted.

'Oh, well, yes – if you like,' but the lady looked a little crestfallen as if she'd much prefer to get things straight in advance.

We were in the area of the great trenchermen of course and when they served you a meal, boy, they served you a meal. No wonder food is the first thing they ask you about.

Oddly enough though, we didn't even see a Yorkshire pudding, not that I'm allowed to eat them these days. But when I was a girl, Yorkshire pudding was a great filler up. We had Yorkshire pudding and gravy before the main course on a Sunday. Then a tiny scrap of meat surrounded by a mound of vegetables and finally to finish, Yorkshire pudding again with jam or sugar and vinegar. It was a good filling meal and I expect the older people still eat it like that.

We phoned the theatre soon after we arrived just to check the arrangements and found the manageress highly perplexed.

'We've had a call from two vicars,' she said. 'They asked if we wanted them to come into the theatre in case anything untoward happened. I didn't know

208

what to say. What do you think? Do you normally have vicars there?'

'No, love, not unless they've bought tickets,' I said, 'but don't worry. Give me the phone numbers and I'll sort it out.'

Well the first vicar was on holiday, so he couldn't have been too worried but the second vicar was at home.

'Hello,' I said, 'it's Doris Stokes here. I understand you've volunteered to come to the theatre. Do you mean you want to come on stage with me?'

'Oh no,' he said, 'I meant did they want me to come and clear out the evil influences afterwards.'

'Evil influences!' I echoed. 'What on earth are you talking about?'

'Well, sometimes, it's happened when we've had people like you here before, it leaves evil influences in the place and we have to go in and clear them out.'

'I can assure you there'll be nothing like that with me,' I said firmly. 'But if you are really so concerned why don't you come on stage with me and warn the people and let them make up their own minds.'

Well he didn't fancy that either but it turned into quite a discussion. He quoted the Bible at me and I quoted the Bible at him, but we weren't really getting anywhere.

'Look,' I said at last, 'I'll tell you what I'll do. I'll give your name and telephone number out so that if anybody is in trouble after seeing me, they can ring you for help.'

There was a small pause. 'Oh, eh – I don't think that would be a very good idea,' said the vicar.

'No? Well that's what you're talking about isn't it? Or do you just want the glory of going into the theatre and doing the whole blessing bit? I thought you were concerned about the people.'

'I am.'

'Well I'll give them your number then,' I said. And I did as well.

But I felt a bit sad as I put the phone down. Why they feel it's wrong to bring joy and strength and comfort to people I don't know. After some demonstrations the love in the air is so thick you can almost see it. How can that possibly be evil?

There wasn't time to dwell on it though because we'd promised to do an interview for Radio Humberside. I'd hesitated at first because I was afraid it might be a long distance to travel, but no they said, they had a studio in Bridlington, we could do it from there.

Well it turned out to be the funniest broadcast I've ever done. The address we'd been given was on the seafront and we pulled up at a strange little building like a cross between a broken down café and a nissan hut. Next door was a funfair and right beside the building a giant swing boat lunged backwards and forwards full of wildly screaming people.

'This can't be right,' said Laurie surveying the place in amazement.

'Well I'm sure this is where they told us to come.' There was a girl at a little tourist information kiosk outside so I asked her.

'Oh yes,' she said, 'there's a studio here. You can go through. I'll give you the key.'

'The key?' I queried my voice going into a squeak. 'Isn't there anyone there?'

'No,' said the girl.

Well we couldn't believe our eyes. We opened the door on a do it yourself studio. It really was radio by numbers. There was a list of instructions: One. Sit comfortably. Two. Pick up the telephone. Three. Dial this number . . . Four. Place yourself in front of the microphone . . .

We were in hysterics. Almost crying with laughter I dialled the number and a young girl answered.

'Oh hello, Doris,' she said. 'The power's by the door. Right, now press that button. Put on the headphones . . .' and so it went on.

The place was double-glazed and absolutely swel-

210

tering that day so we propped the door open with a bucket to get a little air and somehow through our giggles we started the broadcast. Half-way through there was a great clatter. A girl outside had kicked the bucket away.

'Sorry!' she called, 'but we want to use the phone in the other room and we aren't allowed to when this door's open.'

Laurie almost fell off his chair. 'I don't believe this,' he gasped. 'It's *Candid Camera* isn't it? It's not real!'

And over the top of it all, even with the door closed, came the screams from the swing boat.

I don't know what the programme was like but all I can say is I've not had such a good laugh for ages!

On a sadder note it was while we were in Bridlington that the news came of Roy Plomley's passing. We were getting ready to go to the theatre and the television was playing away in the next room, when suddenly I recognized Roy Plomley's voice.

'Roy Plomley's on the television,' I called to John and drifted out of the bathroom to watch. But it was only a recording and afterwards they announced that Roy had passed that morning.

I was very sad because he is such a gentle, loving man. A real old world gentleman. When they showed the list of stars who had been on *Desert Island Discs* I felt very humble and very proud to have been invited. In fact I was one of the last guests on the show. Roy will be sadly missed, not only by his family but by his millions of listeners and by his colleagues at the BBC. He knows now that what I was talking about was true and I hope he has a happy life on the other side. Well I know he will because he was always such a considerate, lovely man.

There was more fun and games when we got to the theatre that night. The dressing-rooms and everything else backstage seemed to be in the basement and when you opened the door from the street, instead of walking forward you went straight down, down these narrow winding stone steps without a handrail. Frightened the life out of me, of course, and I was sure I'd break my neck but I managed it.

Talk about Casey's Court. When it was time to go on stage, there was me holding my long dress up at the front and John holding it up at the back, struggling one in front of the other up these steep steps like some kind of broken down pantomime horse! And when I got on stage and sat down, I nearly shot into the audience! Laurie is a stickler for cleanliness and he'd given the leather seat that had been put out for me, an extra good polish. It looked lovely but it was as slippery as glass and I had to spend the whole evening with my feet braced hard against the floor to stop myself sliding out onto my bum into the auditorium!

Both Bridlington shows were a success thank goodness. I've already mentioned in an earlier chapter Paul Hewson who came to talk to me in my hotel room, but there were many other good contacts. There was a husband who mentioned the £79 his wife had won at bingo. There was ten-year-old Susie who'd been killed in a road accident. 'It was 4.30 and I'd been running, then bang . . . It wasn't fair. I'd only just been to the dentist and I hate the dentist's. I needn't have bothered . . .' There was also a puzzling message about something being rolled up in the toe of a sock.

'Did you find some money in the toe of a sock, or did she use to hide money in a sock. It's something to do with a sock,' I explained.

'I know what that means,' said the young woman at the microphone. 'When I was little we were very very poor and I was hoping for something for Christmas. They got an old sock, filled it with bits of screwed up paper and old hair brushes and things for a joke!'

I also met up with two previous sitters, only one of them was now talking to me from the other side.

'It's Barry,' said a man's voice, 'and I know you.'

I realized then that he must have been for a sitting

212

but I meet so many people I didn't recognize his voice. Barry said he was with Amanda and looking for Margaret. Well when Margaret came to the front I recognized her face. Hers was one of the *Forty Minutes* sittings that didn't ever reach the screen. She'd come with her husband Barry hoping to contact her daughter Mandy who was in the spirit world. But now it seemed as if fresh tragedy had struck, because Barry was also in the spirit world.

'Oh no, he took himself over, darling,' I said in horror. 'He just wants to say he's sorry. I'd upset her two days before and she sulked a bit,' he said, 'but that wasn't it.' And he went on to explain that he was afraid of being made redundant. 'I was redundant once before then I got another job and I thought I was about to lose that as well. I hadn't got the guts to face it . . .'

Most of all he wanted his wife to know that it wasn't anything she'd done, and he still loved her.

During question time a dear little lad came up. He was only two pennyworth and he looked up at me on the stage and said I've read your books and I would like to ask is there room for everyone up there or do we move on?

Well I explained that it takes hundreds of years to move on and there seems to be room for all and he trotted back to his seat, but at the end of the show he came back again with his book to sign and they hoisted him up onto the stage so that I could give him a big hug.

That night they gave me a standing ovation and through the cheers and shouts I detected a familiar chant: 'Doris Stokes . . . Doris Stokes . . .' I looked up at the balcony and there was the girl who'd shown John the cardboard cut-out she'd pinched from the book signing all those months ago. She'd come with a great bunch of friends plus the cut-out and they stood there waving it above their heads as they chanted. Gradually the rest of the audience took up the chant until the whole theatre was swaying to the rhythm of 'Doris Stokes! Doris Stokes!'

It was the most magical moment.

As it turned out I was to have a more lasting reminder of Bridlington and that wonderful evening than my own memories. When I got home there was a letter waiting for me from Kathy Nicholson who'd been in the audience:

Dear Doris, I just felt that I wanted to write to you to say thank you from the bottom of my heart for bringing my little boy Steven to talk to me last night. Everything you said about his accident and how he was put onto a machine to help his breathing, and the fact that he would have been a cabbage if he'd lived, were all so very accurate. His personality came through so very real and I feel so much love towards you because of what you did for me. I would just like to say Doris that right at the beginning of the demonstration you gave us a 'Mrs Roberts' then at one point you said 'Kathy' or 'Katharine' and then later you said 'Caravan' but then you said 'Oh I don't know what all that is about' and there was a group of ladies gathered at the front acknowledging your messages.

I didn't stand up at the time because I was a little confused but I firmly believe now Doris that my Dad, Arthur Roberts, was trying to talk to me. He passed over almost 18 months ago and I have always looked for comfort in the belief that Steven and his Grandad were together in the spirit world because they were very close.

My name is Kathy and at the moment we live in a caravan until we move into our new home. I would be very pleased if you would accept a little gift from me. The cassette enclosed is one I recorded last year. You see I play the trumpet and my Dad was very proud of me and I dedicated my cassette to him. He never got to hear it whilst on the earth plane and I *know* now that he knows all about my recording the cassette and also that he and Steven enjoy listening to it in the spirit world.

God bless you, Doris.

My sincerest best wishes to you and to your dear husband, John,

Yours sincerely
Kathy Nicholson (née Roberts)

Well I played that cassette and it's absolutely beautiful. Kathy is a very talented girl and her music has given me great pleasure. What's more, when I close my eyes and listen to *Danny Boy*, and all the other old favourites, I'm back on that stage in Bridlington surrounded by a great wall of love.

Readers who've got this far will realize that all kinds of wonderful things have happened since my last book! The most exciting of all, however, was being presented to Princess Anne, when she opened the new Bone Marrow Unit at Westminster Hospital.

As I mentioned in a *Host of Voices*, *Woman's Own* magazine launched an appeal to build the unit as part of their support for the Save the Children Fund. Well they raised over a million pounds I believe, and I was able to contribute £12,000 from my own charity shows which was marvellous. The unit was built and on June 6th it was opened by Princess Anne who is president of the Save the Children Fund.

Naturally I'd been looking forward to the ceremony for months and months. I'd got my clothes sorted out. I was going to wear a mandarin style dress in spiritual colours of swirling blues and mauves.

Then just the day before the ceremony I had a slight stroke. I was horrified, not so much by my physical condition as the fact that I might miss the presentation and also two appearances I was supposed to be doing in Brighton immediately afterwards. My right arm was clumsy and almost useless and when I tried to speak it came out as a terrible stammer.

'There is no way you can stand up on a stage and talk to people,' said my wonderful doctor when I finally stuttered out what was worrying me. 'You are not to do any work whatsoever. But I don't see why you shouldn't go to the presentation. It'll do you good because you'll enjoy it and you won't have to do any work. Afterwards, though, I want you in hospital for a check-up.'

Sadly, I had to cancel my Brighton appearances but I did struggle along to Westminster Hospital and I'm so glad that I did.

They looked after me marvellously. Professor Hobbs met me at the door and arranged for a nurse to be with me throughout. Then they took me into the boardroom and let me sit there in a chair intended for a lady-in-waiting, until Princess Anne arrived.

She looked breathtaking. I don't know how to describe her; chic, elegant, immaculate – nothing quite captures the way she looked. She was wearing a cream skirt with a navy blue jacket and her hair was swept up and topped by a cream hat with navy blue spots.

She really is a lovely girl. Very slim and upright with a serious expression until she smiles, and then it's like magic. Her whole face lights up with such radiance that you can see how beautiful she really is.

I was last in line to be presented. In front of me were other fund raisers; Miss Jackie Berger, Pauline and Brendan McAleese from Northern Ireland and then me.

I was terrified I might fall over or do something stupid before she got to me, and as she moved along the line my heart was crashing in my ears so loud I thought everyone in the room must be able to hear it. And then, there she was.

'May I present Doris Fisher Stokes, ma'am, who is a medium, writes books and who has worked unstint-

216

ingly for the Save the Children Fund,' said Iris Burton editor of *Woman's Own*, while I tried to do a little bob.

The Princess looked directly into my eyes so that the rest of the room disappeared.

'Have you lost any children with this?' she asked, referring to the blood diseases that would be treated.

'No, ma'am,' I said, 'I lost four children when I was young but I just love kids, so I try to do what I can.'

She smiled, 'You look a little bit tired.'

She was observant too. 'Well I don't work as hard as you, ma'am.'

'Oh it's a little bit different for me!' she said giving a lopsided grin as if to say it's all laid on for me. I don't have to work like you do.

And then it was over and she was moving towards the platform for the speeches. I think perhaps I didn't pay quite as much attention to the speeches as I should, because we were standing the whole time. The chairman offered Princess Anne a chair but she said, 'No I will stand,' and so everyone else had to stand up too.

It seemed endless. I braced my back against the wall and I didn't know whether to stand with my legs pressed together or apart to balance myself. It went on and on and the room grew very hot yet Princess Anne never moved once. Everyone else got a bit fidgety and even the man on the platform was fanning himself discreetly with his programme behind the Princess's back. Princess Anne, however, didn't move a muscle, she didn't perspire. She simply stood relaxed, attentive and as cool as if there was a pleasant breeze blowing.

I looked at her and I thought, my God, that's breeding, that's royal training for you. You can't buy what that girl's got.

The ceremony moved on. The Princess unveiled a blue and gold commemorative plaque and she was presented with a bouquet of flowers and a plate by a little girl and a little boy.

217

The boy turned out to be Mark, the first boy to have had a successful bone marrow transplant. He'd been at the Dorchester when we launched the appeal and he remembered me. Down came the blue rope that separated us and he came over to give me a hug.

'Did I do it right?' he asked. He'd been told to bow and he'd given a quick duck of his head.

'You did it beautifully,' I told him.

Afterwards we went off for a buffet tea and dear Professor Hobbs had arranged for a table to be carried in for me with my own waiter and waitress to bring me the goodies so that I wouldn't have to stand in the queue.

Mr and Mrs McAleese from Northern Ireland were at my table and I thought they were a wonderful couple. They'd lost their little boy before the unit was built but they'd gone ahead to help raise money so that other children could be saved. And they'd managed it all despite the fact that Brendan was unemployed.

I wasn't supposed to be working of course but while we were chatting I suddenly heard the name David and a little boy's voice said something about his sister.

I didn't want to jump in until I was sure so I asked Pauline innocently if she had any other children.

'Oh, yes, a little girl,' she said.

That was it, I must be talking to her son.

'Who's David?' I asked.

'Why that's my little boy's name!' she said.

'He tells me you got a red sweater out of his drawer the other day and buried your face in it.'

She looked stunned. 'Yes I did, two days ago. But nobody knows about that. I didn't even tell Brendan.'

'Well David was with you love,' I said.

I had to be careful not to go into a sitting of course but I was able to give her a few more words of comfort including the fact that David knew his sister was staying with her Auntie Marie while her parents were in London.

218

Strangely enough we were joined by a very nice young man who'd raised a lot of money in Germany. His name was Flight Leutenant John Foster who worked for the Ministry of Defence. When I told him about my visit to Scampton he said what a pity it was that he hadn't met me then.

'I could have got you in,' he said. 'Just let me know if there's anywhere you'd like to go and I'll arrange it,' and he left me his telephone number.

They were a cheeky lot on our table. They wanted to smoke so they shouted, 'Doris Stokes wants to smoke!' And immediately an ashtray was brought.

Then a bit later somebody wanted to go to the loo. They went out and found they weren't allowed through because Princess Anne was coming down the stairs. So back they came and said: 'Doris Stokes wants to go to the ladies' room!'

'That'll be all right,' they said.

Of course I had to go then but this blonde lady tucked on behind me.

'What did you do that for?' I asked her, 'I could have waited.'

'Well I wanted to go, too,' she said, 'but nobody knows me. Everybody knows you!'

After tea Professor Hobbs came to take me up to see the unit. I'd read in my programme that the unit contained seven special cubicles, five of which are laminar flow cubicles, each with its own filter system bathing the patient with germ free air. There was also a sterile kitchen and utility room.

It sounded very impressive but it was even more impressive when you saw it. There were all these filters and big germ free bubbles.

'Put your hand just there, Doris,' said Professor Hobbs and when I did as he asked I felt a great rush of sterile air pushing against my hand.

There was one little boy in the unit who had already had his transplant and didn't need to be kept in isolation.

219

'This is Matthew,' said Professor Hobbs.

'Hello, Matthew darling,' I said. He was a dear little boy of about three who was lying on his bed with his head on his Daddy's knees. His hair was just beginning to grow back like a little haze of fur all over his head.

'Tummy's going down now isn't it Matthew,' said Professor Hobbs. 'He had a big tummy a little while ago.'

'Aren't you lucky,' I said, 'I've got a big tummy and mine's not going to go down!'

There was a photographer hovering about and he asked if I could get on the bed with Matthew for the picture.

'Yes that's all right,' said Professor Hobbs.

'Can I sit on the bed with you, Matthew?' I asked.

'Yeth.'

'Can I give you a big hug?'

'Yeth,' he said again, so, of course, I did.

It only remained for me to present the doll from Cornwall, now named Anne and resplendent in a red velvet dress and bonnet with underclothes and panties and shoes and socks that all came off and then it was time to go.

I suddenly realized I was exhausted but I wouldn't have missed it for the world.

So here I am in my hospital bed, a bit battered and bruised and playing Kathy's tape to cheer myself up. The doctors shake their heads and tell me I should slow down but I'm busy doing my arm exercises and singing away to get my voice back. I'm determined to be on my feet again soon.

I'm not getting any younger, of course, and I don't know how much longer I've got, none of us does, but I've got a strange feeling that there's still something else I have to do. I can't think what it can be because I've done private sittings, public demonstrations, television, radio and newspaper interviews. Yet I still feel there's something I must do.

No doubt the spirit world will show me what it is in their own good time – and when I find out – you'll be the first to know!

For more information On Mediumship, Contact:
Inner Quest Foundation
PO Box 934, Depot 3
Victoria, B.C.
V8W 2R9